D0776882

The Black Book
of the American Left

The Black Book
of the
American Left
The Collected Conservative Writings
of David Horowitz

Volume II
Progressives

Second Thoughts Books
Los Angeles

First American edition published in 2013 by Second Thoughts Books.

Manufactured in the United States and printed on acid-free paper. The paper used in this publication meets the minimum requirements of ANSI/NISO Z39.48 1992 (R 1997) *(Permanence of Paper)*.

Book design and production by Catherine Campaigne; copy-edited by David Landau; research provided by Mike Bauer.

FIRST AMERICAN EDITION

LIBRARY OF CONGRESS CATALOGING-IN-PUBLICATION DATA

Horowitz, David, 1939–
   The black book of the American left : the collected conservative writings of David Horowitz / by David Horowitz.
   volumes   cm.
   Includes bibliographical references and index.
   ISBN 978-1-886442-95-5 (hardback)
   1. Social movements—United States—History.   2. Radicalism—United States. 3. Anti-Americanism—United States.   4. Horowitz, David, 1939– Political and social views.   I. Title.
HX86.H788 2013
335.00973   2013000496

10   9   8   7   6   5   4   3   2   1

Contents

Progressives

All the volumes in this series of my collected writings called *The Black Book of the American Left* are about individuals who call themselves progressives. This volume focuses on the nature of the progressive outlook and its real-world consequences.

The progressive label is one that its adherents wear proudly. It appeals to their *amour propre*, identifying them as people who are forward-looking, therefore enlightened and modern. "Progressive" fits their sense of themselves as apostles of hope and change, in fact as a species of social redeemers. Consequently, the basic premise of their politics is that "forward" is necessarily a good direction, and that a fundamental transformation of social relationships is both possible and desirable. As an expression of this self-image, progressives commonly refer to themselves as being "on the side of history," as though history was steadily moving towards beneficent ends. Inevitably, the term "progressive" has the added advantage of putting the best face on their collective achievements, although these have frequently entailed consequences that were destructive on an epic scale. It also leads them to make alliances both formal and informal with the enemies of the relatively enlightened democracies in which they actually live.

In addition to examining an outlook that leads to such regrettable results, the essays in this volume pay particular attention to the connections between progressive movements of the present and their antecedents in the past. Bearing these continuities in mind and retaining a sense of past results are essential to understanding the real-world consequences of the progressive faith.

No greater obstacle to clarity about current progressive move-ments exists than the habit of detaching them from their ideologi-cal antecedents, specifically those in the Communist past. A common attitude regards Communist ideas as passé, and any attempt to link them to present company as politically dangerous. But this lazy thinking (to put the best face on it) makes any under-standing of contemporary progressives impossible. When they are in their own company, progressives themselves are not shy about their debts to Marx and his disciples. When they are in position to determine academic curricula, they give the Marxist tradition pride of place. Their politics are directly and self-consciously inspired by the intellectual tradition—Marx, Hegel, Gramsci—that produced the totalitarian results. Many of today's progressives, and certainly their teachers, were actively involved in supporting and defending the 20th Century's totalitarian "experiments" and in opposing the anti-Communist cold warriors who helped to bring them to an end.

Progressives have an understandable interest in separating themselves from the destructive consequences of their past behav-iors. But conservatives should not contribute to their efforts by referring to them as "liberals," or regarding their own differences as merely policy matters that can be compromised and adjusted, rather than as the result of a philosophical divide that leads to con-sequences both predictable and tragic.

Part I: The Mind of the Left

The essays in this volume begin with an introductory section, "The Mind of the Left," which re-establishes the missing connec-tions between current progressive movements and their Commu-nist predecessors.[1] Through profiles of some of its prominent intellectual figures, this introduction traces the continuities between the Communist left of the Stalin era, the New Left that

---

[1] An earlier version of this essay appeared in my book *Unholy Alliance: Radical Islam and the American Left,* Regnery, 2004. It has been revised for inclusion in this volume.

followed, and the contemporary left that emerged following the fall of the Communist empire.

These intellectual portraits are set in the context of the events of September 11, 2001, when Islamic jihadists launched a surprise attack on American soil, killing three thousand civilians. Progressives responded to this heinous assault by organizing protests directed not at the perpetrators but at their own country. The protesters opposed an American military response, and justified the enemy's aggression by attributing it to "root causes" that could be traced to America's imperial ambitions. Not all progressives joined the initial opposition, which was organized by a radical element. But a year later, as hundreds of thousands of activists poured into the streets to protest America's war against Islamists in Iraq, the opposition spread through the entire progressive spectrum to include the leadership of the Democratic Party.[2]

If an inability to grasp the left's historical antecedents is one obstacle to understanding its behavior, a close second is the failure to appreciate the connection between its utopian and nihilist agendas. The belief in a perfect future inevitably inspires a passionate (and otherwise inexplicable) hatred towards the imperfect present. The first agenda of social redeemers is to dismantle the existing social order, which means their intellectual and political energies are focused on the work of destruction. Several passages in "The Mind of the Left" explore this theme.

Antagonism towards the existing social order inevitably leads to uncertain loyalties towards the body politic, and then to uncertain loyalties towards one's country at war. This is a subject that makes everyone uncomfortable, but cannot be simply ignored because of that. Along with the opening section, several essays deal with the issue of patriotism, including "The Future of the

---

[2]The left's opposition to the war in Iraq is explored more fully in Volume III of this series, *The Great Betrayal*, and in two of my books, *Unholy Alliance: Radical Islam and the American Left* (2004), and *Party of Defeat: How Democrats and Radicals Undermined America's Security Before and After 9/11* (2008) co-authored with Ben Johnson.

Left," "Spies Like Us," "Spy Stories," "The Lawyer Who Came in From the Cold," and "The Left on Trial." Another, "The Trouble with *Treason*," recounts my differences on this subject with conservative author Ann Coulter in her book of that name.

Between Past and Present

The essays in Parts II & III are arranged in chronological order and begin with the text of a presentation I made to an Accuracy in Academia conference in 1987, titled "Activists Then and Now." It was written just after Peter Collier and I held our Second Thoughts Conference for former radicals. In this text I describe the continuities between the New Left and the then current left, stressing what I thought conservatives should understand about the protesters and probably did not. It is a theme that runs through the course of the present volume.

This is followed by the text of a speech I gave at Dartmouth University, where I had been invited by conservative students to join a panel defending *The Dartmouth Review*, a student paper under attack for its conservative opinions by the Dartmouth administration. The panel included Peter Collier, Michael Medved, and one other conservative. My remarks were focused on the warm welcome the Dartmouth administration had given the communist Angela Davis who had recently spoken there. At the time the Dartmouth administration was conducting a virtual war against the conservative students who ran *The Dartmouth Review* for transgressing the boundaries of "political correctness," i.e., the progressive party line. Despite its leftist sympathies and censorious attitude, the Dartmouth administration was universally referred to as "liberal." This environment—supportive of totalitarian agitators like Davis and hostile to conservative students—was in my experience typical of most universities, and reflected the general tenor of the intellectual culture.

The essay, "Mercy for a Terrorist," describes how the broad progressive community is ready to embrace domestic terrorists if the motivation for their criminal activity is "progressive." A variation on this theme appears in "The Destructive Romance of the Intellectuals," which is a review of Martin Amis's book about Stalin, and his conflict with Christopher Hitchens over the latter's lingering romance with the totalitarian "comrades."

Tom Hayden was a leader of the New Left and a violent revolutionary who advocated guerrilla war in America's streets and organized a riot at the Democratic Party convention in 1968. Shortly after that riot destroyed the electoral chances of Hubert Humphrey, Hayden led a generation of radicals into the Democratic Party with the idea of transforming it into a party of the left. As a direct result of their success, Hayden was awarded the Medal of Freedom by Democratic president Jimmy Carter and became a Democratic assemblyman in the state of California. After being term-limited from the Assembly he ran unsuccessfully for mayor of Los Angeles, which was the occasion for an op-ed column I wrote, called "Tom Hayden, Los Angeles and Me," which opposed his candidacy. In achieving this acceptance by mainstream Democrats, Hayden had not jettisoned his radical views, including his fundamental hostility to America and its social framework. It was thus the Democratic Party that had undergone a significant change, not him.

In "The Future of the Left," I examine another revealing case of the progressive mind-set. Its subject, Richard Rorty, was born into the Trotskyist left but was philosophically an anti-totalitarian skeptic. Rorty wrote a book criticizing the left for its lack of patriotism and corrosive hostility towards American society, both of which he regarded as counter-productive. But in the end Rorty remained a prisoner of the same attitudes because he could not let go of the fantasy of a utopian future and its ancillary hostility for the unredeemed present. The full flowering of this hatred is manifest in all the works of Noam Chomsky, whose intellectual dishonesty is dissected in the essay, "Guru of Anti-Americanism."

A hallmark of the left is its reliance on deception both in the presentation of its agendas and in its attitude towards the past.

Because of the religious nature of its ambitions these deceptions are intrinsic and not merely calculated. Animated by the fantasy of a future perfection, the left depends on extreme myths to sustain its salvationist illusions. Facts that do not fit its indictments must be made to do so; historical records that question its vanguard status must be challenged or suppressed. Several examples of the historical falsifications that flow from these imperatives are explored in the essays "I, Rigoberta Menchú, Liar," "Three Political Romancers," and "Progressive Education: Panther Style."

When members of the progressive faith do break ranks and dissent from its myths, they are immediately shunned, and often summarily cast out. "The Secret Power of the Leftist Faith" explores this ritual in the case of Christopher Hitchens, although Christopher, a double agent of sorts, was ultimately able to retain his progressive bona fides. A related essay, "Ordeal by Slander," illustrates how the left—in this case represented by the editor of Slate, a *Washington Post* publication—insulates its mythologies from damaging scrutiny by labeling its critics "McCarthyites" and witch-hunters. The result of these maneuvers and the fear they induce is a hermetically sealed intellectual environment that prevents progressives from considering alternative views.[3] This phenomenon is explored in "Guilt of the Son," which tells the story of one of the children of the Rosenberg spies who embarked on a quest to prove his parents' innocence and wound up embracing their guilt.

In 2012, the film director Oliver Stone produced a ten-part television series and 750-page text titled *The Untold History of the United States.* Co-authored by leftist professor Peter Kuznick, this so-called history regurgitated the Stalinist version of the Cold War's origins and conduct, and then the views of America's Marxist and Islamic enemies. It was shocking enough that a major net-

---

[3]The closed intellectual universe of American institutions of higher learning at this time is explored in Volume VII of this series, *The Left in the Universities.*

work would fund and promote a propaganda project like this. But its absurd fabrications were embraced with only a handful of dissents by the progressive culture and its academic establishment. The essay "Oliver Stone's Communist History" reviews the Stone-Kuznick phenomenon as a watershed moment in the devolution of American liberalism and the American left.

The final section, "Identifying the Left," reviews the ferocious reaction that occurred in February 2005 when I published an online encyclopedia of the left. The encyclopedia was called "Discover the Networks," and provided a database of progressive individuals and organizations, ranging from radical to moderate. The three essays that conclude this volume were my responses to leftist critics who focused their attention on an index of individuals accompanied by thumbnail photos, which were featured in the database. This index was subsequently removed for reasons unrelated to the controversy, when leftists began filing copyright infringement complaints over the use of the photos. Since the index was an incomplete listing, designed merely as an advertisement for the contents, it seemed prudent to simply remove it. But the reaction itself was revealing, showing how sensitive the left is to having its agendas and networks described.

PART I

The Mind of the Left

I

Introduction

During a 2003 Columbia University teach-in against the war in Iraq, Professor Nicholas DeGenova told the protesters: "peace is not patriotic [but] subversive."[1] This is a good starting-point for understanding the warped perspective of "antiwar" radicals. DeGenova went on to explain: "Peace anticipates a very different world than the one in which we live—a world where the U.S. would have no place."[2] This is an arresting formulation. It goes to the heart of the questions previously raised by antiwar demonstrators, whose protests took place within two weeks of the attacks of 9/11 and were directed at preventing an American response. How could so many Americans be so quick to oppose their country's response to an unprovoked attack? How could the same "progressives" who claimed to support democracy and oppose imperialism, then go out to defend the totalitarian, expansionist state of Iraq? How could they oppose America's war for Iraqi freedom?

Almost as instructive as DeGenova's remarks in providing answers to these questions were the mild rebukes he received from other speakers at the Columbia teach-in. These rebukes came from critics concerned that DeGenova's description of peace as "unpatriotic" was a phrase too far, exposing them to unfriendly

---

[1]Ron Howell, "Radicals Speak Out At Columbia 'Teach-In,'" *NewsDay*, March 27, 2003
[2]The date of the teach-in was March 26, 2003.

fire. Among the critics, the most significant voice belonged to Columbia's most famous radical faculty member, Eric Foner. While DeGenova was an obscure assistant professor, Foner was an academic lion, a former head of the two principal historical associations as well as chairman of the Columbia History Department, and winner of the Bancroft Prize for historical writing. Foner was also a founding member of Historians Against the War.[3]

In distancing himself from DeGenova's declaration, Foner explained, "I refuse to cede the definition of American patriotism to George W. Bush. I have a different definition of patriotism, which comes from Paul Robeson: 'The patriot is the person who is never satisfied with his country.'"[4] By citing Paul Robeson as an authority on patriotism, Foner provided a revealing commentary on his own allegiances. Robeson was a Communist Party icon, a winner of the Stalin Peace Prize while Stalin was alive. Robeson's passport had been lifted by the State Department because of his overt loyalty and service to the Soviet enemy. At a time when Soviet tanks were supporting police-states in occupied Eastern Europe, Robeson led a Kremlin-inspired campaign to distract attention from its own crimes, in particular Stalin's purges of Communist leaders who happened to be mainly Jews. In 1951, while these purges and executions were in progress in Eastern Europe, Robeson brought a petition to the U.N., which charged the United States with committing "genocide" against American Negroes.[5] Two years before, Robeson had caused an uproar by

---

[3]For a description of this organization, see Greg Yardley, "Historians Against History," *FrontPage Magazine*, July 11, 2003. http://archive.frontpagemag.com/readArticle.aspx?ARTID=17539

[4]David Horowitz, "Moment of Truth (for the anti-American Left)," *Jewish World Review*, March 31, 2003, http://www.jewishworldreview.com/cols/horowitz033103.asp

[5]The petition was entitled, "We Charge Genocide." http://en.wikipedia.org/wiki/We_Charge_Genocide. The Wikipedia entry omits the fact that this was a Communist petition and that all the signers were Party members and fellow-travelers.

declaring that "American Negroes" would not fight for the United States in a war with the Soviet Union.[6]

Throughout his career, Robeson's attitude towards the liberties and opportunities afforded by America was as unrelentingly critical as his attitude towards oppression in the Soviet bloc was lax and forgiving. In this he resembled his Columbia admirer, who could trace his own intellectual roots to American Communism. Eric Foner grew up in a family of well-known Communist Party members. His uncle Philip was the Party's "labor historian" and edited the speeches and writings of the Black Panthers and of Paul Robeson himself. Another uncle was the head of a Communist-controlled union. Foner began his own political career writing for *The National Guardian,* a paper whose editorial line was Maoist and whose editors, Cedric Belfrage and James Aronson, were Communist Party members as well.

In a lengthy review of Foner's academic work, the liberal intellectual historian John Diggins wrote: "[Eric] Foner ... is both an unabashed apologist for the Soviet system and an unforgiving historian of America."[7] Theodore Draper, also a historian and democratic socialist, caustically dismissed Foner's history of the United States, *The Story of American Freedom,* as a work more accurately described as "the story of unfreedom." Writing in *The New York Review of Books,* Draper characterized Foner as "a partisan of radical sects and opinions" and described his narrative as "a tale of hopeful efforts that failed and of dissident voices that cried out in the wilderness." A distinctive feature of Foner's history, Draper said, was his attempt "to rehabilitate American Communism,"

---

[6]"It is unthinkable ... that American Negroes would go to war on behalf of those who have oppressed us for generations ... against a country [the Soviet Union] which in one generation has raised our people to full human dignity of mankind."—*The New York Times,* April 4, 1949; Philip S. Foner, ed., *Paul Robeson Speaks,* Secaucus, 1978, p. 537 n.1

[7]John P. Diggins, "Fate and Freedom in History: The Two Worlds of Eric Foner," *The National Interest,* Fall 2002; http://nationalinterest.org/article/fate-and-freedom-in-history-399

concluding that "from [Foner's] account it would be hard to understand why so many millions of immigrants should have come to the United States for more freedom."[8]

This background is essential for parsing Foner's definition of patriotism as "never being satisfied with [one's] country." It is not dissatisfaction with this or that particular American institution but with the American narrative itself, and it invites a further question. Since Communists like Robeson were dissatisfied with their country to the point that they were unwilling to defend it, what were the conditions—if any—under which Foner and Columbia's protesters would be willing to defend their country against America's enemies? How fundamental were the changes they would demand before experiencing a sense of loyalty to the actual society in which they lived? How did their views actually differ in practice from DeGenova's belief that in a peaceful world the America we know would not exist? Not one of the Columbia speakers spoke to this issue. Implicit in DeGenova's statement (and their silence) was that America—by which they meant American imperialism—was the *cause* of the wars it faced. That was the reason that, in their view, "the U.S. would have no place" in a world at peace.

---

[8]Theodore Draper, "Freedom and Its Discontents," *The New York Review of Books*, September 23, 1999. Foner even "pays tribute to Communists for enlarging the scope of American freedom."

2

The Forerunners

amuel Johnson's famous scoundrel who finds a last refuge in patriotic fervor has a counterpart in radicals like DeGenova and Foner who cloak their revolutionary agendas in the flag and the values they intend to subvert. A generation of American Communists, like Robeson, rationalized their disloyalty to America as a higher loyalty to the socialist revolution that would one day transform America into something entirely different. In defending Soviet Communism, they believed they were actually building "a better America." In the 1930s, the American Communist leader, Earl Browder, fashioned this fantasy into a Party slogan: "Communism is Twentieth Century Americanism."[1] Through this distorted lens, American Communists viewed their loyalty to the Soviet Union as loyalty to a future America that would be built on their Communist principles. Through this surreal lens, they were able to view *anti*-Communism as a treason to America.

Albert Lannon was a Communist leader who was tried under the Smith Act for conspiring to teach the overthrow of the American government. As a Communist, his first loyalty was to the Soviet Union. He regarded America as his enemy. Yet, when he appeared in court, he was able with complete sincerity to invert these relationships and the values that would normally be associated with patriotism:

---

[1]*Encyclopedia of U.S. Labor and Working-Class History*, Eric Arnesen (Ed.), p. 192, Routledge, 2006

I consider disloyal and traitors those who foment war, those who
try to deprive Americans of their democratic rights, those who
live on the blood and sweat of the American working class, those
who have instigated this and other trials of Communists and progressives to stifle the great voice of my beloved Communist
Party.[2]

Obviously, not every critic of American policy—even wartime
policy—has treasonous intent, a distinction that can be blurred in
times of national peril. It is a problem that led to well-known
abuses during both World Wars, as well as to the period of the Cold
War associated with Senator McCarthy. However, the fact that
some leftists were on the receiving end of these abuses did not prevent the Communists themselves from accusing those who dis-
agreed with them of treason. During the Second World War, when
America and the Soviet Union had a common enemy, the Communist Party denounced labor leader John L. Lewis and civil-rights
leader A. Philip Randolph as "American traitors" because they
refused to subordinate labor battles and civil-rights struggles to the
war effort, and therefore to the defense of the Soviet Union.[3] On
the other hand, it is also a fact that many American Communists
were active traitors, working as agents and spies for the Soviet
Union, and operating in secret Communist Party apparatuses that
were set up to serve Soviet interests.[4]

Belatedly, some American leftists have owned up to this reality. "Among the most remarkable revelations that emerged from
the [opening of the Soviet archives]," wrote two of them, "was the
extent to which the Communist Party USA was itself embroiled

---

[2]Albert Vetere Lannon, *Second String Red: The Life of Al Lannon*, American Communist, Lanham, 1999, p. 151. The author is Lannon's son.
[3]Lewis refused to take a "no-strike" pledge, while A. Philip Randolph
refused to call off the 1943 March on Washington; Lewis Coser and Irving
Howe, *The American Communist Party*, New York, 1974.
[4]John Earl Haynes and Harvey Klehr, *Venona: Decoding Soviet Espionage
in America*, New Haven, 1999. See Appendices A and B for lists of
"Americans and U.S. Residents Who Had Covert Relationships with
Soviet Intelligence Agencies."

in Soviet espionage. That individual spies like Julius Rosenberg were Communists is not exactly news. But that the Party helped on a regular basis to recruit spies and vet their political reliability did come as a surprise, as did the indication that some of its top leaders, including wartime general secretary Earl Browder, actually ran espionage operations."[5]

Why did these Americans willingly betray their country? Many of them were European immigrants who had come to America seeking refuge from persecution abroad. Why would they be willing to work for the enemies of a nation that had given them opportunity and freedom? While many students of the left have reflected on this question, few have done so as astutely as the philosopher Gerhardt Niemeyer. "In Communist eyes," Niemeyer wrote, "the future is more real than the present." For Communists, he added, the future was "closed."[6] What Niemeyer meant was that radicals imagined the future as an already determined reality, however improbable this may seem. In this surreal vision, once the chains of oppression had been removed—once the means of production had passed into the hands of "the people"—the natural goodness of human beings would assert itself and the traditional dilemmas of power would no longer obtain. With the abolition of private property, the progressive future would be characterized by "social justice," and there would no longer be troubling questions about the dispensations of authority. In this future, questions of process and means would no longer be important—since the cause of social injustice, private property, would no longer exist. Thus for Marxists there was only the end result, the socialist revolution, which justified everything. For Communists there was the revolution

[5]Maurice Isserman and Ellen Schrecker, "'Papers of a Dangerous Tendency:' From Major Andre's Boot to the Venona Files," in *Cold War Triumphalism*, New York, 2004, p. 157
[6]Gerhart Niemeyer, *Deceitful Peace: A New Look at the Soviet Threat*, 1971, p. 205; cited in Aileen Kraditor, *"Jimmy Higgins," The Mental World of the American Rank-and-File Communist 1930-1958*, 1988, p. 2.

and then there was the perfect future, which for them had already
been achieved in the Soviet Union.

This explains why American Communists were willing to
betray their country. They were convinced that their comrades in
the Soviet Union had already created the just society. The Soviet
Union was "a heaven ... brought to earth," American Communist
Tillie Olsen wrote in 1934, expressing a general view.[7] For radicals
who shared her belief, the fate of the progressive future rested in
the success of the Soviet regime. For Communist progressives, the
interests of the Soviet state were indistinguishable from the interests of mankind; to serve one meant advancing the other. As one
Communist Party text instructed its adherents: "The USSR is the
stronghold of the world proletariat; it cannot be looked on as
merely a nation or a country; it is the most advanced position of
the world proletariat in the struggle for a socialist world."[8]

For progressives who held these beliefs, betraying their country
was easily justified as benefiting their countrymen at the same
time. It was a "higher" form of patriotism. For Communists and
other progressives, treason to America was loyalty to humanity—
and to a truer, better America.[9]

---

[7]Cited in John Earl Haynes and Harvey Klehr, *In Denial: Historians, Communism and Espionage*, San Francisco 2003, p. 53; Cf. Aileen Kraditor,
op. cit.

[8]Ibid. The statement is from a book written by one of the Communist
Party's leading trainers of *cadre*.

[9]The same idea was recently extended by post-Communist radicals to
include racial issues. "Treason to whiteness is loyalty to humanity," runs
the motto of the magazine *Race Traitor*, which is edited by Harvard leftists and which progressive icon Cornel West has called "the most visionary courageous journal in America." West's comment is on the
jacket-cover of an anthology by the magazine's editors, Noel Ignatiev (a
Sixties Maoist) and John Garvey; *Race Traitor*, New York, 1996. In the
words of Amazon.com's reviewer, "The journal *Race Traitor* began in
1992 with one lofty ambition: 'to serve as an intellectual center for those
seeking to abolish the white race.'" West was a political consultant to the
Democratic Party campaigns of former Senator Bill Bradley and Al
Sharpton.

In his memoir, *Witness,* Whittaker Chambers described the Communist movement he had served as a new development in the annals of betrayal: "Other ages have had their individual traitors—men who from faint-heartedness or hope of gain sold out their causes. But in the 20th century, for the first time, men banded together by the millions in movements like Fascism and Communism, dedicated to the purpose of betraying the institutions they lived under. In the 20th century, treason became a vocation whose modern form was specifically the treason of ideas."[10]

Chambers was wrong in maintaining that treason for an idea was an entirely new phenomenon. Benedict Arnold could reasonably be considered a traitor motivated by an idea: loyalty to the Crown of England, his first allegiance. By the same token, America's revolutionary founders were traitors to their king in the name of an idea. This is why—having created a democracy—they made treason such a difficult crime to prosecute. Chambers was right, however, in the sense that Communists and Fascists betrayed the institutions they actually lived under in the name of an abstraction—the perfect future—whereas the others had not. Benedict Arnold and other loyalists to the Crown acted to preserve the system they lived under. So did the American founders who fought to defend what they considered "the rights of Englishmen" for Americans, which they believed the Crown had denied them. In other words, they fought not for a future abstraction but to defend a reality they knew. Insofar as they invoked abstract ideals, it was only to articulate the principles they mostly lived by, which the colonial power sought to deny them. But Communists and Fascists were not defending any reality. Like contemporary radicals, they were motivated by abstractions—by the vision of a future that did not exist and had never existed but which they were convinced they could create.

It is this abstraction, this *monde idéal,* that accounts for the otherwise incomprehensible fact that, for Communists, "the future is

[10]*Witness,* 1952, p. 524

more real than the present." The belief in this "reality" is why radicals discount the apparent freedoms and material benefits of the actual world they live in. Their eyes are fixed on a revolutionary future that is perfect and just. Measured by this impossible standard, any actually existing society—including America's—is easily judged deficient, even to the point where it is worthy of destruction.[11] It is the impossible dream that explains the extravagant hatred radicals feel towards their own privileged circumstances. It is an expression of their total rejection of the existing world.

Commenting on the writings of Marx, which are still the wellspring of the radical "critique," Niemeyer observed that Marxism is not a criticism of particular social wrongs but a "total critique of society" itself: "Marx's indictment condemns not this or that concrete choice or a pattern of civil actions, but the entire historical condition of human existence [under capitalism]." This is not so much a "moral" critique as an "ontological" one—a critique that affects the entire social reality. "All that which has gone under the name of reality appears to Marx as a nullity."[12] Not only is the radical's revolution not about the reform of a social reality, and therefore ultimately its preservation. It is the opposite. It is about the total destruction of a social reality. As Niemeyer explains: "By force of the overall definition, in the present society all laws are unjust, all consciousness is false, all relations must be corrupt, all institutions appear oppressive."[13] In Marx's chilling phrase, "Everything that exists deserves to perish."[14] A total critique requires a total solution.

---

[11]Of course they do not apply the same standard to revolutionary movements and regimes, which are struggling to bring a just society to birth. The failures of revolutionary movements and regimes are to be explained by the opposition of the old regimes and their efforts to strangle the revolutionary utopia at birth.

[12]Gerhart Niemeyer, *Between Nothingness and Paradise*, South Bend, 1998, pp.96–7.

[13]Ibid.

[14]Karl Marx, *The Eighteenth Brumaire of Louis Napoleon.* The words are approvingly quoted by Marx from Goethe's *Faust*, where they are uttered by Mephistopheles.

This is the perspective that informs not only the critiques of Marx and his followers but also of post-Communist radicals, including the post-9/11 antiwar left. For those who define the world in this totalitarian way, the problem of determining the morality or justice of particular human actions and particular institutions no longer exists. Because America is an unjust society, all its wars are also unjust by virtue of that alone. America's reasons for entering the war in Iraq are thus tainted before the fact. It does not matter to the radical whether the use of force was authorized by the elected representatives of the American people, as the Iraq War in fact was. In the radical perspective the electoral system is itself a fraud and cannot be a source of legitimacy for any actions, except of course those favored by the left. Formal political democracy merely masks the domination of a corporate ruling-class whose interests the state allegedly serves. It doesn't matter to the anti-American radical if America is the nation under attack, because America is the corporate ruler of the "global system," which radicals view as responsible for the conditions that create the terrorists and inspire their attacks. In other words, whatever the details and regardless of the facts, America is the root cause of the attacks on itself.

In the radical perspective, every aspect of human activity is shaped by the injustice of the prevailing global order. The radical's universe is thus Manichean, his political actions invariably a choice between an oppressive present and the progressive future. This is a religious conception rather than a political one. Radicals see themselves as the army of the saints and their opponents as the party of Satan, a fact that explains their passionate hatred for conservatives, who are the opponents of their faith.

Aileen Kraditor is the foremost scholar of the worldview of American Communists during the Stalin era. A New Left historian and former member of the Communist Party herself, she has written a classic study of "the mental world of rank and file American Communists."[15] An entire chapter of her book on the subject is devoted to "The Rationale of Hate," as the predominant emotion the Party attempted to instill in its members.[16] In *1984*, his futuristic novel about Communism, George Orwell came to the same conclusion and made the "Five-Minute Hate" program a daily ritual in his totalitarian state. One leader of the American Communist Party tasked with instilling these attitudes was its "chief theoretician," Herbert Aptheker, to whom Kraditor devotes several pages. In a text published in 1949, Aptheker described the global capitalist system as "so putrid ... that it no longer dares permit the people to live at all." In a review of Cleveland Amory's book on America's wealthy, he wrote: "[T]hese are the rules as depicted by a court-scribe. They [the members of America's ruling class] have the morals of goats, the learning of gorillas and the ethics of—well of what they are: racist, war-inciting, enemies of humanity, rotten to the core, parasitic, merciless—and doomed."[17]

Aptheker's rhetorical style was typical of Party functionaries and has been characteristic of the pronouncements of hardcore radicals ever since. In 1951, at the height of the Cold War, the Party's general secretary, William Z. Foster, expressed a view of the conflict which in sentiment and tone was not dissimilar to those voiced from antiwar platforms fifty years later: "It is nauseating to listen to the self-righteous big capitalists and their mouthpieces hypocritically blathering about their 'moral leadership of the world.' Goebbels ... was a novice compared with the war propagandists of the United States.... American imperialism, which is the organization of the most ruthless gang of fascist-minded capitalists on earth, is insolently pictured by its orators and penpushers as the champion of democracy, the defender of world peace, the moral guardian of mankind."[18]

Foster died before the Cold War ended; but Herbert Aptheker lived to see its conclusion, remaining an unrepentant Communist all

---

[15]Aileen Kraditor, *"Jimmy Higgins:" The Mental World of the American Rank-and-File Communist, 1930-1958*, 1988
[16]Kraditor, op. cit. pp. 60–61
[17]Herbert Aptheker, *History and Reality*, 1955, p. 112; cited in Kraditor, op.cit. p. 62
[18]Kraditor, op. cit. p. 62

his life. His ideological venom would only be of historical interest if it were not for the fact that the next generation of radicals—including the organizers of the antiwar movement—embraced him as an intellectual model. In the 1990s Aptheker was given appointments as a visiting professor at Bryn Mawr and at the University of California's Boalt Hall, one of the nation's most prestigious law schools. His writings have been praised by leading figures of the historical profession in its leading professional journals. Before his death in 2003, he was formally honored as a scholar by the Columbia University History Department through the auspices of his friend and admirer, Eric Foner.[19]

One can see the core elements of Aptheker's political perspective on display in the demonstrations against the war in Iraq—in their demonizing of the Bush administration as a terrorist regime and "the real axis of evil," and in their extreme slogans: "Bush is the Disease, Death is the Cure," "We Support Our Troops When They Shoot Their Officers." And in their speeches as well: "The president wants to talk about a terrorist named bin Laden," declaimed a keynote speaker at the Capitol antiwar demonstration. "I don't want to talk about bin Laden. I want to talk about a terrorist called George Washington. I want to talk about a terrorist called Rudy Giuliani. The real terrorists have always been the United Snakes of America."[20]

One could also see these elements present in the fact that the "antiwar" movement was created in the wake of 9/11, thereby defining itself as a movement to attack one's country when one's country is attacked.

---

[19]Also present were Communist professor Angela Davis and History Department member Manning Marable, who had been a member of the Committee on Correspondence, a faction of the American Communist Party led by Davis that had been expelled because of its opposition to the attempted *coup* against Mikhail Gorbachev in 1991.

[20]Horowitz, "America Under Siege," *FrontPage Magazine*, http://archive. frontpagemag.com/readArticle.aspx?ARTID=20218. The speaker was Malik Shabazz, a graduate of Howard University, a lawyer and the leader of the New Black Panthers.

3

The Transition

The collapse of the Communist system, which brought the Cold War to an end, was a watershed event in the life of the international left. The catastrophe of Communism included the creation of a totalitarian state, the reintroduction of slave labor on an epic scale, politically-induced famines, government-created poverty of unprecedented proportions, political purges and mass executions resulting in the deaths of an estimated 100 million individuals.[1] These were the direct results of a system, based on socialist theories, which provided no rational method for allocating resources, no effective incentives to work or create wealth, and no guarantees of individual rights.

The unique cause of the system's failure was the socialist idea, which had resulted in a continent-sized society that did not work.[2] A Czech writer, Joseph Skvorecky, asked: "Has there ever been a case in history of a political system collapsing overnight, not as an aftermath of a lost war or bloody revolution but from its own inner rottenness?"[3] The answer was that there had not. The Soviet system and its political empire were the products of a self-conscious effort to create a social order based on false intellectual doctrines. It was the artificial nature of the regime that explained the unprecedented circumstances of its fall.

---

[1]Stephanie Courtois and Mark Kramer, *The Black Book of Communism*, Harvard, 1999
[2]"The Road to Nowhere," in Horowitz, *The Politics of Bad Faith*, 1998; Martin Malia, *The Soviet Tragedy*, 1994
[3]Paul Hollander, *Discontents: Post-Modern and Post-Communist*, New Brunswick, p. 272

The Soviet catastrophe should have been a moment of reckoning for the progressive movements that had based their hopes on the socialist future, and had guided their actions by its theoretical perspectives. But the paramount fact overriding all others was that the catastrophe gave rise to no such reflections. Although their solution had failed, progressives continued to embrace the political culture that had produced it, and to guide their political ambitions by the same fallacious assumptions.

In America's universities now dominated by the political left, Stalinists like Antonio Gramsci, Gyorgy Lukacs, Walter Benjamin, Herbert Marcuse and Eric Hobsbawm became iconic names. The Cuban Stalinist Che Guevara was resurrected as a saint of the popular culture, along with the Rosenberg spies who were elegized as martyrs in the high culture—among whose expressions was a celebrated theatrical epic, *Angels in America*, which won the Pulitzer Prize. Its author, Tony Kushner, was not surprisingly a signer of the "Not In Our Name" petition against the war in Iraq, circulated by the Revolutionary Communist Party.

For seventy years, the international progressive left had supported the efforts of Soviet Marxists to create socialist states in Russia, China, Cuba and Vietnam. A significant exception was the "Second Socialist International," whose member organizations, particularly the British Labor Party and the German Social Democrats, played important roles in bringing down the Soviet regime. The head of the North Atlantic Treaty Organization (NATO), the principal anti-Soviet alliance, was in fact a Belgian socialist named Paul-Henri Spaak. But in the United States, anti-Communist socialists remained marginal factions of the political left, grouped around tiny political magazines like *Dissent*, having no effect on the direction of its mainstream.

After Khrushchev's denunciation of the crimes of Stalin in 1956, a "New Left" emerged in Europe and America. Hoping to escape the taint of the Stalinist past, these leftists rejected what they regarded as Communist deformations of the socialist dream, but not the Marxian theories that had led to them. In contrast to the socialists of the Second International, they refused to embrace a politics that was anti-Communist or to support the democratic West in its Cold War conflict. New Leftists proclaimed themselves "*anti*-anti-Communists" and continued their antagonism to the capitalist world. Their support for new Communist revolutions, along with their steadfast opposition to America's Cold War agendas, reflected their primary hostility to the democratic West and their continuing commitment to the fantasy that communism could be made to work.[4]

In the normal course of events, the collapse of the Communist states and the bankruptcy of their Marxist economies ought to have thrown the left into a profound crisis of faith. It should have caused radicals to re-think their Marxist critiques of democratic capitalism and their ideas about the revolutionary future. It should have caused them to re-evaluate their opposition to American policy and their support for regimes that had murdered tens of millions and oppressed hundreds of millions more. But such reassessments did not take place. Instead, in articles, manifestoes and academic texts, leftists the world over claimed that the Marxist economies they had supported and defended did not represent "real socialism" and were not what they had meant to defend.[5] The system that had dominated world events and their own political imaginations for nearly a century was dismissed as merely "actually existing socialism," therefore of no particular interest to them now that it was gone, and irrelevant to their political agendas.[6] Jutta

---

[4]Cf. Horowitz, "The Road to Nowhere," op. cit.

[5]Of course, after 1956 their defense of Communism was qualified. New Leftists generally referred to their "critical support" of the Soviet bloc to signal its qualified nature. Such support was summed up in a famous article of the Sixties by Andrew Kopkind called "Two Cheers for the Soviet Union."

[6]E.g., Daniel Singer, "1989: The End of Communism?" in George Katsiaficas, *After the Fall*, 2001, pp. 13, 15, 128, 130, 134, 144. Again the caveat must be made that not all leftists took this view, in particular those who had supported the anti-Communist Cold War effort of the United States and the Western powers.

Ditfurth, a member of Germany's Green Party, articulated the general leftist denial with admirable directness: "There simply is no need to re-examine the validity of socialism as a model. It was not socialism that was defeated in Eastern Europe and the Soviet Union because these systems were never socialist."[7]

In the absence of serious second thoughts, leftists continued to base their political agendas on the same Marxist premises that history had discredited. Even when they acknowledged the need for reappraisal, they avoided the reality of what actually had happened. After the Soviet regime fell, Samuel Bowles, a professor of economics at the University of Massachusetts Amherst, told *The Wall Street Journal* that "Marx wrote almost nothing about socialism and communism," from which he concluded that there was a need for "rethinking about socialist economies but little about capitalist economies."[8] But of course the entire edifice of Marxist theory and its critique of capitalism had been built on the premise that a socialist economy was a practical, viable alternative. This was the very presumption that the Soviet experience had discredited.

The socialist ideal provided Marxists with their standard for measuring every shortcoming and failure of capitalist societies and for explaining what was wrong with them. The falsification of Marxist theories of socialism could hardly be separated from the Marxist view of capitalism, since they were and are two sides of the same analytical coin. If Marx's economic theories do not work in a socialist economy, how can they be said to explain *any* economy? If socialism is not a viable system and capitalism is the only system that can produce wealth and freedom in a modern technological environment, what does this say about the revolutionary project itself? In the absence of a practical alternative to the

---

[7]Paul Hollander, *Discontents: Post-Modern and Post-Communist*, op. cit., p. 281; cf. two typical collections with the same name: Robin Blackburn, ed., *After the Fall*, Verso, 1991 and George Katsiaficas, *After the Fall*, Routledge, 2001.
[8]*The Wall Street Journal*, November 25, 1991

capitalist system, the revolutionary project is a nihilism—the will to destroy existing societies without an idea of what to do next.

The persistence of the revolutionary illusion without the revolutionary fact has given rise to what should properly be called a neo-communist movement—one that has learned nothing from the failures of Communism but has not abandoned the cause itself. Neo-communist radicals add new dimensions of oppression to the Marxist model, like racism and "sexism." But it is the same Marxist model that divides the world into oppressors and oppressed, identifies capitalism as the root cause of global problems, and regards the United States as the global system's guardian-in-chief. Consequently, like the Communist perspective it has replaced, the contemporary radical outlook opposes America's wars and opposes America's peace. All that really distinguishes this neo-communist perspective from its Communist predecessor is its ad-hoc attitude towards the revolutionary future, and the nihilistic agenda that follows.

As an expression of its nihilism, the contemporary left defines and organizes itself as a movement *against* rather than *for*. Its components may claim to be creating egalitarian futures in which racism, "sexism" and corporate dominance no longer exist and in which "social justice" prevails. But unlike Communists, the neo-coms are not committed to even a rudimentary blueprint as to what such an order might be. It is this lack of programmatic consensus that leads some leftists to deny that there even is a "left," and makes it possible for a fragmented coalition of neo-coms—including anarchists, eco-radicals, radical feminists, "queer" revolutionaries, Maoists, Stalinists, and vaguely defined "progressives"—to operate side by side in improbable coalitions like the antiwar movement. It is why they can do so in ways that benefit such anti-egalitarian allies and regimes as Islamic radicals and the Baathist, fascist state of Iraq.

Neo-Communists may or may not reject the Leninist idea of a vanguard party; they may depart from particular aspects of the Communist future like the "dictatorship of the proletariat" or the "central plan." But they are inspired by the same hostility to private property and the market economy, and to the corporate structures that produce society's wealth. It is this common enemy, capitalism, which unites them in the battles they join whether against the structures of "globalization" or the war on terror. The continuity between the generations of the Communist and neo-communist left is, in fact, seamless. It is the product of a leftist culture that openly embraces the intellectual forerunners, political traditions and anti-capitalist perspectives of the Communist past.

An illustrative example of this mentality is provided in the career of Eric Hobsbawm, who was a revered figure of the post-9/11 intellectual left. Hobsbawm joined the Communist Party in 1930 and remained a Communist until after the fall of the Berlin Wall, when he let his membership-card lapse out of pique because the Party didn't ask for his renewal.[9] An unrelenting apologist and devoted servant of the most oppressive and repulsive empire in human history, Hobsbawm is today one of the most honored professional historians among the leftwing faculties of universities in Europe and America.[10] Hobsbawm's last historical work, *The Age of Extremes*, is probably the most highly-praised effort to understand the 20th century and the events about which he was—and remains—so profoundly wrong. The final installment of Hobsbawm's four-volume study of industrial capitalism, hailed by one reviewer as "a *summa historiae* of the modern age," has been translated into 37 languages. This in itself is a testament to the vitality of the neo-communist outlook in the international culture of the left.[11]

The Age of Extremes appeared in 1995, four years after the fall of Communism, and is an elaborate defense of the twin illusions in

---

[9]According to Christopher Hitchens, a friend of Hobsbawm and of this writer to whom he told the story

[10]Author David Caute, for example, has called him "arguably our greatest living historian—not only Britain's, but the world's." Jacket blurb, *Interesting Times*, op. cit.

[11]A reference to Hobsbawm's four-volume history of industrial capitalism, from a review by Joseph Keppler, *Seattle Times*, April 16, 1995

whose name the left wreaked so much havoc during the 20th century: first, the inherent evil of capitalist democracies and second, the humanitarian promise of the socialist future. *The Age of Extremes* is in fact an elaborate and perverse defense of the very illusions that spawned the Communist nightmare.[12] Although the Communist cause left a greater trail of victims than any other in historical memory, Hobsbawm's attitude towards its enormities remains, revealingly, one of sadness and "nostalgia" rather than outrage and guilt. In an autobiography published in 2002, Hobsbawm told his readers: "To this day I notice myself treating the memory and tradition of the USSR with an indulgence and tenderness."[13]

These are his sentiments towards a regime that enslaved and slaughtered tens of millions, and reduced hundreds of millions to lives of unimaginable misery. Imagine a historian expressing the same sentiments towards the memory and tradition of Nazi Germany, which inflicted its damage over twelve years rather than 74, and over one continent instead of several. Such an intellectual would be treated as a moral pariah in the world of letters, and would hardly be accorded scholarly respect. Yet the opposite is true of Hobsbawm, whose tributes issue from the highest reaches of the academic culture, and whose denial and nostalgia are the widely-shared attitudes of the intellectual left.[14]

As a young man in Berlin in the 1930s, Hobsbawm joined the Communist Party and embraced a faith that has never left him. "The months in Berlin made me a lifelong Communist, or at least a man whose life would lose its nature and its significance without the political project to which he committed himself as a schoolboy,

[12]An analysis of the book is contained in Horowitz, *The Politics of Bad Faith*, 1998, pp. 17 et seq.
[13]Hobsbawm, *Interesting Times: A Twentieth Century Life*, New York, 2002, pp. 55–56
[14]Cf. John Earl Haynes and Harvey Klehr, *In Denial: Historians, Communism and Espionage*, San Francisco 2003, which analyzes the responses of American historians to the fall of Communism and the opening of the Soviet archives. Tony Kushner's *Perestroika* provides a cultural expression of the nostalgia progressives feel towards their failed and criminal past.

even though that project has demonstrably failed, and as I know now, was bound to fail. The dream of the October Revolution is still there somewhere inside me."[15]

Hobsbawm's reflection is striking, and provides crucial insight into the mindset of the left. Even though he now claims to "know" that the Communist project "was bound to fail," the dream of Communism lives on inside him. In other words, his belief in an alternate world to replace the one into which he has been born is not connected to any reality. It is an acknowledgment—albeit unintended—of the religious nature of radical belief.

Hobsbawm's other admission is also striking: that his life would "lose its nature and its significance" without the revolutionary project—the project of destroying the world he has been born into. While the destruction of the present social order is justified by the desire to create an alternative one, the practical reality of such an alternative is not an issue for Hobsbawm or for the millions of leftists like him, who proceed with the destruction without regard for what will follow. So strong is the psychological need for the utopian illusion and its project of destruction, it does not matter to Hobsbawm that the noble future to which he devoted his life and talent did not work and could not have worked, or that when put into practice it created monstrous injustice. After this history had run its course, and the corpses of its victims were piled high, Hobsbawm still refused to relinquish his revolutionary fantasy, remaining a dedicated enemy of the democracies that he and his comrades had set out to destroy. Even though the utopian future is an impossible dream, and has been the cause of immeasurable human unhappiness, it remains the center of his intellectual and political life.[16]

---

[15]*Interesting Times,* op. cit. Cf. also Geoffrey Wheatcroft's review of the autobiography in *The New York Times,* September 5, 2003, entitled "Still Saluting the Red Flag After the Flag Pole Fell."

[16]This is evident in his final work, *The Age of Extremes,* in his post-Communist articles (see following footnote) and in the interviews he has given in the last decade

This is an admission by Hobsbawm that for him, and radicals like him, the revolutionary project is less about creating the future than it is about their war against the present. *This* is what gives their lives meaning. Hobsbawm claims that he had doubts about the Soviet system all along. But his enmity towards the democracies of the West, which provided him with a privileged life, was far greater than those doubts. In 1991, the year that ended the Soviet nightmare, Hobsbawm wrote down his reflections. He called the article "After the Fall" and in it expressed not his relief or joy but his *concern* that the Soviet Union's oppressive empire was now a thing of the past. In his eyes, the Soviet Union, creator of tens of millions of innocent victims, was the lesser of two evils; and it was the greater evil that had emerged victorious. "Capitalism and the rich have, for the time being, stopped being scared. Why should the rich, especially in countries like ours where they now glory in injustice and inequality, bother about anyone except themselves? What political penalties do they need to fear if they allow welfare to erode and the protection of those who need it to atrophy? This is the chief effect of the disappearance of even a very bad socialist region from the globe."[17]

In other words, as far as Hobsbawm is concerned, the "chief effect" of the disappearance of a system that murdered 100 million people *in peacetime,* and imposed dictatorships and terror on a billion souls, is this: *The capitalist democracies of the West and the rich who rule them will no longer have this regime to check their predatory designs.* "The world may yet regret[!]," Hobsbawm observes elsewhere, "that faced with Rosa Luxemburg's alternative of socialism or barbarism, it decided against socialism."[18] In this view, capitalism—the system that supports the democracies of the West and has raised the living standards of hundreds of

---

[17]"After the Fall," in Robin Blackburn, ed., *After The Fall: The Failure of Communism and the Future of Socialism,* London 1991, pp. 122-3; *Interesting Times,* p. 280

[18]*Interesting Times,* pp. 280–281. Luxemburg famously said that mankind was faced with a choice between "socialism or barbarism."

millions of human beings to levels that only royalty enjoyed in the past—is *barbarism*, while the system that murdered millions and impoverished whole continents is *civilization*. This is also the conclusion of Hobsbawm's *summa historiae:* "We have reached a point of historic crisis.... If humanity is to have a recognizable future, it cannot be by prolonging the past or the present. If we try to build the third millennium on that basis we shall fail. And the price of failure, that is to say the alternative to a changed society, is darkness. In short, the choice before mankind is exactly what Rosa Luxemburg thought it was in 1917—socialism or capitalist barbarism."[19]

This is also the core belief of the neo-Communist left. Even after the catastrophes to which the quest for a Communist utopia led, they believe that the destruction of the democracies of the West is required for the sake of humanity and its survival.

An illuminating parallel to Hobsbawm's trajectory is found in the life and work of historian Gerda Lerner, a pioneer of radical feminism and a bridge between the New Left and the Old. Like Hobsbawm, Lerner began her political career as a Communist in Central Europe and emigrated to the United States in the late 1930s to escape Nazism. Unlike Hobsbawm, she withdrew from the Communist Party 20 years later, joining the New Left to become one of its intellectual leaders. As a professor of history at the University of Wisconsin, Lerner was a shaping influence on New-Left feminism, writing one of its canonical texts, *The Creation of Patriarchy*. In 2003, during the conflict in Iraq, she was one of the founding members of Historians Against the War.[20]

Lerner abandoned the Communist Party in 1956 following Khrushchev's revelations about the crimes of Stalin, which were revelations only to Communists who had long since closed their minds

---

[19]Eric Hobsbawm, *The Age of Extremes: A History of the World, 1914–1991*, Pantheon, 1995
[20]Greg Yardley, "Historians Against History," *FrontPage Magazine*, July 11, 2003; http://archive.frontpagemag.com/readArticle.aspx?ARTID= 17539

to the facts. But even Khrushchev's revelation of the crimes she had been complicit in—monstrous as they were—did not cause Lerner to rethink her commitment to the revolutionary cause. Instead, she continued her radical career as an "anti-anti-Communist," condemning the democracies of the West, opposing their Cold War against the Soviet Union and pursuing her revolutionary agendas as before. Lerner's arc is especially instructive because her career spans three radical generations and because, unlike Hobsbawm, she made the transition to each new revisionist version of the progressive cause without reservations.

More than 30 years after being apprised of Stalin's crimes and joining the "New Left," she experienced a second metaphysical lurch when the entire Communist enterprise collapsed. In 1991, the fall of the Soviet Union and the opening of the Soviet archives forced her to examine the lies that had governed her life for more than 50 years. In a memoir, published in 2002, she acknowledged: "Had I written this account twenty years ago, I would have focused on the rightness of my position and on explaining to the post-Vietnam generation that the Old Left has been unduly maligned and its achievements have been forgotten. That still seems partially true to me, but now everything has become far more complex and disturbing."[21]

As a historian, Lerner felt she could not simply shrug off the facts that had managed to penetrate her ideological Iron Curtain. "I have striven to lead a conscious, an examined life and to practice what I preach. It now appears that, nevertheless, I failed in many ways, for I fell uncritically for lies I should have been able to penetrate and perceive as such." But like others who went through the same crisis and did not give up their political faith, Lerner was ultimately unwilling to confront the lies she had lived by for so long. When it came to what she refers to as "disturbing" realities, her text becomes minimalist and fails to make any serious

---

[21]Gerda Lerner, *Fireweed, A Political Autobiography*, Philadelphia. 2002, p. 369

attempt to deal with them. The entire passage of her self-
examination occupies a mere four pages of the 373-page book she
calls her "political autobiography." This is a pretty accurate measure of how willing she is to allow these facts to confront and possibly reshape her views of the world.

Lerner manages to concede one lie in particular that she promoted in her service to the progressive cause. This was her acceptance of the Nazi-Soviet Pact, a traumatic event for activists who
had prior to the pact regarded themselves in the front line of the
struggle against Nazism. It should have been especially difficult
for a Jew to swallow this lie, but when the Kremlin signed a "non-
aggression" agreement with Hitler, Gerda Lerner adapted to the
new political reality overnight. She and her comrades rationalized
the Soviet alliance with Hitler as a pact against Western imperialism, and formed an antiwar left inside the Western democracies to
oppose the "militarist" policies of allied nations like Britain and
the United States, which were attempting to resist the Axis
powers.[22]

In Lerner's account of her about-face, none of the ironies of her
current opposition to an Anglo-American coalition fighting a fascist dictatorship in Iraq enters her consciousness. Instead she
focuses exclusively on the past, recalling her studied disregard for
the evidence available at the time, which showed that Stalin
actively colluded with Hitler in dividing up Poland. These facts
were easily accessible in the pages of The New York Times and 50
years later in the history of those events recorded in Harrison Sal-
isbury's book on the siege of Leningrad, which she admits she read
but did not believe. It was only when the Soviet archive itself was
opened, and she was presented with official Soviet documentation
of the collusion, that she was finally able to acknowledge the
truth. Even though she had left the Communist Party in 1956, she

---

[22]Technically, of course, the United States was neutral. But American
sympathies clearly lay with Hitler's victims, while the aim of the Communist peace movement was to keep America neutral. See Harvey
Klehr, The Heyday of American Communism, op. cit.

had to wait another 35 years for an imprimatur from the defunct Soviet regime to accept the facts. In other words she was still a Communist, and the Communist Vatican, now defunct, was still for her the final arbiter of the truth.

As with Hobsbawm, the progressive faith is for Lerner a creed that she identifies with the very core of her being. "Like all true believers, I believed as I did because I needed to believe: in a utopian vision of the future, in the possibility of human perfectibility ... *And I still need that belief, even if the particular vision I had embraced has turned to ashes.*"[23] (emphasis added) After a lifetime of lies, her psychological need for a utopian solution is so great, so fundamental to her identity, that her political choices remain the same: hostility to the capitalist democracies of the West and faith in the fantasy of a socialist future. It is the same illusion that led to her commitment to Communism in the first place. She clings to it in the face of the monstrous crimes her activities and devotions made possible, and the total bankruptcy of the societies and regimes she believed in. Her anti-Communist opponents were right all along about the commitments she made and the world she believed in; but Gerda Lerner remains their determined and passionate enemy. In regard to the conflict in Iraq, it does not matter to her that Saddam Hussein did not even pretend to advance the cause of "social justice" as Stalin did. It just matters that his antagonist was America, an incarnation of the Great Satan.

Her politics are still based on the hope that the next socialist revolution will turn out differently from all the ones that failed. Even though she can't identify or describe the utopia of her dreams, she is still convinced that a "socially just" system is

---

[23]Lerner, op. cit., p. 370. In her catalogue of utopian ideas, Lerner includes "idealism and heroism." But this is just typical radical bad faith. The idea of human perfectibility—of a society embracing the ideals of social justice—is integrally connected to the Communist catastrophe. But in what way does a belief in the possibility of individual heroes and/or noble aspirations lead to Marxist *gulags*? They don't. Nor are they concepts specific to Marxism and Communism.

waiting to replace the capitalist democracies she is determined to destroy. Since her belief in the Soviet Union and in the socialist-bloc states was never grounded in reality, there can be little difference between the beliefs that inspire her activities in the present and those that inspired her Stalinist agendas in the past, or her New Left causes. At the end of a long political life, Gerda Lerner is still pledging her allegiance to an irrational creed.

The utopian longing for an alternate reality that is "truly human" is the religious wellspring of the neo-communist left, just as it was of the Communist left that preceded it.[24] And it is this vision of perfection that inspires contempt and hatred for the real world that lacks it. Asked by an interviewer whether she saw any parallels between the Nazism she experienced in her youth and the America that provided her refuge and freedom, she is as ready to make the comparison as when she was a follower of Stalin: "I see many very frightening signs. I see us creating a deviant 'out-group' once again. For example, the treatment of the Afghan prisoners, whom we are taking halfway across the world without a trial, without investigation. We are removing them from their homeland, we are putting them in open cages, like animals. It's horrible. And I think the only reason for doing it is that the government wishes to create this terror group as the new scapegoat for everything that's wrong with society. It is very dangerous. I also see the automatic, knee-jerk 'patriotism,' in quotation marks, in response to the terrorist attacks, and the immediate demand for conformity, so that anyone who questions whether bombing Afghanistan was the proper response will be treated as a traitor. That's familiar ground, I've been there before."[25]

---

[24]For example, Leo Pannitch and Sam Ginden, "Transcending Pessimism: Rekindling Socialist Imagination" in George Kastiaficas, ed., *After the Fall: 1989 and the Future of Freedom*, 2001, p. 179: "The socialist 'utopian' goal is built around our potential to be full human beings."

[25]Interview with Joan Fischer, *Wisconsin Academy Review*, Spring 2002 Vol. 48, No. 2; http://digicoll.library.wisc.edu/cgi-bin/WI/WI-idx?type= div&did=WI.v48i2.i0005&isize=text

What has this historian learned from the perverse realization of her Communist dreams and their self-implosion? By her own account, virtually nothing. "I have called myself a post-Marxist," she writes, pointedly avoiding the term *ex*-Marxist. "I came to that stance as soon as I became a feminist. Ever since the late 1950s I believed that the so-called errors of Communist leadership in the Soviet Union were structural and built into the very fabric of Marxist doctrine." This might seem like the prelude to a jettisoning of her false beliefs. But when Lerner explains her revision, it is evident that no such rationality is in the offing. "Basically, I came to the conclusion that Marxist thought was in error in regard to race and ethnicity in its insistence that class subsumed these categories. As for gender, Marxist thought, while giving lip service to the 'woman question' ... reduced patriarchal dominance to economic dominance."[26] This is the extent of her second thoughts: the failure of Marxism, of Communism, consists of a gap in its indictment of capitalism.

In other words, Marxism failed to provide a proper map to the socialist future not because it was based on false economic assumptions or utopian delusions about human possibilities, or on a failure to understand the link between liberty and property; but because Marxist theory gave inadequate attention to race and gender oppression. How this accounts for the human catastrophe of Soviet Communism she doesn't attempt to explain. It doesn't even occur to her that an explanation might be in order. There is no lack of thoughtful analysis available on the question of why the socialist idea turned out so badly; but Professor Lerner seems entirely ignorant of this literature and wholly uninterested in the issue itself.[27] Her mind is as firmly shut as when she was a Stalinist (and no "post-Communist" progressive intellectual in the world of academic feminism appears to have entertained such questions

[26]Op. cit., p. 371
[27]E.g., Martin Malia, *The Soviet Tragedy*, 1995 and Leszek Kolakowski, *Main Currents in Marxism: The Breakdown*, Vol. III, Oxford, 1981

either). Her observations about gender and race are all she has to offer about the failure of a system to which she dedicated 50 years of her own life, and which destroyed hundreds of millions of others.

In sum, far from instilling humility in progressives like Gerda Lerner, the collapse of socialism has served to revive their self-righteousness and re-energize their assault on the democratic West. The collapse of the Soviet system has had only one consequence of note for them. It has lifted the burden of having to defend—however critically—an indefensible regime that is now defunct. Because their utopian vision is no longer anchored in the reality of an actually-existing socialist state, the left has been freed to indulge its nihilistic agendas and destructive impulses without constraint.

4

The New Left

Gerda Lerner was in her thirties when the New Left launched itself in the wake of Khrushchev's speech about Stalin's crimes. She was young enough to join the new political generation as one of its mentors. Her easy assimilation to the New Left, and its reciprocal embrace of her as a political authority, reflected the strong bonds that linked the new movement to the Communist past. Its official charter, the 1962 "Port Huron" statement, was written in language that eschewed the traditional Bolshevik style of such manifestos and was self-consciously "American." Its authors employed the words "participatory democracy" to define their goal, which replaced the Communist term "Soviet power," a concept identical in meaning.[1] It was all designed to create an indigenous radicalism that would avoid the foreign loyalties that had discredited their predecessors.

Yet, by the end of the decade, the "new" left had become indistinguishable from the old, was a reliable ally of international Communism, and employed a political vocabulary virtually indistinguishable from that of the Communist states.[2] It opposed

---

[1]On the new terminology as an attempt to speak American, see James Miller, *Democracy Is in the Streets*, 1988. On the similarity in the meaning of the concepts, see Horowitz, "Port Huron and the War on Terror," Glazov, ed. *Left Illusions: An Intellectual Odyssey*, Dallas, 2003. This article is included in the present volume (part III, chapter 5, below).
[2]See Oglesby's speech "Name the System," Miller, *Democracy Is in the Streets*, op. cit., and Horowitz, "Hand-Me-Down-Marxism," in *Left Illusions*, op. cit.

the anti-Communist Cold War and regurgitated Marxist "critiques" of American society. Like its Communist predecessors, it viewed America as the imperial guardian of a global system of exploitation that plundered the poor. It sent "*Venceremos* brigades" to Cuba under the watchful eye of Cuban intelligence to shore up the Castro dictatorship; it parroted the propaganda of Communist North Vietnam and gave "critical support" (its term of choice) to the Soviet bloc which, like Hobsbawm, it regarded as a check on the predatory ambitions of the United States.

These attitudes continued through the next decades as the left focused its energies on "solidarity" organizations to aid Communist movements and regimes in Central America, and on domestic "peace movements" to disarm the West in the face of the continuing Soviet threat to Western Europe. This devolution of the left can be traced in the career of one of its pioneers who more than 40 years later co-authored a UCLA faculty resolution denouncing America's "invasion" of Iraq.

In 1960, Maurice Zeitlin was a Marxist graduate student at Berkeley and a founding editor of *Root and Branch*, one of three journals that helped to launch the new radical movement.[3] With fellow-editor Robert Scheer, who later became a columnist at the *Los Angeles Times* and a prominent opponent of the war in Iraq, Zeitlin visited Cuba in 1960, the second year of the Communist revolution. The two wrote one of the first books hailing the triumph of the Castro regime.[4]

On his trip to Cuba, Zeitlin conducted an interview for *Root and Branch* with Che Guevara, the minister of industries and number-two man in the Communist regime.[5] In the interview, Zeitlin challenged Guevara's attitudes towards unions as a litmus

---

[3]I was also an editor of *Root and Branch.* The other journals were *Studies on the Left* and *New University Thought.*

[4]Robert Scheer and Maurice Zeitlin, *Cuba: Tragedy in Our Hemisphere,* 1961. (I helped edit this book.) Scheer is also a lecturer at the Annenberg School of Communications at USC.

[5]*Cuba: Tragedy in Our Hemisphere,* 1961

of the intentions of the revolutionary state. As a New Leftist, Zeitlin was concerned that the socialist movement not repeat the "mistakes" of the Stalinist past. He questioned Guevara about the control of unions by the state, and asked him about the role they should play in a socialist society. Should they be appendages of the revolutionary state as Lenin and then Stalin had made them in Soviet Russia? In asking the question, Zeitlin reminded Guevara that the elimination of independent unions had paved the way for the Soviet police-state and its infamous *gulags*. Guevara did not answer. The question angered him. He would not criticize the Soviet Union or even discuss its policies, and abruptly changed the subject. Zeitlin had put Guevara to the test and the Cuban leader had failed. Guevara's reaction showed that he was a Stalinist.

Zeitlin and the other *Root and Branch* editors understood exactly the significance of what Guevara had said, and its implications as well. The intention of Cuba's revolutionary leaders was to make Cuba a totalitarian state. Zeitlin and the editors of *Root and Branch* were New Leftists committed to breaking with the Stalinist past. But they continued to support Cuba's Communist regime. Despite Guevara's clear commitment to a totalitarian state, we rationalized our support by telling ourselves that it was America's opposition to the Cuban revolution that was forcing the Castro regime to pursue a totalitarian course, even though the interview had taken place before the Bay of Pigs and before the regime had declared itself a socialist state.

This incident is typical and even emblematic of New Left politics, which applied a double standard to Western democracies and the Soviet bloc: unrelenting criticism of the former, a wide berth for the latter. When "revolutionary" regimes came into conflict with the United States, the New Left's political allegiances were always clear, its attitudes were invariably defensive of the Communist side. At the end of the Sixties, Zeitlin wrote a critique of the Castro government's repressive practices for the New Left magazine, *Ramparts*. But like his progressive comrades and despite his criticisms, he continued to support the Castro dictatorship and defend it against his own country's efforts to promote freedom in Cuba. When the Communist empire collapsed in 1989, Zeitlin remained committed to the utopian cause and to the anti-American agendas that resulted from this commitment. Communist Cuba survived the collapse. More than 40 years after the revolution, its *caudillo* was the longest-surviving dictator in the world; its economy had slid from being the second-richest in Latin America in per-capita income to a place as the second-poorest, slightly above Haiti and below Honduras and Belize.[6]

In these years Zeitlin had become a professor of sociology at UCLA, specializing in Chile and writing about its "dominant classes." In 1997, he spoke at a UCLA symposium on 20th-century utopias, where he returned to the subject of Che Guevara. Thirty years earlier, Guevara had resigned his position in the Cuban dictatorship to take up arms as a revolutionary in Bolivia, where he was killed. His purpose in instigating the guerilla campaign, as he announced in a famous 1967 declaration, was to incite an international civil war, creating "two, three, . . . many Vietnams." Despite the catastrophes of Soviet and Cuban socialism, Zeitlin used the occasion of the UCLA seminar to declare his continuing faith in the Communist cause for which Guevara had died. "Che [Guevara] was above all a revolutionary socialist and a leader of the first socialist revolution in this hemisphere," Zeitlin told his college audience. "His legacy is embodied in the fact that the Cuban revolution is alive today despite the collapse of the Soviet bloc. . . . No social justice is possible without a vision like Che's."[7]

More than 40 years after his confrontation with Che Guevara over the totalitarian future of the Cuban revolution, Zeitlin was celebrating Guevara as a hero of "social justice" and a prophet of

---

[6]CIA World Fact Book, http://photius.com/wfb1999/rankings/gdp_per_capita_o.html

[7]Argiris Malapanis, UCLA Symposium, "LA Symposium Debates Che and the Cuban Revolution," *The Militant*, November 24, 1997. *The Militant* is an organ of the pro-Castro Socialist Workers Party (SWP).

the utopian future. In other words, despite the bankruptcy and collapse of the Communist bloc, despite the failure of every Marxist program and regime that Guevara had supported, despite the mass murders, Zeitlin remained—like Eric Hobsbawm, Gerda Lerner and an entire generation of New Left radicals—a small-'c' communist: a fantasist of the socialist future and a determined enemy of the democratic West. And while praising the Communist future, Zeitlin was simultaneously leading the attack on America's "invasion of Iraq"—blind to the fact that, even as he did so, Iraqis were dancing in the streets of Baghdad, pulling down statues of the former dictator and cheering the American troops that had come to liberate them.

Zeitlin's return to his Communist roots is instructive precisely because he was once an intelligent dissenter from that past, and thus an authentic member of what had started out to be a "new" left. There were plenty of other leftists who were never embarrassed by that past and who continued its agendas as Communists proper, Maoists and members of various Trotskyist sects.[8] They were even referred to as "MLMs" or Marxist-Leninist movements within the left. It was a prominent member of these Communist sects named Leslie Cagan who emerged as the primary leader of what *The New York Times* and other left-leaning media described as the "moderate" peace coalition against the war in Iraq.[9] According to the *Times* article on the coalition, a group of leftwing activists, meeting under the auspices of People for the American Way, selected Cagan to head "United for Peace and Justice" and organize the mass demonstrations against the war. According to its leftwing organizers, United for Peace and Justice was created as a public-relations effort to deflect criticism of the existing antiwar movement, which was a coalition run by the self-styled Bolsheviks of International ANSWER, who were aligned with Communist

---

[8]An appropriate term for these groups might be "paleo-communists."
[9]Chris Hedges, "A Longtime Antiwar Activist, Escalating the Peace," *The New York Times*, February 4, 2003

North Korea and had organized all of the national protests up to that point.[10]

Leslie Cagan was a Sixties radical who entered the Communist movement in college, breaking American laws to travel to the Communist World Youth Festival in Bulgaria in 1968. The following year she joined the first *Venceremos* brigade, a project of Cuban intelligence, which recruited American leftists to help with the sugar-cane harvest. Cagan was a leader in other institutions of the left including the Pacifica radio network; she was an organizer of demonstrations for the Soviet-inspired nuclear-freeze movement and for solidarity with Communists in Central America in the 1980s. She was also a protester against the 1991 Gulf War that had prevented Saddam Hussein from annexing Kuwait. For seven years, Cagan was the director of the Cuba Information Project, which promoted the Communist dictatorship and worked closely with its official agencies. In 1997, she coordinated the U.S. delegation to the World Youth Festival in Cuba, once again in defiance of U.S. law.[11] Then, in 2001, she was chosen to lead the mainstream left opposition to the War in Iraq—the "moderate coalition" in the revealing words of *The New York Times*.

Cagan's view of America was as permanently dark as that of Hobsbawm and Lerner, with whom she shared a direct political lineage. In 1998, the sixth year of the administration of Democrat Bill Clinton, Cagan wrote: "I cannot recall a period in my lifetime as bad as this. The accelerated concentration of wealth and power in everything from the mass media to manufacturing to health-care and banking; the ever-widening gap between the world's poor and wealthy; the global environment crisis; xenophobia, racial and religious violence; an epidemic of violence against women,

---

[10]Kate Zernike and Dean E. Murphy, "Antiwar Effort Emphasizes Civility Over Confrontation," *The New York Times*, March 29, 2003; Michelle Goldberg, "Peace Goes Mainstream," Salon.com, January 20, 2003
[11]Leslie Cagan, "It Should Be Possible, It Has to Be Possible," June 1998, http://www.zmag.org/zmag/articles/caganjune98.htm; communication from Ronald Radosh who was familiar with Cagan in the 1960s

children and sexual minorities; the influence and power of religious fundamentalism in all its variations."[12]

Cagan was not being exactly candid when she identified "religious fundamentalism in all its variations" as one of her nightmare fears. Islamic fanatics were not on her radar-screen. When religious fundamentalism took an anti-American turn, she and her comrades were quite prepared to form alliances with forces they otherwise professed to abhor. For Cagan and her comrades, it was anti-Americanism that defined the party line. This was the core of their revolutionary agenda, taking precedence over all other issues and values. It is what allowed them to make a *de facto* alliance with a regime as oppressive, misogynistic and bloodstained as the regime in Iraq. The Iraq dictatorship was a fascist regime that had murdered 300,000 Iraqis; but this fact did not prevent leftists from marching to defend it against their own country, which was a liberal democracy with a vibrant Bill of Rights.

---

[12]Cagan, op. cit.

5

The Utopian Idea

The worldview of the radical left is shaped by a Manichean dualism that unites its disparate factions and shapes a common agenda. At the heart of this worldview is the belief in a utopian future that is just, and the rejection of a dystopian present that is oppressive and evil. Todd Gitlin, a former president of Students for a Democratic Society and a historian of the Sixties, was one of the speakers at the Columbia teach-in against the war in Iraq.[1] Like his New Left comrades, Gitlin was a self-declared "anti-anti Communist," choosing not to support the West in its Cold War against the Communist police states. After the 9/11 attack, however, Gitlin draped an American flag from his New York apartment window, and felt a tinge of patriotism for the first time in his political life—and suffered the opprobrium of his comrades for his transgression. In an essay entitled "Varieties of Patriotism," Gitlin examined his feelings about this episode and attempted to explain it.[2]

During the Cold War, he wrote, he had not identified with the Soviet Union, but he did expect the utopian idea to be realized in Vietnam or Cuba or some other revolutionary state. His alienation from his own country and rejection of patriotic feeling came not from a positive identification with America's enemies but from a revulsion inspired by the Vietnam War. According to Gitlin,

[1] Todd Gitlin, *The Sixties: Years of Hope, Days of Rage,* 1987
[2] From an article entitled, "Varieties of Patriotism," included in *The Fight Is for Democracy: Winning the War of Ideas in America and the World,* edited by George Packer, Harper Perennial, 2003

49

Vietnam was something like an American original sin. "The war went on so long and so destructively, it felt like more than the consequence of a wrong-headed policy. My country must have been revealing some fundamental core of wrongness by going on, and on, with an indefensible war."[3] Because of this "fundamental core of wrongness," Gitlin recalls, "the American flag did not feel like my flag, even though I could recognize—in the abstract—that it made sense for others to wave it in the antiwar cause." Gitlin "argued against waving the North Vietnamese flag or burning the Stars and Stripes"—or at least he did at first.[4] "But the hatred of a bad war, in what was evidently a pattern of bad wars—though none so bad as Vietnam—turned us inside out. It inflamed our hearts. You can hate your country in such a way that the hatred becomes fundamental. A hatred so clear and intense came to feel like a cleansing flame. By the late '60s, this is what became of much of the New Left."

Gitlin summarizes the anti-American feelings of his generation of radicals in these words: "For a large bloc of Americans, my age and younger, too young to remember World War II—the generation for whom 'the war' meant Vietnam and possibly always would, to the end of our days—the case against patriotism was not an abstraction. There was a powerful experience underlying it: as powerful an eruption of our feelings as the experience of patriotism is supposed to be for patriots. Indeed, it could be said that in the course of our political history we experienced a very odd turn about: The most powerful public emotion in our lives was *rejecting* patriotism."[5]

Gitlin's reflections are rare among leftists for their introspection and frankness. But they remain disingenuous in the end. The

---

[3]Ibid., p. 119
[4]This is a revealing slip. The Vietnamese flags present in the antiwar demonstrations were Vietcong flags—the flags of the Communist-controlled South Vietnamese National Liberation Front—not North Vietnamese flags. There would not have been North Vietnamese flags since the left maintained (falsely) that the Vietnamese liberation struggle was a struggle for self-determination by the South Vietnamese.
[5]*The Fight Is for Democracy*, op. cit.

rejection of patriotism, the identification with the Communist enemy, and the hatred of one's country were not reactions to a "bad" war in Vietnam (and what other bad wars could Gitlin be referring to—the Cold War?). These were staple attitudes of the left long before the Vietnam War began. It was not an action by the United States in Vietnam or anywhere else that inspired this hostility and alienation; it was the utopian idea.

Unlike Leslie Cagan, Gitlin was brought up in a liberal household and while still impressionably young was drawn into the radicalism of the 1960s. The shapers of this movement, its intellectual leaders and leading institutions, were already anti-American and had rejected patriotism long before Todd Gitlin came of age. During the early Cold War years, they had supported Stalin and then Mao and finally Fidel and Ho, whom they defended by employing the usual double standards of the left. The Vietnamese Communists, for example, were to them "national patriots" and bearers of "rice-roots democracy" to a people "oppressed" by American imperialism.

There was, in fact, nothing inherent in the Vietnam War that should have caused any American to turn against his country. Every year that has passed since the war's end has brought new testimonies to this fact. The most eloquent of these come from disillusioned leaders of the victorious side who have testified that the National Liberation Front of South Vietnam was not an indigenous vanguard but a creation of Hanoi; that far more North Vietnamese soldiers were involved early in the conflict than even Washington had claimed; that Communist North Vietnam had conducted a conquest rather than a liberation of the South, imposing a regime that was ruthless, reactionary and oppressive.[6] Far from being an "indefensible war" as Gitlin describes it, America's intervention in Vietnam was driven by honorable objectives.

---

[6]Bui Tin, *From Enemy To Friend: A North Vietnamese Perspective On The War*, Annapolis, 2002; Truong Nhu Tang, *A Viet Cong Memoir*, New York, 1985. Truong was Minister of Justice for the NLF. Col. Bui Tin was one of the architects of the Ho Chi Minh Trail, the path of the *(cont.)*

America's failure to win the war, a failure Gitlin and the left worked hard to bring about, was a national tragedy for the *Vietnamese.*

Colonel Bui Tin was a leader of the Communists' conquest, an architect of the "Ho Chi Minh Trail" through which they accomplished their invasion of the South. In 1995 he wrote: "Nowadays the aspiration of the vast majority of the Vietnamese people, both at home and abroad, is to see an early end to the politically conservative, despotic and authoritarian regime in Hanoi so that we can truly have a democratic government of the people, by the people, for the people."[7]

In understanding the mind of the anti-American left, it is interesting to note how, once the United States was defeated in the war, the Vietnamese—whom leftists had claimed to love with all the passion they denied their own countrymen—disappeared from their consciousness and also from their consciences. When America withdrew from Indochina, tens of thousands of innocent South Vietnamese and millions of Cambodians were murdered by the Communists. The Communist victors reduced the nations they had conquered to impoverished *gulags.* But these sufferings of the people of Cambodia and Vietnam evoked no outrage or cries of compassion from activists who had once made them the center of their political concerns. The defining difference was that their oppressors now were Communists. Today, the aspirations of the Vietnamese themselves are as invisible to these radicals as are the testimonies of the Iraqis freshly liberated from the prisons and torture-chambers of the Saddam regime.

Gitlin's fixation on Vietnam as the symbol of an American essence—an evil essence—is unrelated to any factual reality. It is merely an inverted expression of the utopian idea. Vietnam was a metaphor that served to justify the already-formed radical world-

---

(cont.) Communists' conquest of the South. He was a leader of the Hanoi regime and a personal friend of Ho Chi Minh. Truong Nhu Tang was a founder of the National Liberation Front.

[7]Bui Tin, *Following Ho Chi Minh,* 1995, p. 192

view he had adopted.[8] It did not create it. Gitlin is also less than candid in attributing his own anti-patriotic feelings to America's role in the Vietnam War. According to his account, these feelings lasted for more than 30 years until 9/11. By the same account, his patriotic fervor—if it can be called that—was quite short-lived. A "few weeks" after 9/11 he took down his American flag, because "leaving the flag up was too easy, too easily misunderstood as a triumphalist cliché. It didn't express my patriotic sentiment, which was turning toward political opposition.... "[9] Patriotism by this tormented logic is expressed in opposing one's country rather than supporting it. It is exactly the logic embraced by Paul Robeson, and Eric Foner and Albert Lannon.

Gitlin's opposition hardened as President Bush declared war on America's al-Qaeda attackers and identified three states—Iran, North Korea and Iraq—as an "axis of evil." In Gitlin's words, "By the time George W. Bush declared war without end against an 'axis of evil' that no other nation on earth was willing to recognize as such—indeed, against whomever the President might determine we were at war against, ... and declared further the unproblematic virtue of pre-emptive attacks, and made it clear that the United States regarded itself as a one-nation tribunal of 'regime change,' I felt again the old estrangement, the old shame and anger at being attached to a nation—*my* nation—ruled by runaway bullies, indifferent to principle, their lives manifesting supreme loyalty to private (though government slathered) interests, quick to lecture dissenters about the merits of patriotism."[10]

Ignoring the particular (and particularly hysterical) claims in this indictment, one might ask in what way could these particular faults be ascribed not to "wrong-headed policies" but to "some fundamental core of wrongness" in America's Constitution? Put

---

[8]Peter Collier and David Horowitz, "A Decade Overrated and Unmourned," in Collier and Horowitz, *Deconstructing the Left*, Los Angeles, 1995, p. 9. See Volume I, Part II in this series.
[9]Gitlin, op. cit., p. 133
[10]Gitlin, op. cit., p. 134

another way, why does the fact of Gitlin's turn "toward political opposition" preclude a continued display of the flag—which is to say, an embrace of his nation—particularly when that nation is a democracy that protects opposition and embraces dissent? It seems that Gitlin learned very little from his brief identification with his country at war. It is certainly possible to love one's country and identify with it even when one judges an individual policy or a series of policies or an entire political administration to be wrong. That is what a democracy is about. The war against terror or the war in Iraq could easily be criticized on many grounds that would be recognized as patriotic and should not result in alienation from one's flag, or cause one to experience "shame and anger at being attached to a nation."

Perhaps the Iraq war was the wrong war fought at the wrong time. Perhaps the policies pursued were counterproductive and, far from strengthening national security, incurred more risks. Since the policies in question—the decision to go to war and to pursue regime-change—were ratified by both political parties, they were not the whims of "runaway bullies" and could be changed by pursuing a different electoral result. But Gitlin's rejection goes much deeper, and can only have been inspired by hostile assumptions about America itself, *in its fundamental core.*

This is precisely the case. In describing his hatred for America as a Sixties radical, Gitlin recalls encounters he had with Communists in Cuba. "Those of us who met with Vietnamese and Cuban Communists in those years were always being told that we had to learn to love our people. In my case, it was a Communist medical student in Cuba who delivered the message in 1967. Love our people! How were we supposed to do that, another SDSer and I argued back, when our people had committed genocide against the Indians, when the national history was enmeshed in slavery, when this experience of historical original sin ran deeper than any class solidarity, when it was what it meant to *be* an American."[11] (emphasis in original)

---

[11]Todd Gitlin, *The Intellectuals and the Flag,* Columbia University, 2006, p. 133

This litany—typical for American radicals—is an expression of Gitlin's core antipathy for his country rather than a reasonable accounting of observable facts. It is based on a utopian standard with no anchor in any existing historical reality. There was no such genocide (in any meaningful sense of the word) against American Indians, many of whom fought on the side of the settlers in the frontier wars and more of whom are alive today than were alive when the first Europeans set foot on the continent. Moreover, these "exterminated" people now live on vast areas of land, which were set up for them and are financially supported by the United States government, which also affords them full citizenship rights. Somewhat different from *genocide*.

One might feel that the provision made for these people is insufficient, or regret the past that led to such results, but to regard America as a genocidal nation because of them is irrational bigotry. There is no nation on earth that was not created through some original aggression. Why should America, which has been more generous than other nations to those it conquered, be singled out for total condemnation? The same question can be asked in regard to Gitlin's rhetorical flourish about the institution of slavery. Historically, America was a more important force in ending slavery than it was in participating in an institution that was embraced by all European, Latin American and Islamic states, and by Africans themselves. The historical record refutes Gitlin's claim that these injustices are somehow the American essence; or that they make this country less worthy than, say, Gitlin's favored Cuba, which in fact imported more African slaves than all of England's North American colonies or the United States.[12]

Gitlin summarizes the case against patriotic attachment to America in these terms: "Worst of all, from this point of view,

---

[12]A response to the general radical indictment of America is to be found in Dinesh D'Souza, *What's So Great About America?* (Washington, 2002). America accounted for less than one per cent of the world slave trade in Africans. For data on American slavery, see Horowitz, *Uncivil Wars: The Controversy Over Slavery*, San Francisco, 2001, p. 111.

patriotism means obscuring the whole grisly truth of America under a polyurethane mask. It means covering over the Indians in their mass graves.[13] It means covering over slavery. It means over-looking America's many imperial adventures—the Philippine, Cuban and Nicaraguan occupations, among others, as well as abuses of power by corporations, international banks, and so on. It means disguising American privilege, even when America's good fortune was not directly purchased at the cost of the bad fortune of others, a debatable point. So from this point of view, patriotism betrays the truth."

One could hardly ask for a more acid expression of the utopian view and the irrational hatred it inspires. Is there an actually exist-ing nation that has had *no* war of conquest in its past, embarked on no imperial adventures, experienced no abuse committed by its private institutions, enjoyed no privileged status of one kind or another, or received no good fortune at some other people's expense? There is no such country. On what grounds, therefore, would this litany persuade one to renounce his native land, partic-ularly a land as generous and free as America? Insofar as these claims are justified, they reflect human problems, not specifically American ones. Gitlin's rejection of America can be explained only by the illusions of a worldview based on an imaginary future that has no anchor in any past or present human reality, and whose complaints, therefore, can never be assuaged or redressed. Gitlin's leftist critique and the political alienation it promotes are identical in nature to the critiques of his Communist predecessors. The term "progressive" aptly describes their common utopianism, which is the striving towards an unattainable future whose sole practical effect is to provide a measure by which they can con-demn the present.

---

[13]What graves is he talking about? There were indeed isolated massacres of Indians, just as there were isolated massacres by Indians. But "mass graves" representing actual genocides? This is a charge more readily put to the Aztecs than to the European settlers in North America.

6

The Nihilist Left

Noam Chomsky is a cult figure among contemporary radicals and their leading intellectual, celebrated throughout the leftwing culture. A *New Yorker* profile identified him improbably as "one of the greatest minds of the twentieth century," while the leftwing English *Guardian* has referred to him as the "conscience of a nation."[1] No individual has done more to shape the anti-American passions of a generation. When Chomsky speaks on university campuses, which he does frequently, he draws ten times the audiences that other academics do. Abroad he has attracted individual audiences as large as 10,000. According to the academic indexes that establish such rankings, Chomsky is one of the ten most quoted sources in the humanities, ranking just behind Plato and Freud. His most recent tract on the events of 9/11 sold 200,000 copies in America alone, despite the fact that it is not really a book but a series of rambling interviews. Of the hundred or so "books" on current-affairs subjects he has published, all but a handful amount to collections of table talk, a further indication of the cult-like nature of his influence and of the general cultural decline.

Chomsky claims to be an anarchist, which frees him from the burden of having to defend any real-world implementation of his ideas. In fact he does not take his "anarchist" ideas very seriously,

---

[1]Larissa MacFarquhar, "The Devil's Accountant," *The New Yorker*, March 31, 2003; *Guardian* quote cited in Keith Windschuttle, "The Hypocrisy of Noam Chomsky," *The New Criterion*, May 2, 2003

either as a program or as intellectual doctrine. His comments on the subject, in a political career spanning nearly half a century, amount to mere fragments—an article here, an isolated passage there. Moreover, his commitment to anarchist principles, which would presumably entail the rejection of all forms of social hierarchy and coercion, is highly selective. He is more than willing to support "centralized state power" when it is mobilized against private businesses, and he defends Marxist dictatorships in Nicaragua, Cuba, Vietnam and other Third World countries—like Iraq—when they are engaged in conflicts with the United States.[2] Even considered strictly as ideas, Chomsky's anarchist thoughts, if they can be dignified as such, are at base authoritarian and therefore incoherent.[3] The utility of Chomsky's anarchism is to provide an impossibly perfect model of freedom by which to judge the democracies of Western societies as "fascistic" and "oppressive."

The destructive antipathy of radicals like Chomsky towards the existing social order in the West is a nihilism manifest even in Chomsky's prose style. "To read Chomsky's recent political writing at any length is to feel almost physically damaged," observed journalist Larissa MacFarqhuar in a *New Yorker* profile. "The effect is difficult to convey in a quotation because it is cumulative. The writing is a catalogue of crimes committed by America, terrible crimes, and many of them; but it is not they that produce the sensation of blows: it is Chomsky's rage as he describes them. His sentences slice and gash, envenomed by a vicious sarcasm.... He uses certain words over and over, atrocity, murder, genocide, massacre, murder, massacre, genocide, atrocity, atrocity, massacre, murder, genocide.... Chomsky's sarcasm is the scowl of a fallen world, the sneer of Hell's veteran to its appalled *naifs*."[4] It is in fact a form of literary fascism, bludgeoning the reader into acceptance.

---

[2]Noam Chomsky, *Class Warfare*, 1966, pp. 122–3

[3]Barry Loberfeld, "The Coercive Anarchism of Noam Chomsky," *Front-Page Magazine*, January 31, 2003; http://archive.frontpagemag.com/readArticle.aspx?ARTID=20016. Loberfeld is a libertarian.

[4]Op. cit., p. 73

MacFarqhuar's *New Yorker* profile made its appearance in May 2003, barely two weeks after the successful liberation of Baghdad. It began with a characteristic Chomsky observation, reflecting a worldview that is not interested in criticizing particular American policies but in condemning America's essence:

> When I look at the arguments for this war, I don't see anything I could even laugh at. You don't undertake violence on the grounds that maybe by some miracle something good will come out of it. Yes, sometimes violence does lead to good things. The Japanese bombing of Pearl Harbor led to many very good things.[5]

These comments are noteworthy both for their calculated malice, and their misrepresentation of historical events. The interview was conducted before the war had started. The Saddam regime was toppled in three weeks, perhaps the swiftest and most bloodless such victory on record. Obviously, the military planners of "Operation Iraqi Liberation" did not count on a "miracle" to achieve a positive result—the removal of the dictator, and the closing of his torture chambers—but had reasonable expectations that their objective was practical and worthwhile. (The failures in Iraq were those of the political planners.) The very absurdity of Chomsky's claim reveals the irrational nature of his attack.

The second half of Chomsky's statement is, if possible, even more perverse. There are innumerable cases Chomsky might have offered as examples of justifiable violence. The sneak attack on Pearl Harbor is not one of them. Even the Japanese concede that. Pearl Harbor, as Chomsky is well aware, has been invoked as a historical precedent for 9/11. By using the parallel, Chomsky intends to reverse the meaning of both events. Like 9/11, Pearl Harbor is an event symbolizing America's shattered innocence and its resolve to fight back. Praising Japan's act of infamy is Chomsky's way of denying the innocence and assaulting America's right to

---

[5]Op. cit., p. 64

defend itself. In reversing the meaning of both events, Chomsky is expressing the loathing he feels for his own country.

Chomsky's view of Pearl Harbor parallels Osama bin Laden's rationale for 9/11. Bin Laden claimed that the attack was a response to America's "invasion" of the holy lands of Islam. Chomsky explains how Pearl Harbor led to good things: "If you follow the trail, [Pearl Harbor] led to kicking Europeans out of Asia—that saved tens of millions of lives in India alone. Do we celebrate that every year?"[6]

In point of historical fact, Pearl Harbor led to the expulsion of the Japanese empire from Asia, where its brutal rule had left behind a trail of atrocities in China, Korea, Malaya and elsewhere. But acknowledging these realities would undermine Chomsky's case. His reference to tens of millions of Indian lives saved by independence, which had nothing to do with Pearl Harbor or its effects, is another Chomsky fiction standing history on its head. One of the recognized achievements of British rule in India was to establish internal peace in place of intercommunal violence that had existed previously and has recurred since. Whatever else may be said of British rule, it *saved* Indian lives that would otherwise have been lost to this indigenous violence, a fact epitomized in the communal slaughter that broke out at the precise moment the British departed. A million Indians were killed in the civil strife that erupted between Hindus and Muslims on the eve of independence, leading to the partition of the country and the creation of a Muslim state in Pakistan.

It is difficult to know if Chomsky believes his own fabrications. In the same *New Yorker* profile, he indicates—without acknowledging any irony or contradiction—that kicking Europeans out of Asia in his view actually led to very bad results. In a comment condemning the Bush family for inviting foreign dictators to Washington, Chomsky names several leaders of postwar

---

[6]*The Anti Chomsky Reader,* edited by Peter Collier and David Horowitz, Encounter, 2004

Asia he despises: "[A gangster] they loved was [Indonesia's] General Suharto. Another they adored was Marcos of the Philippines. In every single one of these cases, the people now in Washington supported them right through their worst atrocities. Are these the people you would ask to bring freedom to Iraqis?"[7] These gangsters, who were elected leaders, were the *products* of independence. Marcos was subsequently ousted by the United States, and Deputy Secretary of Defense Paul Wolfowitz, one of the planners of Operation Iraqi Freedom, was one of the architects of the new democracy in the Philippines that followed Marcos's exit.

Chomsky's twisted history reflects the core belief of anti-American radicals that the United States can do no right. Assailing the victim of Pearl Harbor is only a small part of Chomsky's distorted account of World War II. To complete a credible picture of American perfidy, he must also deny the United States its role in the allied victory over Nazi Germany. The *New Yorker* profile reports the following Chomsky comment to a college audience: "The United States and Britain fought the war, of course, but not primarily against Nazi Germany. The war against Nazi Germany was fought by the Russians. The German military forces were overwhelmingly on the Eastern Front."[8]

To say that larger German military forces were committed on the Eastern front of World War II is correct, but to say that "the war against Nazi Germany was fought by the Russians," as though they fought it alone, is absurd. Without massive support from the United States, it is doubtful that Russia would have survived. The fact that the United States defeated Germany's axis partners Italy and Japan, and that Britain vanquished Hitler's African legions, was hardly incidental to the allied victory. Chomsky's ignorance of the Normandy invasion, the defeat of Hitler's European armies, and the liberation of three-quarters of the German homeland by American arms displays a mind committed to hate.

---

[7]*The Devil's Accountant*, Larissa MacFarquhar, *The New Yorker*, March 31, 2003
[8]Ibid.

Disturbed by the perverse implications of this argument, a student in his college audience offered an objection to his comments: "But the world was better off" because of America's intervention. Even this concession Chomsky was unwilling to make. He responded to the student by blaming the allies for Hitler's victims. "First of all, you have to ask yourself whether the best way of getting rid of Hitler was to kill tens of millions of Russians. Maybe a better way was not supporting him in the first place, as Britain and the United States did." In fact, Britain and the United States didn't support Hitler. But Russia did. American isolationism and British appeasement in the 1930s may have been helpful to the Germans by underestimating their aggressive ambitions; but it was not the same as the direct support provided by the Russians through the Stalin-Hitler Pact, which actually launched the war in Poland.

Chomsky was not content with the insinuation that Britain and America were Hitler's sponsors and allies. He had to make them responsible for the Holocaust as well. "By Stalingrad in 1942, the Russians had turned back the German offensive, and it was pretty clear that Germany wasn't going to win the war. Well, we've learned from the Russian archives that Britain and the U.S. then began supporting armies established by Hitler to hold back the Russian advance. Tens of thousands of Russian troops were killed. Suppose you're sitting in Auschwitz. Do you want the Russian troops to be held back?"

There is no evidence to support this accusation. Some academics puzzled by the bizarre nature of Chomsky's claim have suggested that he was alluding to Bandera's Ukrainian nationalists, who had every reason to detest *both* Hitler and Stalin.[9] But there is

---

[9]See H-Diplo March 2003 logs. Confronted by John Williamson with the untenability of his statements, Chomsky claimed that he had never made them and that the *New Yorker* reporter, Larissa MacFarquhar, had merely made them up. In fact, the entire event, including the exchange cited by MacFarquhar, was videotaped by C-Span, and the tape showed that Chomsky was lying. John Williamson, "Chomsky, Linguistics and Me," in Peter Collier and David Horowitz, eds., *The Anti-Chomsky Reader*, Encounter Books, 2004

no evidence to support Chomsky's contention of allied support for Bandera or any anti-Soviet military forces until 1948, which was during the Cold War and three years after the liberation of Auschwitz.[10] Even the historical premise of Chomsky's claims is a falsification. However important Stalingrad was as a military victory, it was hardly equivalent to winning the war, and no one but Chomsky thinks it was—not even the Russians, who begged the allies to open a "second front" to save them from defeat.

These are not simple intellectual lapses but keys to a worldview that is shaped by one overriding imperative—to demonize America as the fount of global evil. This agenda entails a revision of history as ambitious as that of Holocaust deniers, with whom Chomsky has had an unsavory relationship.[11] Their purpose is not to understand the history in question but to refashion it so as to portray America as a satanic monster.

Chomsky's influence can be detected in the prevalence of this theme among protesters against America's actions after 9/11 and during the conflict in Iraq. For Chomsky, the 9/11 attacks represented a turning point in the war against American imperialism. "For the first time, the guns have been directed the other way. That is a dramatic change."[12] It was the first time the "national territory" had been attacked since the War of 1812. In Chomsky's summation, in the intervening years "the US annihilated the indigenous population (millions of people), conquered half of Mexico, intervened violently in the surrounding region, conquered Hawaii and the Philippines (killing hundreds of thousands of Filipinos), and in the past half century, particularly, extended its

---

[10]In fact, the evidence is that there was *no* contact before 1948.

[11]Werner Cohn, "Chomsky and the Holocaust Deniers," in Collier and Horowitz, eds., *The Anti-Chomsky Reader*, op. cit.

[12]Alexander Cockburn and Jeffrey St. Clair, "Interviewing Chomsky," September 18, 2001; http://www.counterpunch.org/2001/09/18/interviewing-chomsky/; Christopher Hitchens, "Of Sin, the Left and Islamic Fascism," *The Nation*, October 8, 2001; http://www.thenation.com/article/sin-left-islamic-fascism

resort to force throughout much of the world. The number of victims is colossal."[13]

Anyone accepting Chomsky's words at face value could almost feel the justice of al-Qaeda's malignant death-squad that struck thousands of innocents in the World Trade Center. The premise of Chomsky's texts is that whatever evil is committed against America by others pales in comparison to the evil that America has committed against them. In Chomsky's telling, America is the "Great Satan," the power responsible for all the oppressions and injustices of the modern world. Nor does he shrink from contemplating the practical imperatives that flow from such a view. In Chomsky's post-9/11 talk he declared: "The people of the Third World need our sympathetic understanding and, much more than that, they need our help. We can provide them with a margin of survival by internal disruption in the United States. Whether they can succeed against the kind of brutality we impose on them depends in large part on what happens here."[14]

Chomsky revealed just how seriously he meant his incitement to treason when America finally launched its military response to the 9/11 attacks. On October 18, eleven days after U.S. forces began strikes against the Taliban, Chomsky told an audience at MIT that America was the "greatest terrorist state" and was planning a "silent genocide" against the people of Afghanistan. Chomsky made this malicious charge in an almost casual manner to emphasize its horror: "Looks like what's happening [in Afghanistan] is some sort of silent genocide," is what he said.[15] His

---

[13]Alexander Cockburn and Jeffrey St. Clair, op. cit. Pearl Harbor doesn't count in Chomsky's calculus of attacks on the national territory because Hawaii was a "colony" at the time. The fact that it was a benignly-run colony and is now a proud state of the Union counts for nothing, it seems, in Chomsky's view.
[14]Noam Chomsky, *What Uncle Sam Really Wants*, Odonian Press, 1992, p. 100
[15]Noam Chomsky, *The New War Against Terror*, October 18, 2001, http://www.chomsky.info/talks/20011018.htm

speech at MIT to 2,000 listeners was viewed and heard by millions via satellite, the Internet, and C-Span TV.

According to Chomsky, not only was America planning a genocide in Afghanistan, but America's cultural elite knew it, and were unconcerned. They were unconcerned because they were racists and the targets were Third World peoples. "It also gives a good deal of insight into the elite culture, the culture we are part of. It indicates that whatever, what will happen we don't know, but plans are being made and programs implemented on the assumption that they may lead to the death of several million people in the next few months very casually with no comment, no particular thought about it, that's just kind of normal, here and in a good part of Europe."

As usual, Chomsky's defamation was based on an inversion of the facts, and a readiness to make the most far-fetched assumptions about the malignity of American motives. It was true that in Afghanistan the food situation was dire, and that *prior to America's intervention* a famine was predicted for millions. But thanks to the determination and generosity of the American government, help was already on the way. Through massive food transports conducted by the American military, the famine was soon averted. The plans for this rescue mission had been publicly announced *before* Chomsky delivered his address. The reason there was no comment—press or otherwise—on the planned genocide was not because of the immoral indifference of Americans and Europeans, as Chomsky suggested, but because the crisis was about to be solved and there was no basis whatsoever for Chomsky's allegation. As Laura Rozen reported in the online leftwing magazine *Salon.com* on November 17, 2001: "Aid experts say that . . . alarms about the impact of the U.S. military campaign against the Taliban have ignored the fact that more food has been reaching Afghanistan since the U.S. bombing began than was before—a lot more."[16]

---

[16]Cited in David Horowitz and Ronald Radosh, "Noam Chomsky's *Jihad Against America*," in Collier and Horowitz, *The Anti-Chomsky Reader,* op. cit. The relief agencies' alarm was not unrelated to the leftwing politics of the relief community and the charges of Chomsky himself.

Given the military uncertainties when the fighting was just getting underway, and the distrust sown about America's intentions by people like Chomsky, the myth of the "silent genocide" could still seem plausible to the uninformed. This was as true in Cambridge, where he made his false charges, as it was a month later in countries bordering Afghanistan, where he went to spread them to much larger Muslim audiences.[17] In this campaign of lies against his own country, Chomsky traveled to New Delhi and Islamabad, where he made front-page news with claims that the United States was the world's "greatest terrorist state" and was planning to conduct one of the largest genocides in history on a neighboring Muslim population.

In Islamabad the situation was particularly volatile. Pakistan was an unstable nation armed with nuclear weapons and ruled by a military dictatorship whose security forces had set up the Taliban. While the international press worried about the problematic future of the Islamabad regime, and tens of thousands of pro-terrorist demonstrators filled the streets of the capital, the prestigious MIT professor made the front pages of the local press with attacks on his own country, calling it a genocidal threat to Muslims. It was Chomsky's personal effort to "turn the guns around."

---

[17]http://www.frontlineonnet.com/fl1825/18250190.htm

7

The Anti-American Cult

Noam Chomsky's demonic views and seditious actions would be of little interest—intellectual or otherwise— but for the fact that they have such a wide following.[1] Critics of the Chomsky phenomenon often fail to appreciate that this is not so much the cult of an individual—Chomsky is a remarkably boring speaker and middling writer—but of an anti-American cult among progressives to whose primitive hatreds Chomsky speaks. Chomsky did not spring into being *de novo*. He is the product of a leftwing culture that had already traveled far down the path of fanaticism and was imbued with the conviction that a nation conceived in liberty and dedicated to the proposition that all men are created equal is really a Great Satan—an empire built on slavery, oppression and imperial conquest.

The scope of this cult is indicated by the proliferation of lesser Chomskys who feed the hunger of movement activists for anti-American litanies and rationales. Most prominent among these is Chomsky's intellectual twin, the popular historian Howard Zinn, a lifelong expounder of Communist myths and adherent of Communist causes. Like Chomsky, Zinn has produced a corpus of

---

[1]An impressive array of leftwing media-outlets provides platforms for Chomsky's views. In addition to bibliographical Internet sites devoted to his work, they include *The Nation, The Progressive, The Boston Review of Books*, Zmag.org, indymedia.org, counterpunch.org, commondreams.org, antiwar.com, the Pacifica Radio network and PBS, to name a few. Chomsky's influence is discussed in Richard Posner, *Public Intellectuals: A Study of Decline*, 2003.

work that is a cartoon version of the nation's past, pillorying America as an evil predator. Zinn has even published a Chomsky-like tract of table talk about 9/11, blaming America and its alleged crimes for the terrorist attack and characterizing the victim as a terrorist state.[2]

Like Chomsky, Zinn is a rambling, unimpressive speaker and a pedestrian writer who has attained an intellectual celebrity few can match. His signature book, *A People's History of the United States,* is a raggedly conceived Marxist caricature that begins with Columbus and ends with George Bush. It has sold over a million hardback copies, greatly exceeding that of any comparable history text. Like Chomsky's rants, Zinn's book has been incorporated into the academic curriculum of universities and secondary schools. *The New York Times Sunday Book Review* gave it this imprimatur: "Historians may well view it as a step toward a coherent new version of American history." The reviewer was Eric Foner.

As with Chomsky, Zinn's readership extends far into the popular culture as well. He was invoked as a "genius" by the lead character in the Academy Award-winning film *Good Will Hunting* (the film's co-writer and star Matt Damon grew up as a Zinn neighbor and is a Zinn enthusiast). Both he and Chomsky have been heavily promoted to youthful rock audiences by mega-bands such as Rage Against the Machine and Pearl Jam, even while they are also icons of intellectual journals like *The Boston Review of Books,* which is edited by Joshua Cohen, an MIT professor and Chomsky disciple.[3]

The express methodology of *A People's History of the United States* is political rather than academic. In an afterword, Zinn explains to the reader that he has no interest in striving for objectivity

---

[2] Howard Zinn, *Terrorism and War,* Seven Stories Press, 2002. Like Chomsky's *9-11,* which sold 200,000 copies and was translated into many languages, Zinn's tract is a slender one-volume interview about these themes.

[3] Professor Joshua Cohen, shared this information with the author in a private communication.

because his intention is to expose American history as a conspiracy of rich white men to oppress and exploit "the people"[4]—meaning Indians and other minorities, especially blacks ("there is not a country in world history in which racism has been more important, for so long a time, as the United States"), women and the industrial proletariat.[5] Zinn launches his narrative not with the settling of North America or the creation of the United States, as one might expect, but with a lengthy chapter on Columbus's "genocide" against the native inhabitants, an event which—even if it had happened as Zinn describes it—was committed by agents of the Spanish empire more than a century before the English settled North America and nearly three centuries before the creation of the United States. It is an emblem of the tendentiousness of Zinn's entire project, which is really not a *history* of the American people but an indictment of white people and American capitalism.

The perspective that shapes the nearly seven hundred pages of *A People's History* is a plodding Marxism informed by the preposterous idea that nation-states are a fiction and that economic classes are the only real social actors. "Class interest has always been obscured behind an all-encompassing veil called 'the national interest.' My own war experience [World War II], and the history of all those military interventions in which the United States was engaged, made me skeptical when I heard people in high political office invoke 'the national interest' or 'national security' to justify their policies. It was with such justifications that Truman initiated a 'police action' in Korea that killed several million people,

---

[4]Zinn, *A People's History*, Harper Perennial, p. 646: "Objectivity is impossible, and it is also undesirable. That is, if it were possible it would be undesirable, because if you have any kind of a social aim, if you think history should serve society in some way; should serve the progress of the human race; should serve justice in some way, then it requires that you make your selection on the basis of what you think will advance causes of humanity." Cited in Dan Flynn, "Master of Deceit," a review of Zinn's book, *FrontPage Magazine*, June 3, 2003; http://archive.frontpagemag.com/readArticle.aspx?ARTID=17914
[5]Ibid., p. 23

that Johnson and Nixon carried out a war in Indochina in which perhaps three million died, that Reagan invaded Grenada, Bush attacked Panama and then Iraq, and Clinton bombed Iraq again and again."[6]

Zinn's summary of events illustrates the continuity of leftwing myths in shaping the consciousness of radical generations. A Stalinist in his youth, Zinn retains into his seventies the same ideological outlook. America's defense of South Korea was not an aggressive act by the United States, as the Communist propaganda machine maintained at the time. It was a response to a Communist aggression initiated by Stalin himself.[7] The war and subsequent American support for the South Koreans resulted in their liberation from both poverty and dictatorship. South Korea was in 1950 one of the poorest countries, with a per-capita income of $250, on a level with Cuba and South Vietnam. Fifty years of American protection, trade and investment have made South Korea a First World industrial nation with a reasonably stable democracy. By contrast, North Korea, which was the industrial heart of the Korean peninsula and which the American armies failed to liberate—thanks to Zinn's political allies at the time—is an impoverished totalitarian state that has starved more than a million of its inhabitants in the last decade, while its Communist dictator hordes use their scarce funds to build an arsenal of nuclear intercontinental ballistic missiles. The rest of Zinn's examples consist of equally vacuous communist propaganda points.

Not surprisingly, Zinn describes the founding of the American Republic—the world's most successful democratic experiment—as an exercise in the tyrannical control of the many by the few for greed and profit. "The American Revolution ... was a work of

---

[6]Ibid., pp. 658–9
[7]"Scattered Soviet materials have shown that Soviet involvement in preparing and planning an invasion after Stalin gave his reluctant endorsement in January 1950 was higher than previous writers had thought"—Bruce Cumings, *Korea's Place in the Sun*, 1998, p. 263. As it happens, Cumings is a leftwing historian.

genius, and the Founding Fathers deserve the awed tribute they have received over the centuries. They created the most effective system of national control devised in modern times, and showed future generations of leaders the advantages of combining paternalism with command."[8] In Zinn's account, the Declaration of Independence was not so much a revolutionary statement of rights as a cynical means of manipulating popular groups into overthrowing colonial rule for the benefit of the rich. The rights it appeared to guarantee were "limited to life, liberty and happiness for white males"—and actually for wealthy white males—because they excluded black slaves and "ignored the existing inequalities in property."[9] This is an absurd (and absurdly unhistorical) view of the Declaration and the Republic to which it gave birth; but it is the entrenched belief of the political left for whom Zinn is an icon and his tract canonical.

The attack on the American Founding is crucial to the outlook shared by Zinn, Chomsky and their followers. It is central to understanding the left's animus against America, and the fact that no particular event—least of all a foreign-policy event like the war in Iraq—is required to generate the kind of hatred on display during the "antiwar" protests. There is nothing original in Zinn's book, nor has he engaged in any serious research other than to dot the i's and cross the t's of Communist clichés. *A People's History of the United States* reflects a leftwing culture that despises its native land.

As a result of the left's colonization of the academic social sciences, this anti-American culture is now part of the educational curriculum of America's emerging elites, and as much an element of the cultural mainstream as any other historical tradition. In 2004, the Organization of American Historians devoted an evening at its annual convention to honor Zinn and his work. Todd Gitlin, a former president of SDS and now professor of Sociology and

---

[8]Zinn, op. cit. p. 59
[9]Ibid., p. 73

Journalism at Columbia University, summed up the academic triumph of the left in these words: "My generation of the New Left—a generation that grew as the [Vietnam] war went on—relinquished any title to patriotism without much sense of loss.... The nation congealed into an empire, whose logic was unwarranted power. All that was left to the Left was to unearth righteous traditions and cultivate them in universities. The much-mocked 'political correctness' of the next academic generations was a consolation prize. We lost—we squandered—the politics, but won the textbooks."[10]

Entire fields—"Whiteness Studies," "Cultural Studies," "Women's Studies," "African-American Studies," "American Studies" and "Peace Studies," to mention a few—are now principally devoted to this radical assault on American culture and society and to the "deconstruction" of the American idea. The study and teaching of American Communism at the university level is now principally in the hands of academics who, in the words of two political scientists who are experts in the field, "openly applaud and apologize for one of the bloodiest ideologies of human history."[11] Even the study of the law has been subverted by political ideologues with ferociously anti-American agendas. Consider the following passage from a legal text on the Fourteenth Amendment—the statute which establishes equal rights for all Americans—written by a professor at Georgetown, one of the nation's most prestigious schools of law: "The political history of the United States that culminated and is reflected in the [Constitution] is in large measure a history of almost unthinkable brutality toward slaves, genocidal hatred of Native Americans, racist devaluation of nonwhites and nonwhite cultures, sexist devaluation of women and a less than admirable attitude of submissiveness to

---

[10]"Varieties of Patriotic Experience," op. cit., p. 120
[11]John Earl Haynes and Harvey Klehr, *In Denial: Historians, Communism and Espionage*, Encounter Books, 2003, p. 1

the authority of unworthy leaders in all spheres of government and public life."[12]

These ignorant and repellent views are replicated in whole libraries of texts written by the academic left. They present an American reality shaped by the intellectual traditions of Communism and characterized by the crude economic determinism and historical distortions of writers like Chomsky and Zinn. It is hardly surprising, given the orthodoxies of American universities, that hundreds and perhaps even thousands of faculty-led anti-American demonstrations, justifying the attacks of 9/11 and denouncing America as "imperialist" and "racist," were held on campuses during the wars in Afghanistan and Iraq. From this point of view, observes Gitlin, "the attacks of September 11, 2001 revealed a symmetry that the hard-bitten Left had long expected. America was condemned by its history. The furies were avenging, chickens were flying home, American detonations were blowing back." The left had "little hardheaded curiosity to comprehend a fanatical Islamist sect that set no limits to what and whom it would destroy. Whoever was killed in America, Americans must still end up the greatest of Satans."[13]

Despite the fact that as a self-described "democratic socialist" Gitlin dissents from the most extreme views articulated by Chomsky, Zinn and others, he nonetheless shares their disturbingly negative perspective on America's history and world role. "Read history with open eyes and it is hard to overlook the American empire.... You need not subscribe to the Left's grandest claims that America from its birth is essentially genocidal and indebted to slavery for much of its prosperity to acknowledge that white colonists took the land, traded in slaves, and profited immensely thereby; or that the United States later lorded it over Latin America (and other occasional properties, like the Philippines) to

---

[12]Robin West, *Progressive Constitutionalism: Reconstructing the Fourteenth Amendment*, Durham 1994, pp. 17–18
[13]Gitlin, op. cit. p. 122

guarantee cheap resources and otherwise line American pockets; or that American-led corporations (among others) and financial agencies today systematically overlook or, worse, damage the freedom of others."[14]

This selective memory obscures the reverse side of the ledger; it fundamentally distorts the impact of America's development and the meaning of its history. America was a pioneer in ending slavery (which was a drag on the nation's economy rather than the source of its prosperity as Gitlin maintains) and has liberated hundreds of millions of people from totalitarian tyrannies. Its national narrative encompasses expanding spheres of tolerance and inclusion. Its war against terror is being led by a Secretary of State and national security advisor who are African-American, and by a military force in Iraq under the command of an Arab-American and a Hispanic-American. Its policies in Iraq ended one of the most brutal tyrannies on record. Its corporate institutions have led the world in technological innovation; its economic order has lifted billions out of poverty, liberating them from unbearable social conditions. If the glass is half empty, it is also half full.

The negative animus of the left was on display in a post-mortem analysis of the Iraq War by the celebrated author Norman Mailer, which appeared in *The New York Review of Books*, the paper of record for the intellectual class. Mailer began his political life as a prominent literary figure in the Communist-orchestrated Progressive Party campaign of Henry Wallace in 1948. The political focus of the campaign was opposition to the "Truman Doctrine," America's early Cold War effort to resist Stalin's conquest of Eastern Europe. The Wallace "peace candidacy" was, in fact, a prototype of all the postwar "peace" campaigns against America's efforts to resist totalitarian aggression. Twenty years later, Mailer was a leading literary figure in the anti-Vietnam War movement of the 1960s, writing a highly praised book, *The Armies of the Night*, which celebrated the famous "March on the Pentagon." *The New*

---

[14]Ibid., p. 120

York Review of Books is a magazine of the literate, somewhat moderate left. Its editors stopped publishing the writings of Chomsky in the 1970s, when he veered too far over the political edge by dismissing early reports of the Communist genocide in Cambodia and defending a Holocaust-denier in France.[15] Yet the *New York Review* editors were perfectly comfortable with Mailer's article, which was acidly titled, "The White Man Unburdened;"[16] as though America's war in Iraq—whose leadership included two African-Americans, an Arab-American and a Hispanic-American, and which immediately turned over authority to an Iraqi government—was nonetheless an expression of racial imperialism.

In its accusatory title, as in its bill of specifics, Mailer's article was actually indistinguishable from the less artful screeds of Chomsky and Zinn. It illustrated the metaphysical dimension of the anti-American worldview, which enables its adherents to accumulate disinformation with every new event in order to construct demonic images of America's practices and purposes. The fact that on 9/11 America was the victim of an unprovoked attack by religious fanatics is no more discouraging to the anti-American hysteria of these critics than is the fact that, in April 2003, American forces liberated Iraq from one of the bloodiest tyrannies of the modern world. That is because their anti-American attitudes are built on three irreducible assumptions, each of which was exemplified by Mailer's article in *The New York Review of Books:* first, America can do no right; second, even the right America appears to do is wrong; third, the wrongs are monstrous.

Approaching the question of Iraq, Mailer asks, "Why did we go to war?" He begins by addressing facts that might seem to justify the war, like the discovery of the mass graves of Saddam's victims. The uncovering of these graves, writes Mailer, appears to show that "we have relieved the world of a monster who killed untold

---

[15]Stephen Morris, "Whitewashing the Cataclysm," in Collier and Horowitz, eds., *The Anti-Chomsky Reader*, op. cit.
[16]Norman Mailer, "The White Man Unburdened," *The New York Review of Books*, July 17, 2003; http://www.nybooks.com/articles/16470

numbers, mega-numbers of victims." But such appearances are wrong, according to Mailer, because it is America that is responsible for those murders. "Nowhere is any emphasis put upon the fact that many of the bodies were of the Shiites of southern Iraq who have been decimated repeatedly in the last twelve years for daring to rebel against Saddam in the immediate aftermath of the Gulf War [of 1991]. Of course, we were the ones who encouraged them to revolt in the first place, and then failed to help them."[17] Having shifted the blame for Saddam's slaughter to America, Mailer explains why Washington failed to help Iraq's Shiites in a way that compounds American culpability. A successful Shiite rebellion, he writes, "could result in a host of Iraqi imams who might make common cause with the Iranian ayatollahs. Shiites joining with Shiites!" Racists and imperialists, of course, would want none of that.

This is a warped view of why America might have feared an alliance between Shiites in Iraq and Iran. The Iranian revolution of 1979 spawned a revival of radical Islam and began with the seizure of the American Embassy by Iranian revolutionaries a million strong, chanting "Death to America." To support its hatred of America and the imperial ambitions of radical Islam, the Iranian regime developed long-range missiles and planned to tip them with nuclear warheads. It created Hizbollah, the largest terrorist army in the world, which in 1983 blew up a U.S. marine barracks in Lebanon, killing 245 servicemen, and whose leaders promised death to the American Satan. If the Iraqi Shiites had overthrown the regime of Saddam Hussein in 1991 and forged a radical alliance with Iran, this would certainly have posed a threat to America—one that had nothing to do with Mailer's racial paranoia.

There was another consideration behind America's decision not to overthrow Saddam in 1991. The first Bush administration did not want to proceed without U.N. authorization or without authorization from its Arab coalition partners, who were unanimously

---

[17]Ibid.

opposed to toppling Saddam. It may be argued that the first Bush should have ignored these considerations and proceeded unilaterally, but not by a progressive like Norman Mailer who opposed the Gulf War on exactly those grounds—that it was America's war and no one else's. Mailer also represses any memory of the opposition by the Democratic majority in Congress to the Gulf War, and thus to any regime-change in Iraq. Although Bush formed the Gulf War coalition in faultless multilateral fashion, his war policy was still opposed by the Democrats and he was barely able to secure the congressional authorization required to reverse Iraq's conquest of Kuwait. Although he assembled an international coalition of 40 nations, only ten Democratic senators finally voted to authorize the use of force—even for the limited goal of liberating Kuwait. Moreover, three of those senators, Al Gore among them, did so reluctantly and at the last minute. In other words, Norman Mailer and the political left he represents were opposed to the very war that he now complains did not go far enough and lead to the removal of Saddam.

What is Mailer's own accountability—or the accountability of those who share his politics—for positions that led to Saddam's massacre of the Iraqi Shiites? He concedes none. The consequences of his past oppositions to American interventions don't even occur to him. This is because his intent is not to understand the war but to make America responsible for Saddam Hussein's killing-fields. "Today [the Shiites] ... may look upon the graves that we congratulate ourselves for having liberated as sepulchral voices calling out from their tombs—asking us to take a share of the blame. Which of course we will not." In other words, in addition to being mass murderers, we are hypocrites. "Yes, our guilt for a great part of those bodies remains a large subtext and Saddam was creating mass graves all through the 1970s and 1980s. He killed Communists *en masse* in the 1970s, which didn't bother us a bit."[18]

---

[18]Ibid.

This Mailer accusation is not only tendentious but downright puzzling. What other nation, it could be asked, would be held accountable for not rescuing its own enemies? Of course, for progressives like Mailer, Communists are not enemies. The events Mailer is referring to were a series of power-struggles between fascists and Communists who *both* wanted Americans dead and America destroyed. What was Mailer suggesting with his accusations? That America should have intervened in a Soviet sphere of influence and risked nuclear war to rescue the foot soldiers of the Communist bloc?

Mailer next accuses America of "supporting" Saddam in his war with Iran in the 1980s, a common charge of the antiwar left: "[Saddam] slaughtered tens of thousands of Iraqis during the war with Iran—a time when we supported him." But this is to confuse *Realpolitik* with affection. What America did was to tilt to Saddam's side—supplying him with weapons—at a juncture in the Iran-Iraq War when it looked as if Iraq was going to be defeated by the fanatical, anti-American Shiite regime in Iran. America did not want to see a totalitarian Iran with three times Iraq's population dominating the Middle East. If Iran had prevailed in the war, the ayatollahs would have taken control of the majority of the world's oil reserves; and the empire of radical Islam—with terrorist armies operating in Europe and elsewhere—would have become a global force. To prevent this by aiding Saddam was realism, not endorsement. Moreover, the military equipment America supplied to Iraq in the war was designed to balance the arms Iran received from the Soviet empire, which also would have benefited handsomely from an Iranian victory. What would Mailer have had American planners do? If they had failed to take any action at all, Mailer would have blamed America for the deaths Iran inflicted on Iraq, and for the disastrous consequences that would ensue from its victory. Instead, American arms contributed to a military stalemate and to a peace that saved hundreds of thousands of lives. But this reality is off Mailer's radar-screen.

When it comes to adding up the balance-sheet of America's efforts in Iraq, Mailer does it with steely disdain: "A horde of those newly discovered [Shiite] graves go back to that period [of the Iran-Iraq war]. Of course, real killers never look back."[19] Real killers; in other words, Americans. In sum, America can do no right; even the right America does is wrong; and the wrongs are monstrous. This syllogism captures the entire logic of the anti-American mind.

---

[19]Ibid.

8

The Great Satan

A crucial aspect of the worldview of American radicals is not only the monstrous nature of America's essence but the belief in American omnipotence—the ability of America's leaders to control the circumstances of their international policies without regard to the interests of allies or the threats of adversary powers or the constraints imposed by domestic political forces. Radicals never see America as reacting to a threat that cannot be ignored, or to a set of circumstances whose outcome it cannot determine. A typical expression of this can be found in James Weinstein's book *The Long Detour,* which is about the re-emergence of the American left. Weinstein was a Communist in the 1940s, a founder of the New Left in the 1960s, and an advocate of the idea that socialists should work within the Democratic Party to achieve their ends. In his book, which was published two years *after* 9/11, Weinstein wrote: "The realistic military threat to the United States from any other nation, of course, is near zero."[1]

A corollary of the view that America is the master of world events is the idea that America has no worthy enemies, only rebellious subjects. America's adversaries are only reacting to America's own aggressions. In an interview on March 31, 2003 as U.S. troops entered Iraq, Noam Chomsky posed a rhetorical question to himself—"Has Saddam ever posed a threat to the US?"—and answered

---

[1]James Weinstein, *The Long Detour: The History and Future of the American Left,* p. 225. Weinstein was a founding editor of *Studies on the Left* and the founder and publisher of the socialist newspaper *In These Times.*

it: "The idea verges on absurdity."[2] Three months before the Iraq war, Daniel Ellsberg, leaker of the Pentagon Papers on Vietnam and a protester against the impending conflict in Iraq, had been asked: "What threat does Iraq now pose or could pose in the future to essential U.S. objectives in the Middle East or globally?" Ellsberg's answer: "No threat at all, so long as Saddam is not faced with overthrow or death by attack or invasion."[3] In other words, Iraq posed no dangers to American security that America itself did not provoke. This is the perfectly circular, self-validating logic of the anti-American cause.

It is also perfectly preposterous. Even a backward and impoverished nation like Afghanistan under the Taliban had shown it could pose a serious threat to the lives of American citizens—not to mention the American economy—through its support for the Islamic terrorists who conducted the 9/11 attacks. Estimates of the economic damage caused by 9/11 range as high as $600 billion; whole industries—airlines and travel being the two most obvious—were threatened with bankruptcy. If 9/11 had been followed by similar attacks in the United States and Europe, the possibility of global economic instability with attendant civil and political disruption would have been a real, and daunting, prospect.

The assumption of America's omnipotence flows from the religious nature of the radical worldview. A favored text of activists opposed to the Iraq war is *Rogue State* by William Blum, a former State Department employee and a featured speaker at university "teach-ins" against the war on terror after 9/11. The "rogue state" in Blum's title is the United States. His book is subtitled, "A Guide to the World's Only Superpower," and comes with encomiums from authors as disparate as Gore Vidal and Noam Chomsky on the one hand, and Thomas Powers and former *New York Times* Saigon bureau-chief A.J. Langguth on the other. This is the way

---

[2]"Chomsky on War," *Zmag.org*, March 31, 2003
[3]"Daniel Ellsberg on Iraq," *Zmag.org*, January 31, 2003; http://www.zcommunications.org/daniel-ellsberg-on-iraq-by-daniel-ellsberg

Blum's text begins: "This book could be entitled *Serial Chainsaw Baby Killers and the Women Who Love Them*."[4] In the author's view, the chainsaw baby-killers are American officials and their agents, while the women who love them are supporters of American foreign policy.

In fairness to Powers and Langguth, their praise for Blum was based on a volume published prior to *Rogue State* called *Killing Hope: US Military and CIA Interventions Since World War II*. But while the tone of that book is more dispassionate, the irrational animus towards the United States is the same. Blum begins his introduction to the 1995 edition of *Killing Hope* with these words: "In 1993, I came across a review of a book about people who deny that the Nazi Holocaust actually occurred. I wrote to the author, a university professor, telling her that her book made me wonder whether she knew that an American holocaust had taken place, and that the denial of it put the denial of the Nazi one to shame.... Yet, a few million people have died in the American holocaust and many more millions have been condemned to lives of misery and torture as a result of U.S. interventions extending from China and Greece in the 1940s to Afghanistan and Iraq in the 1990s."[5] In other words, America is worse than Nazi Germany (and it would have been better for the world if the Communists had won in Greece, as it was that they did win in China).

From its opening image, *Rogue State* proceeds to dismiss the idea that the Cold War was a conflict between nuclear superpowers or a contest between totalitarianism and freedom. Instead, Blum presents the Cold War as the concoction of a single omnipotent power—a power whose ends are predatory and evil—able to manipulate events in order to establish its global rule. "For

---

[4]William Blum, *Rogue State: A Guide to the World's Only Superpower*, Common Courage Press, Monroe, Maine, 2000, p. 1
[5]William Blum, *Killing Hope: US Military and C.I.A. Interventions Since World War II*, Common Courage Press, 1995, p. 1. Blum speaks widely on American campuses and abroad; his website is killinghope.org.

seventy-nine years the United States convinced much of the world that there was an international conspiracy out there. An *International Communist Conspiracy* [italics in original] seeking no less than control over the entire planet for purposes which had no socially redeeming values. And the world was made to believe that it somehow needed the United States to save it from communist darkness. 'Just buy our weapons,' said Washington, 'let our military and our corporations roam freely across your land, and give us veto power over whom [sic] your leaders will be, and we'll protect you....'"[6]

There is no discernible difference between this view of America's role in the Cold War and the crudest Communist caricature manufactured by the Kremlin leaders at their height—between the Stalinism of a Herbert Aptheker and the "anarchism" of a Noam Chomsky or the "progressivism" of a Howard Zinn—or the views expressed on scores of Internet websites like indymedia.org, commondreams.org, counterpunch.org, dailykos.com and zmag.org, which serve as the organizing venues of the "antiwar" movement.[7] When it comes to the perception of American policy and its purposes, these views are substantively the same: American policies and purposes are controlled by a corporate ruling-class whose guiding interest is profit and plunder. External enemies are mythical; they serve merely as a smokescreen for suppressing revolts against the empire. Thus, in a best-selling pamphlet, *What Uncle Sam Really Wants*, Chomsky writes: "[After World War II] US planners recognized that the 'threat' in Europe was not Soviet aggression ... but rather the worker- and peasant-based antifascist resistance with its radical democratic ideals, and the political power and appeal of the local Communist parties."[8]

---

[6]*Rogue State*, op. cit, p. 1
[7]Andrew Boyd, "The Web Rewires the Movement," *The Nation*, August 4, 2003; http://www.thenation.com/article/web-rewires-movement?page=0,4
[8]Noam Chomsky, *What Uncle Sam Really Wants*, Odonian Press, 1992, p. 15

The resistance movements Chomsky refers to, such as those in France and Greece, were organized by Communists; their "radical democratic ideals" were to establish Soviet satellites and totalitarian states. The views of Chomsky, Zinn and Blum, which accurately reflect the political culture of the movement against the war in Iraq, reprise the Stalinist propaganda line during the Cold War and are based on long-discredited Marxist analyses of the democratic West. These views demonize America as a satanic force in the modern world—the force behind a global order of hierarchy and privilege that is responsible for the misery of the world's impoverished masses. As long as America continues to maintain the will and ability to protect what radicals regard as a global order of "social injustice," all reforms and social advances will be illusory. This is the meaning of Nicholas DeGenova's claim that all progressives should wish for the defeat of American power in Iraq and elsewhere, because America can have no place in a world that is at peace and just. It is the credo of the radical left, and its corrosive views have come to permeate the entire spectrum of the progressive cause.

PART II

After the Sixties

I

Activists Then and Now

What does Marxism have to offer the bourgeois univer-
sity? Preferably nothing. That is, Marxism can do nothing
for the university; the real question is what can Marxists
do to and in the university.

—HARVARD PROFESSOR RICHARD LEWONTIN

On April 15, 1980, as invading Soviet armies poured across the Afghanistan border, a thousand students assembled for a "Stop the War Teach-In" on the University of California, Berkeley campus. Their protests were not addressed to the Soviet invaders but to the Carter White House, which had condemned the attack and requested defense increases and a military draft to deter the Soviet aggression. Speaker after speaker in Berkeley rose to denounce both measures as manifestations of a resurgent American militarism and anti-Communist paranoia, as preludes to "another Vietnam" and as threats to peace.

These echoes of the radical past were far from incidental to the event, which served to kick off the activism of a new political decade. Those in the crowd who were too young to make the allusions for themselves were guided by the parade of middle-aged political veterans who mounted the rostrum at the invitation of the protest organizers. Communist Party leader Angela Davis and

·

Speech given at an Accuracy in Academia conference in Washington, D.C., June 27, 1987

Berkeley radical Congressman Ron Dellums, veterans of the Sixties political drama, were center-stage at its Eighties revival. Recalling how similar "teach-ins" and anti-draft protests had changed history in Vietnam, they applauded the symbolism the organizers had contrived. The time had come, they said, to revive the political enthusiasms of the past and its radical discontents.

If the episode revealed the self-conscious effort of Eighties activism to identify itself as a child of the Sixties, it also exposed the contradiction inherent in such a claim. For the radicalism of the Sixties had identified itself as a child without political parents. Its most famous slogan—"You Can't Trust Anyone Over Thirty"— meant exactly what it said. Sixties activism had been born as a self-conscious attempt to reject one tainted politics (Stalinism) and atone for another ("Cold War Liberalism"). Eighties activism was born in an opposite effort to revive the tainted politics that had been previously rejected, while appropriating—illegitimately—the aura of idealism that the rejection had produced. Therein lies its cynicism and deceptive political style. The cynicism is evident in the way today's radicals present themselves as "progressives" and "liberals." Eighties radicals are not only comfortable with these political labels, they insist on them; and they denounce as "McCarthyite" any effort to penetrate their deceptive surfaces.

The Sixties radicals and today's activists are, in fact, successive generations of an American left that is a branch of the international Marxist movement whose own roots lie in the Soviet Revolution of 1917. It is a left that, having been shattered by the traumas following Stalin's death, embarked on a long and painful process of rebirth. Sixties radicals situated themselves squarely within this tradition by identifying themselves as a "New Left"— a term that had been adopted by Communists all over the world who repudiated Stalin's crimes but not the cause that led to them. By calling themselves a "New Left," they declared their intention to distance themselves from the pro-Soviet allegiances of their parents' generation and also to pick up the ideological pieces; in other words, to begin politically where their parents had left off. On the one hand, this meant a renewal of faith in Marxist ideas. On the other, it meant the adoption of a political style that would exculpate them from their Communist past and allow them to present themselves as something new.

Since they had rejected the Old Left's loyalties to Soviet Russia, New Leftists had no need to disguise their agendas or to pose as "progressives" as their Communist parents had done. They could be openly radical and proud of it. They had no desire to infiltrate liberal institutions in order to shape and influence the democratic process. Their declared intention was to confront and reject liberalism, to make "a revolution in the streets." As the Sixties began, these New Leftists were joined by another group of political orphans, the offspring of the Cold War Liberals whose anti-Communist crusade had incurred a debilitating taint in the McCarthy excess. At the outset of the Sixties, the two groups joined one side of a conflict that would define their relationship to the past and determine the course of their political future.

The scene of the conflict was SDS, which was to become the focal point of Sixties radicalism. SDS had begun the decade as the student arm of the Socialist Party, an anti-Communist faction of the left. The conflict, at SDS's founding conference, was over the radicals' determination to include Communists in the SDS ranks and to reject "anti- Communism" as a political principle. This caused a break between the young Turks and the parent organization, in particular with Michael Harrington and Irving Howe. The rejection of anti-Communism was the self-evident truth with which the New Left declared its independence in launching its radical career.

In its early years, as a legacy of its rejection of Stalinism and the influence of the civil-rights movement, this New Left adopted an ethos that was non-violent, democratic, idealistic and "American." But deep in their hearts the radicals regarded the triumphs of the civil-rights movement as worrisome subversions of their real agendas. The democratic passions and non-violent tactics—above all the principle of "integration" into American society—were obstacles to political agendas that were "revolutionary" and could never be satisfied by these means. By mid-decade, America was engaged in a war against Communist aggression in South Vietnam. The unavoidable horrors of this war provided radicals with the rationale they needed to discard the liberal ideals which had made them uncomfortable, and return to their political—chiefly Marxist—roots. By the end of the decade, they had relinquished any commitment they might have had to the purposes and values of American democracy. Proclaiming themselves Marxists and Leninists at war with "Amerikkka," the radicals embraced America's totalitarian enemies and resurrected the Communist loyalties of the past. With these twin betrayals of country and self, the New Left came to an end.

As in the previous era, a radical politics had discredited itself and died. And as before, the radical faith survived. During the Seventies, radicals undaunted by their defeats began a "long march through the institutions" of the American mainstream. While liberals wrestled with their guilt over America's anti-Communist war in Vietnam, leftists came to terms with the Communist heritage they had previously rejected. In a cultural offensive that included films like *The Front* and books like *The Romance of American Communism*, leftists attempted to rehabilitate the discredited forbears whose politics they once had scorned, and they celebrated the old reds whose corrupt, divided loyalties they once had disdained. It is this reunion of subversive generations that has given birth to the left we see before us today.

The Sixties left had no political teachers, but it did have a political guide: the memory of the crimes and treasons its predecessors had justified in the Revolution's name. The Eighties left has no such guide, but it has plenty of teachers in the hardcore survivors of the Sixties who betrayed their own political ideals and embraced a discredited past. The teachers of today's left are the political diehards whose radicalism is defined in solidarity with Communist totalitarianism and in an anti-Americanism immune to the lessons of its own experience. The most dramatic civil-rights revolution in the history of any 20th-century nation, the most spectacular display of democratic process resulting in a self-inflicted defeat in Vietnam, the most expansive demonstration of political tolerance in a postwar amnesty for America's internal enemies who had sabotaged the war effort—these did not cause radicals to have second thoughts but only served to harden their hatred for America.

The Eighties left did not originate, as its predecessor had, in a rejection of Communist politics and the Soviet empire, or in a renewed appreciation for American democracy. Under the malign tutelage of its Sixties elders, the Eighties left began in apologies for Soviet aggression in Afghanistan; in refusals to condemn Communist oppression in Vietnam; in solidarity with Communist revolutions in Central America; and in denunciations of America's battered democracy as racist and militarist and a threat to peace. Where the New Left had begun with traumatic lessons in the nightmare realities of Marxist solutions, and had rejected the Old Left's treasonous loyalties to Marxist regimes, the Eighties left had no such chastening guides. In the political school of its radical teachers, the lessons it learned about Vietnam contained no instruction in the brutal consequences of Communist victories, in the imperialist expansion of Communist empires, or in the costly toll of American defeats.

It has been more than a decade since American armies were at war in Vietnam or anywhere else. But while America has remained militarily passive, the Communist victors have been on the march. In Indochina, Hanoi's armies have blazed a trail of conquest and colonial occupation. In Africa, Cuban expeditionary forces have spread famine and bloodshed and Communist oppression. In Afghanistan, Soviet marauders have torched a nation and made refugees of half a population in one of the most savage invasions of modern times. But from its inception, the Eighties left has been deaf and blind to these events; while through all these years of Communist conquest and human suffering caused by socialist regimes, the United States has remained the only real enemy of

American radicals. In the radicals' university, the lesson of Vietnam is just this: America is the enemy; America can be defeated. *Vietnam Has Won, El Salvador Will Win.* All that is necessary for victory is a Communist guerrilla army backed by the Soviets on the field of battle, and a political force inside the United States that acts in solidarity with them.

The "solidarity left" of the Eighties begins where the movement of the Sixties left off: in a politics of secession from America's democracy and service to the totalitarian cause. Because its politics is Marxist, it is a continuation of the war that was begun in 1917. Because its politics is war by other means, it has no room for candor in its rhetoric or integrity in its agendas. In framing its argument, the left pays lip-service to humane goals and liberal values in order to manipulate the democratic public. But liberality and humanity are not the practical commitments of the American left. Its practical commitments are to American defeats and to Communist victories, as in Vietnam.

The strategy of today's radicals was devised by the old Communist left in its heyday as a fifth column for Joseph Stalin. It is a strategy that forms progressive coalitions for "Peace and Justice in Central America" in furtherance of its real goals, which are to defend a Marxist police-state in Nicaragua and to support a Communist revolution in neighboring El Salvador. The Eighties left invokes democratic principles and America's interests only to promote its covert agendas, which are anti-American and anti-democratic. That is why it is eager to deny democratic rights to its political opponents whenever the opportunity appears. The radical left is a fascist force with a human face.

What can be done to strengthen democracy's defenses against this attack? The Sixties provide a relevant lesson. The Sixties left was numerically small and politically weak. Not one of its political achievements would have been possible through its efforts alone. Its successes were made possible by a factor beyond its control: the collapse of the liberal center of American politics, the surrender of the establishment to which it had laid siege. Crippled by guilt over Vietnam, the liberal center lost the will to defend itself and its traditional values, thus conferring legitimacy on radicals and their political agendas. Instead of maintaining radicals' isolation, the liberal establishment gave them access to the very institutions—the media, the universities, and the Democratic Party—that the radicals had so diligently attempted to destroy.

Today the legacy of this political masochism is everywhere evident, above all in academic institutions. Radicals who violate the canons of intellectual discipline and the principles of academic freedom are not promptly expelled from the community they despise. Instead, their political savagery and contempt for academic values are treated as expressions of an idealistic concern that the academy ought to heed and respect. Administrators at Columbia University have even devised an especially lenient disciplinary code for students whose offenses occur in the course of political protests. In this way, an institution that was brought to its knees by radicals in the Sixties encourages the destructive agendas of their political heirs as an integral part of the educational process. The short-term result is that every spring Columbia radicals find a pretext to lay siege to the university and bring its functions to a halt. A year ago, the occasion was the radicals' desire to inflame a racial conflict in southern Africa. This year, it is to ignite a race war at home. The longer-term result is that the radicals' agendas are accepted as legitimate by the very communities they seek to destroy. By failing to enforce its principles and standards, the academic community not only strengthens its radical enemies but weakens its own foundations and accelerates its decline.

In the last two decades in America, there has indeed been a precipitous decline in academic standards and scholarship. In classrooms across the country, ideological indoctrination has supplanted intellectual inquiry as academic discipline. Marxism, a theory long consigned with flat-earthism to the intellectual mausoleum, has been raised from the dead to a place of respect in the university curriculum. Racial and gender discrimination against

Asians and white males has been institutionalized as enlightened academic policy. Professional associations once devoted to the promotion of scholarship have been turned into political lobbies for totalitarian causes and terrorist elites.

The problem that faces the university is the problem that faces our democracy. A community that refuses to recognize its enemies is a community that is unable to defend itself, and has lost its will to survive. The continuing failure of the liberal center to withdraw the cloak of legitimacy from the illiberal shoulders of the hate-America left is a reflection of the continuing failure of liberal nerve that began with Vietnam. Its root cause is a loss of faith in the liberal values of American society and in the role that American power must play for liberal hopes in the world at large.[1] It is only when liberal America is once again able to believe in itself that it will be able to recognize its radical enemies and join with American conservatives, the contemporary defenders of traditional liberal values, who have begun to wage the battles that must be won if America's democracy is to survive.

---

[1] Of course I use the term liberal in the classical sense, as defined by the American founders and the Constitution.

2

Angela Davis at Dartmouth
(Text of a Speech Given at the College)

Imagine that a group of Dartmouth students had invited a Grand Dragon of the Ku Klux Klan to speak at Dartmouth; that the Grand Dragon agreed to come to Dartmouth for a $10,000 honorarium; that, having come, he had launched into a semi-literate diatribe against women, blacks, and American democracy. Let us suppose, further, that four Dartmouth fraternity presidents were in the audience and stood up to cheer when the Grand Dragon was done. Imagine the reaction.

A similar event actually took place on this campus—except that it was the Dartmouth *administration* and four college *deans* who played host and cheerleaders to the racist demagogue; that she was not only invited, but invited to keynote a major college commemoration; that she was introduced by a college dean as an "example of a committed black woman activist [who] has chosen to make a difference;" that the targets of her bigotry were men, whites, Jews and President Bush; and that the hate-groups she represented play a far more sinister role in America's political life and are implicated in far greater evils globally than the pathetic remnants of the Ku Klux Klan. I am speaking, I need hardly explain, of

---

Speech given at Dartmouth College, November 17, 1988, published as "Dartmouth Dignifies the Hate-Filled Angela Davis," *Human Events*, Vol. 49, No. 12 (1989), p. 10. See also, "Dartmouth Dignifies the Hate-Filled Angela Davis," *Policy Forum (National Forum Foundation)*, Vol. V, No. 1, Jan. 1989.

comrade Angela Davis and the Communist Party and an event that took place on this campus only a month ago.

Angela Davis and Communism are institutions that I know something about, since both my parents were card-carrying members of the American party, whose central committee Ms. Davis now graces. She and I belong to the same political generation. While I was helping to found the New Left in the early Sixties, she was joining the Communist International. A decade later, I helped to create a community base for the Black Panther Party in the East Oakland ghetto. It was a time when she was helping Black Panther Field Marshal George Jackson—then an inmate at San Quentin prison in San Francisco—amass an arsenal for his private liberation army. Equipped with the weapons provided by Davis and others, this army murdered half a dozen people in Marin County, California, in the years 1970 and 1971. I would like to take a moment, therefore, to share with you some insights into the perverse mind of the individual whom your president has seen fit to support so generously with your college tuition, under the rationale of providing for your educational enrichment.

In 1956, when I was 17 years old, the Israeli Mossad smuggled Nikita Khrushchev's secret speech about Stalin's crimes out of the Kremlin and delivered it to the Central Intelligence Agency and *The New York Times,* which printed the text in full. Only today, 30 years later and thanks to *glasnost,* can citizens of the Soviet Union also read what Khrushchev said at that time. In the West, the significance of the Khrushchev Report lay not in its revelation of Soviet crimes—about which the world was already informed—but in the fact that the Communist pope had finally confirmed what conservative anti-Communists like William F. Buckley had been saying for two decades and more. And what Communists and fellow-traveling progressives had been denying and denouncing as red-baiting lies for all of that time.

It is important to remember what the socialist crimes of the Stalin era actually were: mass murders on a scale that exceeded those of Adolf Hitler. Tens of millions of people deliberately starved and brutally slaughtered; tens of millions more incarcerated in the infamous gulag archipelago, a network of concentration camps whose conditions rivaled Majdanek and Auschwitz.

During the slaughters conducted by the Stalinist police-state, the American Communist Party supplied political emissaries and cheerleaders for the slaughterers. The Communist Party, in whose community I grew to adulthood, always pretended to outsiders that it was just a band of "progressives" who wanted to make the world a better place. In reality it was a conspiratorial fifth column, operating within America's borders on behalf of the Soviet mass-murderers outside. For its Soviet masters, the American Communist Party provided willing intellectuals such as Lillian Hellman to act as propagandists, to smear and discredit those who attempted to tell the truth about the Soviet atrocities, libeling them with accusations that would have put a witch-hunter like Joe McCarthy to shame. The Communist Party provided spies, like Julius and Ethel Rosenberg, to steal the secrets of America's atomic weapons. It infiltrated the Democratic Party and the topmost reaches of the American government with agents like Harry Dexter White and Alger Hiss to further Moscow's imperial cause.

When Khrushchev's speech appeared on the front page of *The New York Times* in February 1956, admitting the terrible crimes that socialism had committed, the faithful were shocked and then demoralized. The Communist movement began to disintegrate. In Hungary, dissidents rebelled against the Stalinist nightmare and Soviet tanks rolled across the border to crush them. In America there were dissidents, too, who spoke out in support of the Hungarian freedom-fighters. They were led by Spanish Civil War veteran John Gates, who wrote an editorial in the Communist *Daily Worker* denouncing the unconscionable Soviet act. But these voices also were crushed. When John Gates and his supporters were silenced by their own party, they decided there was no honorable course but to leave its ranks. So morally bankrupt had Communism become that any Communist with a shred of integrity left the Party at that time.

Overnight, the party, which had numbered 60,000, shrank to a tenth that size. Those who stayed were the Stalinist diehards—morally-comatose political sycophants, unswerving in their loyalty to the Soviet state. The leading toady among them was the party's "theoretician," Herbert Aptheker. While his comrades expressed their outrage at the Soviet betrayal of their socialist ideals, Herbert Aptheker sat down to write a tract called *The Truth About Hungary*, defending the Soviet tanks that had flattened Budapest and killed 30,000 Hungarians; libeling the freedom-fighters as "fascists" and "Nazis;" repeating every lie of the Kremlin line.

I was sixteen the year before these events took place. Herbert Aptheker was my teacher at the Jefferson School of Social Science, which was actually a Communist-run school of Marxism in New York. A few years later, Angela Davis began her own political career while living in the Aptheker household, co-founding a Communist youth front called "Advance" with Aptheker's daughter, her best friend. Although I too had been part of the Communist youth movement, I did not follow the path that took Angela Davis into the party in its most politically corrupt and degenerate hour. Instead, along with many other Communist offspring of my generation, I helped to found a "New Left" which distanced itself from the Party and Stalin's crimes. Through this New Left we hoped to rescue socialism from the clutches of the mass-murderers and their progressive accomplices to make sure that such crimes would not happen again. During the Sixties, or at least the first half of the decade, we New Leftists despised young Communists like Angela Davis and the old Stalinist hacks who had stayed in the party, and we kept them at arm's length. We would not have invited them—let alone bribed them—to speak on our platforms, as Dartmouth's president has recently done.

Ultimately, however, we New Leftists failed in our efforts to create a radical movement that had moral integrity and political independence—a movement that was not in league with totalitarian regimes. As the Sixties came to an end, the New Left was once again becoming a fifth column for Communist powers, supporting new crimes in the name of "solidarity" with socialist police-states. The New Left fell in love with Communist tyrants like Mao Zedong, whose "Great Leaps" took the lives of 70 million people, and Fidel Castro, whose Communist foreign-legions have propped up dictators in Angola and Ethiopia, spreading death and famine among millions more.

At the end of the Sixties Angela Davis became the lover and political comrade of George Jackson, a maximum-security inmate in San Quentin prison who was awaiting trial for murder. At the time, Angela Davis and other leftists—including myself—defended Jackson as an innocent black victim of racist "Amerika." But to intimates on his own defense committee, George Jackson boasted that he was guilty as charged and had killed 12 other men in prison besides. One of his revolutionary schemes was a plan to poison the water system of Chicago, the city where he had grown up.[1] Jackson was awaiting trial for the murder of prison guard John Mills, who had been killed in retaliation for the shooting death of a black convict during a prison brawl. Neither Jackson nor anyone else ever claimed that John Mills had had anything to do with the previous shooting. Jackson murdered him because he was a guard and because he was white.

On August 7, 1970, shortly before George Jackson was scheduled to go on trial, his 17-year-old brother Jonathan entered a Marin County courtroom and kidnapped a judge, an assistant district attorney, and a Marin County juror. He was armed with weapons freshly bought by Angela Davis. The young Jackson intended to use the hostages to set his brother free, but the attempt failed. The judge, Jonathan and two other prisoners were killed, and Angela Davis disappeared from sight. When she was finally caught, she was indicted as an accomplice to murder; but the prosecution was unable to prove that she had given Jackson the weapons or had known his intentions in advance. Radicals

---

[1]See David Horowitz and Peter Collier, "Requiem for a Radical," in *Destructive Generation*, Summit, 1989.

familiar with the Black Panthers and the Communist Party, and with the relationship between Angela Davis and George Jackson, drew conclusions of their own.

A year later, George Jackson attempted to escape from San Quentin. One guard was shot to death and three others were tied up by Jackson and his comrades, who slit their throats with razors. Jackson was killed running towards the prison wall. At his funeral, Angela Davis praised Jackson for dying a hero's death and reaffirmed his declaration of war against the "racist" society that had allegedly killed him. But Jackson's death did not end the trail of those tragic events. Before his escape attempt, Jackson had been defended and made internationally famous by the efforts of a radical attorney named Fay Stender, who was a political ally and friend of Angela Davis. When Jackson asked Stender to provide him with a weapon to launch his escape, she refused. In 1979, she was punished for this "betrayal" by a member of Jackson's prison gang who appeared at her door in the middle of the night and shot her five times at point-blank range. A year later, paralyzed and condemned to a lifetime of pain, Stender committed suicide. Fay Stender had devoted her entire life to radical and feminist causes and to the defense of Huey Newton, George Jackson, and hundreds of other black men in prison who she felt were oppressed. But Angela Davis did not come to her funeral or speak a word in her praise.[2]

One of George Jackson's prison gangsters—a rapist and thug named Fleeta Drumgo—was an accomplice in the assault on Fay Stender. Fleeta Drumgo had helped Jackson murder John Mills but was later released on parole. A drug addict, he attempted to sell information about Fay Stender's assailants to other leftists concerned about her fate. Soon after, he was killed in a gang-style execution. Angela Davis spoke at Fleeta Drumgo's funeral and eulogized him as a "Communist martyr."

The Communist and pro-Communist left for which Angela Davis is a hero and leader is a fanatic, nihilistic, and—given the

---

[2]Ibid.

opportunity—violent movement. The diehards of the left are ideo-logical hate-mongers, more dangerous today because they have the protective goodwill and support of institutions like Dartmouth. And not only Dartmouth, but college faculties across this nation, where Communists and political Marxists and fellow-travelers have already gained an alarming foothold.

Is it an accident that Marxists and Communists should be involved in political assassinations and mass murder from Califor-nia to Cambodia and from Ethiopia to Afghanistan? Or that Com-munist revolutions should result in nation-sized prison camps from Managua to Warsaw and from Havana to Hanoi? After 70 years of bloody history, the answer is obvious. It is no more an accident that Marxist doctrines of class-hatred should have led to the *gulag* than that Nazi doctrines of race-hatred should have led to Majdanek and Auschwitz.

The university in America is now a battleground between those who value the freedoms we have developed in this country for 200 years and the totalitarians of the left, who have been bat-tling for the last 70 to take them away. It is the responsibility of those who cherish free institutions and the culture that sustains them to stand up against the barbarians who are already within the gates.

3

The Peace Movement

Y ou see them every hour at the top of the local news, with
their signs of "No Blood for Oil" and their chants of "Hey,
hey, ho, ho, George Bush has got to go." You watch their
apologists, like aging New Leftist and Columbia professor Todd
Gitlin, squirm uncomfortably at their reckless passion in declaring
America the enemy while failing to condemn the global outlaw
Saddam Hussein. You observe in mounting wonder as they
descend on Washington to hear their balding Sixties heroes—Jesse
Jackson, Daniel Ellsberg, Ron Kovic—call for capitulation on the
battlefield and the impeachment of the president. The troops in
these demonstrations are dressed for battle in the old Movement
issue—jeans and down jackets, lettered T-shirts, even tie-dyes. The
familiar targets are steady in their sights: "big oil," the "Pentagon
war machine" and "American imperialism." As always, they
claim to be sheep in wolves' clothing; despite the war- paint, just
pilgrims for peace. To disarm their critics, they concede some past
"mistakes," like spitting on U.S. soldiers returning from Vietnam.
Simultaneous with their present denunciations of U.S. "death
squads" in Iraq, they proclaim their heartfelt concern for the very
soldiers who have volunteered to carry out the mission and whose
morale they continue to undermine.

Is the glaring contradiction between the belligerence and malice they project, and their claims to good intentions, the result of
mere pig-headedness? An inability to communicate? Or is it the

---

This article appeared in *The National Review,* February 25, 1991.

failure of a political camouflage to conceal the true motives that inform their passion? As a former partisan of similar movements I never in 25 years of political activism marched in a demonstration that did not have militant, Marxist, and anti-American agendas just beneath its pacifist surface. The "Coalition to Stop U.S. Intervention in the Middle East," which staged the January 19 march on Washington, is but another cynical attempt by the now-discredited left to jumpstart the revolutionary engines that have recently stalled.

Do I exaggerate? Can the current mobilization for "peace" be so readily dismissed as an occasion for America-bashing by the unrepentant left? Consider the view of an unimpeachable source, a faithful keeper of the radical flame. The writer is Alexander Cockburn and his column appeared in the December 31, 1990 issue of *The Nation*, as a commentary on the organizers of the Washington march: "I wish people would stop writing to [suggest] that today leftists of principle should espouse the cause of Iraq and eschew criticism of Saddam Hussein. This is Marxism-Leninism-Bonkerism of a sort much savored by the Workers World Party, which seems to be the animating force behind the Coalition to Stop U.S. Intervention in the Middle East, decorated by Ramsey Clark."[1]

Most people will not have heard of the Workers World Party, which according to Cockburn is the organization that has put together this new "antiwar" coalition. But I remember it from the Sixties as the only Trotskyist splinter to endorse the Soviet invasion of Hungary. Thus, the spearhead of this season's "antiwar" demonstrations is a Marxist-Leninist party that defined itself by supporting the bloody invasion that took the lives of 30,000 Hungarians, whose only crime was to want their national independence and freedom.

---

[1]Saddam, Kuwait and Bonkerism, Alexander Cockburn, December 31, 1990, http://www.highbeam.com/doc/1G1-9245346.html

The antiwar coalition favored by Cockburn was the National Campaign for Peace in the Middle East, which held its demonstration a week later on January 26 and was portrayed by the media as the "liberal" peace contingent. But this turned out to be a distinction without a difference. Jesse Jackson, for example, addressed both demonstrations. The "liberal" coalition was organized by the pathetic remnants of the American Communist Party, its fellow-travelers and fronts, like the U.S. Peace Council. Its official coordinator was Leslie Cagan, a veteran New Leftist, and—like the organizations that made up the coalition—pro-Castro, pro-Sandinista, pro-FMLN, pro-PLO, and anti-American.[2] And it is the same story for the rank-and-file across the country. As a warm-up to the Washington demonstrations, activists held "teach-ins" from coast to coast, including one at Los Angeles' Fairfax High School featuring Clark, Ellsberg, Kovic and Jackson. Attended by 1,500 people, the affair was described by the press as the largest "antiwar" demonstration until then. Its official spokesman, Achmed Nassef, told reporters that he had joined the Coalition through the Palestine Solidarity Committee. In other words, the official spokesman for the "peace" coalition was drawn from a group supporting Saddam's rape of Kuwait.

Nassef also explained that the coalition itself had grown out of groups that had been organized to oppose U.S. intervention in Central America—that is to say, of groups that proclaimed themselves "antiwar" when it came to the struggle of Nicaraguans against the Sandinista dictatorship but pro-war when it came to the struggle of Communist guerrillas against an elected democracy in neighboring El Salvador. One of the headliners at the Fairfax High "teach-in" was Blase Bonpane, a defrocked priest who, like all the other speakers over 50, had for three decades, supported every Communist guerrilla war in the world. Bonpane even authored a book with the Orwellian title *Guerrillas for Peace.* In

---

[2] These two coalitions organized all the major demonstrations against the Iraq War without exception.

addition to Achmed Nassef's Palestine Solidarity Committee, the "antiwar" coalition sponsoring the teach-in included the Association of Palestinians for Return and the Committee for a Democratic Palestine—support-groups for the PLO's terrorist war against the Jews of Israel. This led a reporter for *The Jewish Journal* to ask Bonpane whether the gathering was anti-Israel. "Why would someone say the gathering is anti-Israel?" Bonpane replied. "Because we're antiwar? We think that nothing would be worse for Israel than a war in the Middle East. We're horrified that some voices in Israel could be calling for this war." More candid than Bonpane's double-talk were the signs that had appeared at a Santa Cruz "antiwar" teach-in two months earlier, where coalition members carried signs that read "Zionism Kills" and "Palestinian Blood."

These hypocrisies reminded me of the last time the left tried to launch an antiwar crusade, during the Soviet invasion of Afghanistan. It was then called a "Stop the War" movement, and its purpose was not to stop the Soviet invasion but to oppose President Jimmy Carter's call for a resumption of the military draft, which he felt was necessary to counter the Soviet aggression. This should be remembered every time the current peace left hypocritically criticizes the present volunteer military as "undemocratic," since it was the opposition of the left to a military draft during the Vietnam War that led to the creation of a volunteer army in the first place. Of course, what the left really wanted—and what it still wants—is that the United States should have no army at all and should therefore be vulnerable to its Marxist enemies and their Marxist friends.

The Eighties left, which opposed America's stand against Soviet aggression in Afghanistan, was no more "antiwar" than the present left is. It was—like all the lefts that have sprung up since the Sixties—anti-American. As the Soviet legions poured into Afghanistan in 1980, leftist Congressman Ron Dellums, now the leader of the "antiwar" caucus in Congress, told the thousand cheering Berkeley students who had gathered for a "Stop the War" demonstration: "From my vantage point, as your representative, [I believe] we are at an incredibly dangerous moment. Washington D.C. is a very evil place.... While [the White House] professes to see the arc of crises in Southwest Asia as the Balkan tinderbox of World War III, well Ron Dellums sees the only arc of crises being the one that runs between the basement of the west wing of the White House and the war room of the Pentagon."[3]

In other words: America is the source of the world's crises and problems. This is the cardinal axiom of the left. It was also the animating principle of the father of contemporary "antiwar" movements—the one that enabled Pol Pot's victory in Indochina and that of the Hanoi Communists in Vietnam. In the words of a Santa Cruz student active in the coalition: "Obviously, this current antiwar movement takes inspiration from its Vietnam predecessor. Siphoned through 20 years of anti-Vietnam sentiments, my generation enters its movement more cynically than our counterparts of the Sixties...."

More cynically, indeed. For what did those "anti-Vietnam sentiments" accomplish, judged by the passage of 20 years? A communist-sponsored genocide in Indochina that extinguished nearly two million lives and obliterated a national culture; a decade and a half of Communist oppression in South Vietnam that killed more than a half-million civilians, created nearly 1.5 million refugees—unprecedented in Vietnam's 1,000-year history of foreign conquests and domestic tyrannies—and made Communist Vietnam one of the poorest, most repressive and militaristic states on the face of the earth.

This is the real agenda of today's antiwar radicals: to reprise the Vietnam experience of the Sixties in the Nineties. In fact, they can hardly wait to repeat it. "Right now our movement is not as big as Vietnam was," one student organizer breathlessly told a campus

---

[3]*Liberals and Leftists in a Time of War*, David Horowitz, *FrontPage Magazine*, December 10, 2004, http://archive.frontpagemag.com/readarticle. aspx?ArtId=10280

recruit, "[but] I think that as soon as a shooting war starts this will be even bigger than Vietnam." Bigger than Vietnam. This is what every radical for 30 years has dreamed of—an occasion that will trigger an explosion of the left bigger than the Sixties itself. And what is this left? It is no longer a left that pledges its allegiance to Soviet power and worships at the altar of the Soviet state—though it *was* that. It is no longer a left that justifies Soviet expansion into Eastern Europe as a revolutionary beachhead of "peoples' democracies"—though it *was* that. It is no longer a left that celebrates Chinese Communism as a new dawn in humanity's long march into the socialist future or Cuba's *gulag* as a beacon of Latin America's coming liberation—though it *was* (and for some may still be) that.

It is a left that has been temporarily disoriented by the repudiation of its socialist paradise by hundreds of millions of former inhabitants. But it is also a left that has not for a single moment put down its weapons in the permanent war it has been waging since 1917—against the capitalist societies of the democratic West and, in particular, of the United States. Earlier this year, Daniel Singer—*The Nation* magazine's authority on Eastern Europe—lectured leftists as to how they should react to the rejection of socialism by East Europeans liberating themselves from the Soviet yoke: "Our problem is not to convince the Eastern Europeans that they can change regimes by Fabian [socialist] methods.... Our duty, rather, is to go to the heart of the matter and to the fortress of advanced capitalism.... In other words, our task is to spread the conviction that a radical change of society in all its aspects is on our own historical agenda."[4] In other words, damn the disasters our crusades have created in the East, full speed ahead with our plans to destroy the capitalist democracies of the West. Or, as *Time* columnist and Democratic Socialists of America chair Barbara Ehrenreich put it: "As a responsible radical, I believe our first

---

[4]*Revolutionary Nostalgia*, Daniel Singer, *The Nation*, November 20, 1989, http://www.thenation.com/article/revolutionary-nostalgia

responsibility is toward the evil close to home, and stopping that. In any event, I'm more worried in the long run about the belligerence of George Bush than of Saddam Hussein."[5]

We see this destructive left active today in America's universities, striving to discredit the very culture that created American democracy, attempting to smear America's heritage as the imperialist, patriarchal, racist construct of "dead white European males." And we see it in the streets, mobilized to oppose America's own right of self-determination and self-defense in an ongoing, relentless assault on America's military and intelligence communities, which it maliciously portrays as the tentacles of a sinister "national security state." What the left has become—now that its fantasy of a socialist future has been exploded all over the world—is this: a nihilistic force whose goal is to deconstruct and dismantle America as a democracy and as a nation.

Revolution is a form of total war. The radical left sees itself—has always seen itself—as part of an international revolutionary army. The archenemy of this international army is today, as it has been for the last 45 years, the United States. Thus *The Nation*, which is the most prominent organ of the radical left, defined the terms of the current battle over the Persian Gulf in a front-page editorial called "Choose Peace":

> The choice in the Persian Gulf conflict has never been between sanctions and force. It is between peace and war, between life and death. The party of death, which prefers self-descriptions that cover its thirst for conquest with appeals to the great tradition of just wars and lesser evils, has since August 2 seen sanctions as a kind of ritualistic foreplay to the violent penetration of an entire region of the globe. President Bush manipulated the various United Nations sanctions votes as he sent Secretary of State Baker to bribe and buy a favorable "use of force" resolution, putting a specious international gloss on his deadly designs for war.[6]

[5]*Tikkun*, January 1991
[6]"Choose Peace," *The Nation*, December 24, 1990, http://www.highbeam.com/doc/1G1-9240242.html

To *The Nation*'s progressives, America is the "party of death."
That is their moral calculus. George Bush's America—not Saddam
Hussein's Iraq—is the power with the "deadly designs for war."
This is what radicals mean when they preach about peace. Encap-
sulating their heartfelt sentiments about their own country is a
political song composed by "Voices for Peace" activists at Dart-
mouth during the Persian Gulf War, to be sung to the tune of
America the Beautiful:

> *Oh Beautiful,*
> *For racist lies,*
> *For homeless screams of pain;*
> *For purple lesions apathy,*
> *And bombs and acid rain.*
> *Amerika, Amerika,*
> *God cast a curse on thee!*
> *And spill the blood of brotherhood,*
> *That keeps oppressing me.*

4

Tom Hayden and Me

Tom Hayden and I were once comrades-in-arms in a move-ment to overthrow America's democratic institutions, remake its government in a Marxist image and help America's enemies defeat her sons on the field of battle. Now he is running for mayor of Los Angeles and many people are asking me, "Does this past matter?" I think it does.

Tom and I were deadly serious about our revolutionary agen-das. During the Vietnam War, Tom traveled many times to North Vietnam, Czechoslovakia and Paris to meet communist North Vietnamese and Viet Cong leaders. He came back from Hanoi pro-claiming he had seen "rice-roots democracy at work." According to people who were present at the time—including Sol Stern, later an aide to Manhattan borough president Andrew Stein—Hayden offered tips on conducting psychological warfare against the United States. He arranged trips to Hanoi for Americans perceived as friendly to the Communists and blocked entry to those seen as unfriendly, in particular the sociologist Christopher Jencks. He attacked as "propaganda" stories of torture and labeled American POWs returning home with such stories "liars."

Even after America withdrew its troops from Indochina, Hay-den lobbied Congress to end all aid to the anti-Communist regimes in Vietnam and Cambodia. When the cutoff came, the

---

"Hayden: A Revolutionary L.A. Can Skip," *Los Angeles Times*, Metro Section, March 11, 1997; http://www.salon.com/1997/03/03/horowitz 970303/

regimes fell and the Communists conquered South Vietnam and Cambodia, slaughtering 2.5 million people. When antiwar activist Joan Baez protested the human-rights violations of the North Vietnamese victors, Hayden called her a tool of the CIA.

On the domestic front, Hayden advocated urban rebellions and called for the creation of "guerrilla *focos*" to resist police and other law-enforcement agencies. For a while he led a Berkeley commune called the "Red Family," whose "Minister of Defense" trained commune members at firing-ranges and instructed high-school students in the use of explosives.

Why do these facts still seem important? It is not that I think a man cannot learn from his mistakes or change his mind; far from it. I myself have recently published a memoir recounting my own activities in the radical left, a past that I now regret.[1] I find this history relevant not just because Hayden is now proposing himself as the chief executive of one of America's most important cities, but because he has never been fully candid about this past. He has not owned up to the extent of his dealings with America's former enemies or to the true agenda of the Red Family commune, which was little more than a leftwing militia. He has remained silent about the criminal activities—which included murder—of the Black Panther Party, whose cause he promoted at the time.

To be fair, Hayden has admitted to some second thoughts. In an abstract way, he now understands that the democratic process is better than the totalitarian one. He now claims to embrace more modest ambitions about what can be accomplished in the political arena. Yet in all these years he has not found the courage to be candid about what he actually did. His silence on these matters has been coupled of late with ongoing attacks on the FBI, the CIA and other authorities responsible for the public's security and safety.

In his 450-page memoir, published only a few years ago, Hayden included many pages of his FBI dossier, along with sarcastic comments suggesting that the agents who kept an eye on him

---

[1]*Radical Son: A Generational Odyssey*, Touchstone, 1997

were no different from the agents of a police-state trying to suppress unpopular ideas. Just last week, Hayden, along with American communist Angela Davis and other '60s leftovers, led a march on Los Angeles City Hall organized by something calling itself the "Crack the CIA Coalition." Among its demands were "Dismantle the CIA" and "Stop the media cover-up of CIA drug involvement"—a reference to a *San Jose Mercury News* story discredited by the *Los Angeles Times, The New York Times* and *The Washington Post,* which claimed the CIA had flooded Los Angeles' inner-city communities with crack cocaine.

This sowing of boundless suspicion towards legal authority is troubling in a man who proposes himself as the leader of a city like Los Angeles, which has many political, racial and economic fault lines, and where there are visible tensions between its diverse communities. At worst, it fuels the racial paranoia of elements in the inner-city community who are convinced that there is a government plot to eliminate their leaders, not to mention their community itself.

It is only five years since a mob in South Central, inspired by deep suspicion and distrust of public authority, went on a rampage that killed 58 people, burned 2,000 businesses and destroyed a large section of the city. Its citizens cannot afford to have as their chief public official a man who inspires such distrust, and who actively sows suspicion about the institutions of civil law and authority. We cannot afford "the fire next time."

5

Social Justice

It is almost a decade since the Marxist empire began crumbling, yet the crackpot ideas of its founder live on. The notion that wealth is a form of "social injustice" and that redistributing income is a worthy and progressive goal remain persuasive to many in government and out. That is the reason there is a progressive tax-code, and why we still have a capital-gains tax, which specifically targets money earned from the creation of wealth. Such ideas are also very much a part of the language we speak. We refer casually to the "haves" and "have nots," as if in the beginning someone handed out life's goodies to a few and withheld them from the many. By equating "injustice" with unequal wealth, we also imply that one man's bounty can only result from another's deprivation.

Why instead do we not speak of the "cans" and the "can nots," the "wills" and the "will nots," the "dos" and the "do nots?" Everyone can look around and see examples of each. It is will, intelligence, ability, energy and desire that determine individual destinies, and with some exceptions it is the same dimensions of human character that produce economic rewards as well. A recent study shows that most of the families who constitute the richest one per cent of U.S. households (over $2 million in net worth) earned their wealth, and that most of it is in entrepreneurial

Originally published as "Robin Hood Lives," May 24, 1997, http://archive.frontpagemag.com/Printable.aspx?ArtId=24404; http://www.salon.com/1997/05/24/horowitz970524/

assets, unincorporated businesses or investment real-estate. More-over, the list of the richest families changes from year to year, a reflection of the fact that wealth can be lost as well as earned and is not a divine right.

There are, of course, undeserving rich, just as there are deserv-ing poor. But most people with money are busily producing more jobs and conveniences for others, and taking great risks to do it. That's why the market rewards them as it does. And that is why redistributing their wealth—socialism—is simply theft. It uses the force of the state to reach into the pockets of those who have earned their money and give it to someone who has not.

Not only is this not justice, it is destructive to the less fortu-nate. Suppose the government were to confiscate what Bill Gates has—all $20 billion of it at this point in time—and distribute it to the homeless or the inner-city poor. We know what would happen to it, because the government does that every other week with welfare payments, taken from those who work and given to those who don't or won't. It disappears. Sometimes it is used to buy alco-hol and drugs that destroy the purchaser over time. Other times it may be used for food and other necessities. In either case the money disappears or, more precisely, leads to nothing further for the individuals who are given it.

If Gates keeps his capital, on the other hand, there is a likeli-hood he will invest it in ways that create jobs, even whole indus-tries, that never existed before. To prevent Gates from doing that by "redistributing" his income diminishes capital for a growing economy. Redistribution has grave social and psychological costs as well. It sows resentment and distrust. When liberal enthusiasts inveigh against the one per cent of the nation who own 50 percent of the wealth, they are inciting passions against the most produc-tive members of the community. This can have catastrophic con-sequences, as the misery spread over half the globe by Communist revolutions amply demonstrated. In the West, the effects are more subtly corrosive, making it more difficult for entrepreneurs to accomplish their wealth-creating agendas, thus slowing the improvement of conditions for everyone.

The idea of social justice, as Friedrich Hayek observed long ago, is a mirage, a social fiction of the left.[1] There is no "society" that distributes income unfairly, and no "society" that could make the distribution just. Social justice is the rationale for a political elite to appropriate what others have earned and distribute it to their own constituencies to increase their power.

---

[1]Friedrich Hayek, *The Mirage of Social Justice*, University of Chicago, 1978

6

Spies Like Us

Two weeks ago, three leftist radicals from the University of Wisconsin were arrested and charged with spying. The media played the story big, but I still have a question: Why only three?

James Clark, Kurt Stand and Theresa Squillacote were all New-Left enthusiasts, Maoists who had gotten their revolutionary religion in the late '60s. In 1972, they decided to strike a blow at "Amerika" by delivering state secrets to the communist East German dictatorship. Squillacote (code-name "Tina") had become a Pentagon analyst, her husband Kurt ("Ken") a labor union representative, and Clark a private detective who had worked at the Rocky Mountain Arsenal in Boulder, Colorado. In addition to their funneling State Department papers to East German spymasters, in 1995 Squillacote offered the team's services to a South African communist and government official in a letter bemoaning the "horrors" of "bourgeois parliamentary democracy"—such as the one, presumably, presided over by Nelson Mandela.

In fact, many New Leftists collaborated with America's enemies during the '60s and '70s. Why should they have been any different from the Old Leftists like Alger Hiss, Harry Dexter White and Ethel and Julius Rosenberg, who spied for Stalinist Russia in the 1930s and 1940s? I had my own encounters with a KGB agent in London in the mid-Sixties, which I later described in *Radical Son*. I was wined and dined at London's fanciest restaurants, my

October 20, 1997, http://www.salon.com/1997/10/20/nc_20spies/

gracious host plying me with questions about my employer, the philosopher and political activist Bertrand Russell. Lord Russell was a leader of Britain's "peace movement" but something of a thorn in the Soviets' side—having demanded, in one of his more noteworthy news conferences, that Moscow send MiG fighters to North Vietnam to shoot down American planes. An odd position for a self-described pacifist, but in those days Russell was being guided by an American radical named Ralph Schoenman, who was not about to let such small inconsistencies stand in the way of his political agendas.

In addition to working for Russell, I was an instructor for the University of Maryland, which held courses on U.S. military bases scattered about England. After several courses of *coquilles Saint Jacques* and other delights, my dining companion got around to asking me directly if I would supply information to him about what I saw on the bases. I was outraged by his request and told him to get lost. But I observed him hanging around New Leftists in London and treating other activists I knew to similar expensive lunches. How many of them were recipients of his requests to spy for Soviet Russia? How many of them said yes?

Quite a few, I suspect. In fact, the number of New Leftists who actively worked with Communist regimes and their intelligence agencies probably ran into the thousands. The *Venceremos* brigades, composed of New Leftists who went to Cuba ostensibly to harvest sugar-cane, were operated by Cuban intelligence. How many of the Americans came home with more than a cut of cane as a souvenir? The Committees in Solidarity with the People of El Salvador, which were active during the Reagan years, were affiliated with the Communist guerrilla movement there and run by Cuban intelligence as well. New Left radicals like Tom Hayden met in Eastern Europe and Cuba with Communist officials from Hanoi and South Vietnam's National Liberation Front to plot the fall of the "Amerikkkan" empire.

This shouldn't surprise anyone. If one believes, as leftists do, that America is an evil empire, then why not cooperate with its socialist enemies and the governments of America's Third-World "victims?" The Wisconsin three did it; why not others? Everybody in a leadership position in the New Left was aware of contacts like the ones I've mentioned, but only a handful have ever written about them. If those contacts were not seditious, why the continued reticence to speak about them?

7

Progressive Education, Panther Style

One of the more interesting characteristics of progressives is the way they seem to learn nothing from their experience, confounding the very idea of what "progressive" means— a form of enlightened behavior, a process of escaping from the myths of the past. Today, self-styled progressives can be found supporting economic redistribution and state-sponsored racial discrimination, or memorializing the death-anniversaries of totalitarian legends like Che Guevara, just as though the history of the last 50 years had never taken place. And progressives can still be counted on to lend their support to the discredited domestic legends of Sixties radicalism, most notably the Black Panther vanguard.

In Oakland recently, an entity calling itself the Dr. Huey P. Newton Foundation launched a "Legacy Tour" of "historic" Black Panther sites as a step toward making the Panther stronghold into a local monument like Lexington and Valley Forge. On a glistening October day, three busloads of former Panthers and Panther supporters, along with Oakland city officials, began the tour with visits to the former Oakland homes of Huey Newton, Bobby Seale and Panther "Field Marshal" David Hilliard. Hilliard, who was their guide for the day, once spent a year in jail for threatening to kill President Nixon in front of 100,000 antiwar protesters in Golden Gate Park. Now the executive director of the Huey P. Newton Foundation, Hilliard describes himself as a recovering drug-addict and alcoholic. Other sites included various Panther

December 1, 1997, http://www.salon.com/1997/12/01/nc_01horo_3/

headquarters; the street-corner where Newton shot an Oakland police officer in an incident that launched the "Free Huey" movement and made the Panthers a national cause; the shootout scene where a Panther named Bobby Hutton was killed after a Party hit-squad fired at San Francisco policemen in an attempt to "avenge" the assassination of Martin Luther King, Jr.; and the sidewalk where Newton met his long-deserved end at the hands of a crack cocaine dealer he had burned.

Not included in the Legacy Tour were the sites where Newton killed a 17-year-old black prostitute, raped a black mother of three and shot-gunned the doorman of an after-hours club that had refused to cooperate in a Panther shakedown. Also missing were stops at the sites where Party members were "mudholed," whipped with cat o' nine tails or beaten with chains by Newton's goon-squad for infractions of Party discipline. Elaine Brown, an editor of the Black Panther paper, by her own account was bull-whipped for missing an editorial deadline. Absent also was a visit to the house where Panthers tortured former *Ramparts* employee Betty Van Patter before smashing her head with a pipe and throwing her body into San Francisco Bay.

Instead, tour-guide Hilliard stressed the Panthers' "idealism" and explained that "when you fall below history, as happened with women and slaves, you're really nothing. So the point we're trying to make here is to not be written out of history but to be a part of history." The enthusiastic audience for these pieties included the sitting mayor of Oakland, members of the Oakland City Council, the Oakland Board of Education (the same that adopted "Ebonics" as an "official language") and former California governor Jerry Brown, now running for mayor of Oakland.

A straight-faced account of the "Tour of Panther Sites" appeared in the *San Francisco Chronicle* complete with accompanying tour map.[1] It began: "The Black Panther Party for Self-

---

[1]"Tour of Black Panther Sites," Rick DelVecchio, *San Francisco Chronicle*, October 25, 1997; http://www.sfgate.com/news/article/Tour-of-Black-Panther-Sites-Former-member-shows-2825056.php

Defense was about politics, as its name implies, not about destruction." None of the missing pieces of Panther history was alluded to in the *Chronicle* account, nor in similar credulous reports on National Public Radio and in *The New York Times*. This was more than a case of collective amnesia. After all, America is not a police-state as the Soviet Union once was; here, you cannot simply erase the historical record. It's not as if the sordid history of the Panthers, a homicidal street gang with political pretensions, is unknown. But as Michael Kelly recently observed in *The New Republic*, the journalistic ranks are filled with veterans of the counterculture who consider themselves leftists and supported the revolutions of that time. They have taken it upon themselves to protect the Panther myth and, more importantly, the cause it supports. The result is a national media that acts to institutionalize the myth of the Panthers and the progressive Sixties.

This mentality was on full display in the national coverage of Black Panther Geronimo Pratt's release from prison, on a technicality, last July.[2] Although Pratt had been convicted of an unusually cold-blooded murder, not a single reporter interviewed prosecutors on the case, let alone Pratt's chief accuser, a former Black Panther named Julius Butler, to gain a reasonably balanced view. Nor did a single reporter bother to look at the court records, which prove that Pratt did murder elementary-school teacher Caroline Olsen on a Santa Monica tennis court 29 years ago. Instead, the press repeated his defense attorney Johnnie Cochran's fantasies about an FBI-LAPD conspiracy to frame Pratt, despite the fact that the evidence originally presented at trial shows that there could not have been such a conspiracy. While ignoring Pratt's prosecutors, the press reported the claims of his fans, who viewed him as an "American Nelson Mandela" and a new progressive hero. After his release, journalists followed him deferentially on his own tour of college campuses and dutifully reported the book and film deals

---

[2]This case is reviewed in "Johnnie's Other O.J." in Volume VI of this series, *Progressive Racism*.

he was negotiating, which will undoubtedly further lionize his criminal life.

And so history repeats itself, as Marx once said: "the first time as tragedy, the second as farce." Today's progressives are like the Bourbons, of whom it was once said, "They have forgotten nothing and learned nothing."

8

The Loafing Class

There's good news and bad news in higher education today. The good news is that a university education can provide a pass open to all to the incredible bounties of the information-age economy. The bad news is that the price of the pass can be the equivalent of a Ferrari, putting the average student into hock for a good chunk of his or her working life. While the price-tag of a liberal arts degree has gone up, the quality of the product has gone precipitously down. Professors of literature eschewing the classics have taken to teaching courses on racism and imperialism, while sociologists discourse on the "social construction" of scientific truths in which they are equally unlettered. The discredited doctrines of Karl Marx flourish in the academy in the midst of real-world economic forces about which Marx hadn't a clue.

The current issue of the academic journal *Social Text* offers a particularly illuminating example of the state of academic affairs in an article titled with typical professorial arrogance, "The Last Good Job in America." Couched as a personal memoir and written by one of the magazine's editors, the article is a self-portrait of the author, a liberal-arts professor, as slacker-in-residence.

Stanley Aronowitz was a 1960s labor organizer who earned the equivalent of a diploma mill Ph.D. from an Antioch extension program and was recruited to the graduate center of City University by a political comrade already embedded on the faculty. City University is New York's publicly funded higher education opportunity

February 9, 1998, http://www.salon.com/1998/02/09/nc_09horo_3/

for children of the working classes. Like other financially overbur-
dened educational institutions, it is downsizing, replacing full professors like Aronowitz with lower-paid teaching assistants.
Twenty years ago, City University hired Aronowitz "because they
believed I was a labor sociologist." In fact, as he boasts in *Social
Text*, this was a scam: "First and foremost I'm a political intellectual ... [I] don't follow the methodological rules of the discipline."[1]
Following his own looser rules, Aronowitz created—with administration support—the "Center for Cultural Studies" at CUNY, a
broad umbrella under which he could teach Marxist politics at his
leisure on the public dime.

From this base, Aronowitz became an academic star with a six-
figure salary and a publishing *vita* to match. In today's faddish university climate, it is totally in keeping that Aronowitz's *chef
d'oeuvre* is a book called *Science as Power*, which endorses the old
Stalinist doctrine that science is an instrument of the ruling class.
A reviewer for the *Times Literary Supplement* was moved to
remark: "If the author knows much about the content or enterprise of science, he keeps the knowledge well hidden." Connois-
seurs of Aronowitz were hardly surprised last year when he and his
fellow editors at *Social Text* published Alan Sokal's notorious
hoax-essay, designed to demonstrate that the magazine would run
pure gobbledygook so long as it sounded postmodern and politically correct.[2]

Aronowitz pays more respect to reality in his recent *Social Text*
article. In a sense, he does have the last good job in America, at
least from the perspective of someone as intellectually lazy as he
is. "What I enjoy most is the ability to procrastinate and control
my own work time, especially its pace: taking a walk in the mid-

---

[1] "The Last Good Job in America," Stanley Aronowitz, *Social Text*, Febru-
ary 1997
[2] *Fashionable Nonsense: Postmodern Intellectuals' Abuse of Science*,
Alan Sokal and Jean Bricmont, Picador, 1998; The Editors of *Lingua
Franca*, eds., *The Sokal Hoax: The Sham That Shook the Academy*,
Bison, 2000

dle of the day, reading between the writing, listening to a CD or tape anytime I want, calling up a friend for a chat." Easy to do when you teach just one two-hour course a week, a seminar (no surprise here) in Marxism. On Mondays and Wednesdays, Aronowitz doesn't even bother to leave his house. These are days devoted to writing such scholarly pieces as "The Future of the Left" for *The Nation* magazine. And the pay isn't too shabby, either. Aronowitz discloses this coyly, identifying himself, naturally, with the working class. "I earn more by some $5,000 a year than an auto worker who puts in a sixty-hour week." The last time I checked, an auto worker can make up to $40 an hour, which factors out to $1,600 a week (not including overtime) or over $112,000 a year. Then again, your average autoworker doesn't work the assembly-line just two hours a week or only nine months a year.

Aronowitz and his armchair comrades tilt at the windmills of a capitalist patriarchy from whose teat they feed, while trampling on academic standards and abusing the educational aspirations of their young charges. But such contradictions (a favorite term of failed revolutionaries) seem to escape Aronowitz. He concludes his memoir with a call to arms, reproving to his comrades for not advancing their struggle militantly enough: "We have not celebrated the idea of thinking as a full-time activity and the importance of producing what the system terms 'useless' knowledge. Most of all, we have not conducted a struggle for universalizing the self-managed time some of us still enjoy."

Loafers of the world, unite!

9

Eldridge Cleaver's Last Gift

Eldridge Cleaver was a man who made a significant imprint on our times, and not for the best. But I mourn his passing nonetheless. I first met Eldridge when he was *Ramparts* magazine's most famous and bloodthirsty ex-con. "I'm perfectly aware that I'm in prison, that I'm a Negro, that I've been a rapist,"[1] he wrote in a notorious epistle that *Ramparts* published. "My answer to all such thoughts lurking in their split-level heads, crouching behind their squinting bombardier eyes, is that the blood of Vietnamese peasants has paid off all my debts." This sociopathic outburst became an iconic comment for those radical times—a ready excuse for all the destructive acts that radicals like us committed.

No one doubted that Eldridge was the most articulate and colorful tribune of the Panther vanguard. But what he articulated was a limitless, nihilistic rage. Eldridge was indeed a rapist, and possibly a murderer as well; he boasted to Timothy Leary, whom he held hostage in his Algerian exile, that he even had a private graveyard for his enemies. It was Eldridge who accused Panther leader Huey Newton of betraying the radical cause; when Newton reversed his famous summons to "pick up the gun," Eldridge provoked a Panther split and became godfather to the Black Liberation Army, a violent revolutionary faction that murdered several police officers.

May 3, 1998, http://articles.latimes.com/1998/may/03/opinion/op-45871
[1] *Soul on Ice*, Eldridge Cleaver, McGraw-Hill, 1968. Written from Folsom Prison October 9, 1965.

But afterwards, Eldridge had a change of heart, or rather many changes of heart. He became a Moonie, then a Christian and a Republican, and then veered left again. Those of us who knew him saw these various incarnations as a political street-hustle designed to secure new cash-flows. Still, it took a certain integrity to divulge even a part of the truth. It meant, for example, detaching himself from the radical gravy-train, when his comrades were just beginning to cash in on their criminal pasts. His Panther cohorts David Hilliard, Bobby Seale and Elaine Brown were busily taking advantage of a national false memory syndrome that celebrated the Panthers, not as the street-thugs they were, but as heroes of a civil-rights struggle they had openly despised. (In their heyday, Panther leaders liked to outrage their white supporters by referring to its leader as "Martin Luther Coon.") On campus lecture tours, in Hollywood films, and in a series of well-hyped books celebrated by cultural institutions like *The New York Times* and *The Washington Post*, they rewrote their past to fit the legend.

But Eldridge chose the lonely and more honest course of admitting what he had done. His most famous encounter with the law had been a shootout that followed the assassination of Martin Luther King. In this episode, an 18-year-old Panther named Bobby Hutton was killed. It quickly became a famous martyrdom for the New Left, and a ritual occasion to attack as repressive and racist the power structure that had victimized black militants. In an interview with reporter Kate Coleman more than a decade later, however, Eldridge revealed that he had ordered Party members to "assassinate" police as a "retaliation" for the King murder (although police had nothing to do with it), and that he himself had participated in an armed ambush that left two San Francisco police officers wounded. This was why the police were chasing Eldridge when the shooting of Bobby Hutton occurred. Eldridge's revelation took greater courage than has been shown by other New Left leaders who know these facts but still deny them.

It was during his last televised interview on "60 Minutes" earlier this year that Eldridge won my respect. Quiet-spoken as he had never been in his public life, sober, bespectacled and fully grey, he discussed what appeared at last to be truly felt convictions, not designed for anyone but himself. He said that when you looked at this country as compared to others, it was remarkably good to people like himself and to minorities generally, a fact he had not appreciated when he was young. On the other hand, he said, "If people had listened to Huey Newton and me in the 1960s, there would have been a holocaust in this country."

The interviewer didn't acknowledge or perhaps even notice the significance of the remark. But I did. In these words lies the beginning of any real understanding of what the radical left and its Black Panther vanguard were about in the Sixties. For coming to this end-of-life knowledge, Eldridge paid a profound price. In a world where it is so difficult to get a purchase on the truth, we can be thankful to him for providing us with one.

10

The Future of the Left

For years, the philosopher Richard Rorty has been holding court as the foremost leftwing intellectual in America. Now he has come forward with a book that is a heart-felt lament about the state of the left, a movement he describes as anti-American, negative, program-less and politically irrelevant. Damning as this indictment might seem, *Achieving Our Country* is not a work of second thoughts. Rorty has no intention of abandoning a movement in whose causes he has toiled as a lifelong partisan. When all his complaints are registered, the left remains in his eyes the "party of hope," the only possible politics a decent, humane and moral intellectual could embrace. This air of invincible self-righteousness, coupled with his hand-wringing, makes Rorty's book at once a desperate and revealing case, an emblem of the quandary in which the American left now finds itself.

Rorty's own career as a philosophical pragmatist is based on an American skepticism hostile to the grand theorizing and absolute certitudes characteristic of Marxism. Yet Rorty's personal background lies firmly inside the Marxist tradition. His parents, by his own account, began as "loyal fellow-travelers" of the Communist Party, breaking with their comrades in 1932 when they realized how completely the Party was dominated by Moscow. Rorty's father became a leader of American Trotskyism and was lampooned in a 1935 *Daily Worker* cartoon that portrayed him as a

May 4, 1998, http://archive.frontpagemag.com/readArticle.aspx?ARTID=24323; http://www.salon.com/1998/05/04/nc_04horo/

trained seal reaching for fish thrown by William Randolph Hearst. In this environment, the young Rorty grew up as an "anti-Communist red diaper baby," supporting America's Cold War against the Soviet empire while keeping the socialist fires burning at home, a post-modernist *avant la lettre*. With the passing of Irving Howe, Rorty is now the last of the breed, godfather to a small but influential remnant of self-styled social democrats (which after all is how Lenin thought of himself) gathered around Howe's magazine, *Dissent*. While Rorty sometimes seems to understand the real-world failure of the socialist fantasy, he stubbornly clings to socialism in the same way Howe did, as "the name of our desire."

Rorty begins his diagnosis of the American left by comparing national pride to individual self-esteem, declaring it a "necessary condition for self-improvement." This announces his central concern, which is the emergence since the 1960s of a left that openly despises America and everything it stands for. When this left speaks of America, Rorty observes, it does so only in terms of "mockery and disgust." When it thinks of national pride, it is as something "appropriate only for chauvinists." It associates American patriotism with the endorsement of atrocities against Native Americans, ancient forests and African slaves.

In Rorty's view, it was not always thus. In America, there was once a progressive left whose pride in country was "almost religious," and whose aspirations were summarized in Herbert Croly's title *The Promise of American Life*. It was a left that believed in an organic development of America into the country that it should be, and therefore in a politics of piecemeal reform. Into this radical Eden, as Rorty's narrative continues, there came first the serpent of Marxism and then the trauma of Vietnam. Instead of promoting reforms, Marxism was chiliastic and confrontational. It was absolutist instead of skeptical. Instead of aiming at realistic improvements to our benighted condition, Marxists aimed at a totalizing revolution that would transform the world we know into something radically other. This apocalyptic vision made piecemeal reform irrelevant if not positively dangerous, since reforms might co-opt or dampen the revolutionary spirit. Negativism—the use of social criticism as a corrosive acid—became its tactic of choice.

In Rorty's eyes, the Vietnam War was the trigger of this transformation. Vietnam was "an atrocity of which Americans should be deeply ashamed."[1] Along with the "endless humiliation inflicted on African-Americans" throughout American history, Vietnam persuaded the New Left, which had previously recognized the "errors" of Marxism, that something was "deeply wrong with their country, and not just mistakes correctable by reforms." Consequently, they became neo-Marxists and revolutionaries.

But even if Rorty's explanation were correct, these events took place 20 years before the fall of Marxist socialism in 1989. Now everyone can see—or should be able to see—that the Marxist vision is not viable. It was killed by the failures of 20th-century utopias. While Rorty is realist enough to recognize this truth, he still remains wedded to the leftist idea of a redemptive future. In his eyes since Communism is no longer an issue, the utopian idea can be revived and the divided factions of the left can unite in a new version of the Popular Front. According to Rorty, the time has come to drop names like "Old Left" and "New Left," which once reflected differing attitudes towards the Soviet Union, and also to erase the distinction between socialists and liberals, since it is easy to see they share similar agendas once the metaphysical idea of overthrowing capitalism is abandoned.

Just how far Rorty is willing to take these reconciliations is revealed by his roster of icons he includes in his proposed progressive front. "A hundred years from now, Howe and Galbraith, Harrington and Schlesinger, ... Jane Addams and Angela Davis ... will all be remembered for having advanced the cause of social justice," he writes. "Whatever mistakes they made, these people will deserve, as Coolidge and Buckley never will, the praise with which Jonathan Swift ended his own epitaph: 'Imitate him if you can; he

---

[1]*Achieving Our Country: Leftist Thought in 20th-Century America*, Richard Rorty, Harvard, 1998

served human liberty.'" Elsewhere he says, "My leftmost students, who are also my favorite students, find it difficult to take
my anti-communism seriously." Rorty's own readiness to embrace
Angela Davis and other lifetime servants of communist totalitarianism and present them as defenders of liberty, while dismissing
anti-totalitarians like William F. Buckley, shows why.

An obstacle to Rorty's plan to create this popular front is posed
by what he calls the "cultural left," which has disquietingly reproduced the modalities of 1930s fascism and Stalinism on American
campuses. It is a left that Rorty describes as "spectatorial," "dis-
gusted," "mocking" and "politically correct." The nihilism of its
attitude towards America is so total, Rorty laments, that it has no
practical political agenda. After reading works by its icons, Rorty
singles out Fredric Jameson, telling him, "you have views on practically everything except what needs to be done." There are over-
laps between these "post-modernists" and the Old Left. Rorty
notes that Jameson, an armchair Maoist, thinks that "anti-
communists are scum." To Rorty, this is an amusing quirk rather
than a telling political position. But elsewhere, Rorty himself
refers to anti-communist figures like Ronald Reagan with a nasti-
ness that approaches Jameson's own.

Having scolded the cultural left, Rorty then proceeds to praise
them. The older, economically oriented left, he writes, set out to
purge society of "selfishness." The new "cultural left" aims to
purge America of "sadism," an agenda he judges to have been
marked by "extraordinary success." According to Rorty, the
speech-code and sensitivity commissars of the academic left "have
decreased the amount of sadism in our society. Especially among
college graduates, the casual infliction of humiliation is much less
socially acceptable than it was during the first two-thirds of the
century. The tone in which educated men talk about women and
educated whites about blacks is very different from what it was
before the Sixties.[2] ... The adoption of attitudes which the Right

---

[2]Ibid., p. 81

sneers at as 'politically correct' has made America a far more civilized society than it was thirty years ago."

Perhaps it is true that the tone in which "educated" men talk to women and whites to blacks has improved under pressures from the diversity-controllers. But what about the tone in which women talk to men, blacks talk to whites, and women and blacks talk to white men? What about the ritual punishments and humiliations meted out daily in these very havens of cultural sensitivity and concern to those who deviate from the leftist party line, who are subject to political grading and hiring, general ostracism and reflexive hatred because of their race and gender status, or political and religious orientation? The juices of atavistic prejudice have simply been redirected. Now they are aimed, for example, at religious Christians and at Jews, who have been the particular targets of anti-Semitic assaults by Muslim and black supremacists, and anti-Israel progressives. In one of the "Table Talk" threads in *Salon*—in Rorty's schema a center of cultural enlightenment—I was recently named "the most repellent Jew in American history" for the crime of being politically incorrect.

How is one to account for these *lacunae* in the perceptions of an otherwise intelligent person like Richard Rorty? A good bet is that the aging Rorty suffers from being committed to a movement whose younger generations he is loath to alienate. Only this could explain the mash notes he writes to the politically correct, whose agendas he can easily see through: "The cultural Left has a vision of an America in which the white patriarchs have stopped voting and have left all the voting to be done by members of previously victimized groups, people who have somehow come into possession of more foresight and imagination than the selfish suburbanites. These formerly oppressed and newly powerful people are expected to be as angelic as the straight white males were diabolical. If I shared this expectation, I too would want to live under this new dispensation. Since I see no reason to share it, I think that the Left should get back into the business of piecemeal reform within the framework of a market economy."

While delivering dollops of good sense, Rorty nonetheless keeps returning to the idea that a way can be found to achieve the socialist fantasy, despite what history has shown and what he himself knows. This acceptance of conservative truths and avoidance of conservative conclusions marks a critical fault-line in his perspective. In order to preserve his radical faith, Rorty constantly finds it necessary to demonize the conservative Right, and does so in a manner as ham-fisted and unremitting as the demonization of white males and America by his cultural comrades. Here is how Rorty characterizes his conservative peers:

> It is doubtful whether the current critics of the universities who are called "conservative intellectuals" deserve this description. For intellectuals are supposed to be aware of, and speak to, issues of social justice.[3] But even the most learned and thoughtful of current conservatives ridicule those who raise such issues. They themselves have nothing to say about whether children in the ghettos can be saved without raising suburbanites' taxes or about how people who earn the minimum wage can pay for adequate housing. They seem to regard discussion of such topics as in poor taste.[4]

Can it be that Rorty is ignorant of the work of James Q. Wilson, Marvin Olasky, Peter Mead, Glenn Loury, John Dilulio, Robert Woodson, or any of scores of conservative intellectuals who have thought long and hard about the problems of poverty from a perspective of concern? This is a caricature so extreme as to be self-discrediting. On the other hand, the academic purge of conservatives by Rorty's political allies has been so thorough that he need hardly be concerned about being held to account for such a shallow and uncompromising dismissal of his critics.

---

[3]*Richard Rorty,* Michael A. Peters, Paulo Ghiraldelli Jr., Rowman & Littlefield, 2001, p. 145
[4]*Achieving Our Country: Leftist Thought in 20th-Century America,* op. cit. pp. 82–83

Rorty's myopia has a Thirties flavor. "The Right ... fears economic and political change, and therefore easily becomes the pawn of the rich and powerful—the people whose selfish interests are served by forestalling such change." And it is just as far removed from reality. Why would the interests of a Bill Gates or a Marc Andreessen or a Larry Ellison or their community of super-rich Silicon Valley revolutionaries be interested in "forestalling" economic and political change? In recent years, the political right has brought down the socialist empire and unleashed the political and technological future throughout its former satellites. In America, it has stemmed the flow of government red ink that promised to drown future generations in an ocean of debt and has begun the long unraveling of the welfare bureaucracy that for a quarter of a century has stifled personal and economic growth in America's inner cities. The Right is in fact the party of reform—just as surely as the left, hopelessly addicted to its socialist nostalgias, has become a camp of reactionaries clinging to a bankrupt perspective.

The true source of the left's negativism is its guilty recognition that the future it promoted for two hundred years killed tens of millions, impoverished and blighted the lives of hundreds of millions more, and, in the end, didn't work. *Achieving Our Country* is a disappointing book by a man who should know better but doesn't have the intellectual grit to admit that he was wrong.

I, Rigoberta Menchú, Liar

One of the great hoaxes of the 20th century has finally been exposed as a politically motivated fabrication, a tissue of politically-correct lies. It is the story of Rigoberta Menchú, a Quiché Mayan from Guatemala, whose autobiography catapulted her to international fame, won her the Nobel Peace Prize, and made her an international emblem of the indigenous peoples of the Western hemisphere and their purported attempt to rebel against the oppression of European conquerors and the United States. Equally remarkable and instructive regarding the cultural power of the perpetrators of the hoax, exposing it has changed nothing. The Nobel committee has already refused to take back her prize; the thousands of college courses that make her book a required text for American college students will continue to do so; and the editorial writers of the major press institutions have already defended her falsehoods on the same grounds that supporters of Tawana Brawley's similar hoax made iconic: *Even if she's lying, she's telling the truth.*

Made internationally famous by the success of her book and by the Nobel Prize she was awarded in 1992, Rigoberta is now head of the Rigoberta Menchú Foundation for Human Rights and a spokesperson for the cause of "social justice and peace." The 1984 autobiography, *I, Rigoberta Menchú*,[1] which launched this hoax, was actually written by a French leftist, Elisabeth Burgos-Debray.

January 12, 1999; http://frontpagemag.com/2010/david-horowitz/david-horowitz%E2%80%99s-archives-i-rigoberta-menchu-liar/;
http://www.salon.com/1999/01/11/nc_11horo/
[1] *I, Rigoberta Menchu*, Elisabeth Burgos-Debray, Verso, 1984

Elizabeth is the wife of Regis Debray, the Marxist whose theory of guerilla *focos* provided the strategy for Che Guevara's failed effort to foment a war in Bolivia in the 1960s. Debray's misguided theory led to the death of Guevara and an undetermined number of Bolivian peasants; it is also at the root of the tragedies that overwhelmed Rigoberta Menchú and her family.

The story of Rigoberta Menchú, as her autobiography tells it, is a classic Marxist parable. The Menchús were a poor Mayan family living on the margins of a country from which they had been dispossessed by the Spanish conquistadors whose descendants, known as *ladinos,* tried to drive the Menchús and other Indian peasants off unclaimed land that they had cultivated. The child Rigoberta was illiterate. Her peasant father, Vicente, refused to send her to school because he needed her to work in the fields.

So poor was the Menchú family because of their lack of land that Rigoberta had to watch her younger brother die of starvation. Meanwhile, her father was engaged in a heroic but ultimately hopeless battle with the *ladino* masters of the land for a plot to cultivate. Finally, Vicente organized a resistance movement called the Committee for Campesino Unity to advance the land claims of the *indígenas* against the *ladino* masters. Rigoberta became a political organizer too. The resistance movement linked up with a Guatemalan revolutionary force called the Guerrilla Army of the Poor. To suppress an aroused people, the brutal security forces of the conquistadors were called into the fray and eventually prevailed. The family was forced to watch Rigoberta's brother burned alive. Her father, Vicente Menchú, was killed. Rigoberta's mother was raped and also killed.

According to Rigoberta's account, the tragedy of the Menchús is "the story of all Guatemala's poor."[2] It is a plea to people of good will all over the world to help the good but powerless indigenous peoples of Guatemala and other Third World countries to their

---

[2]*Rigoberta Menchú and the Story of All Poor Guatemalans,* David Stoll, Westview, 1999, p. 1

rightful inheritance, and by implication to support revolutionary forces like the Guerrilla Army of the Poor which are trying to liberate them.

Unfortunately for this political fantasy, virtually every significant detail in Rigoberta's account is a lie. They are lies about the central events and facts of her story, and they have been concocted to create a specific political myth. The deceptions begin on the very first page of her text: "When I was older, my father regretted my not going to school, as I was a girl able to learn many things. But he always said: 'Unfortunately, if I put you in school, they'll make you forget your class; they'll turn you into a *ladina*. I don't want that for you and that's why I don't send you.' He might have had the chance to put me in school when I was about fourteen or fifteen but he couldn't do it because he knew what the consequences would be: the ideas that they would give me."[3]

To the unsuspecting reader, this looks like an all-too-perfect realization of the Marxist paradigm in which ruling ideas become the ideas of the ruling class through its control of the means of education. But, contrary to her assertions, Rigoberta was not uneducated. Nor did her father oppose her education because he feared it would indoctrinate her in the values of the *ladino* ruling class. Her father, in fact, sent her to two prestigious private boarding-schools operated by Catholic nuns, where she received the equivalent of a middle-school education. Although it is only a hypothesis, it was probably in this Catholic school that she was recruited to the Marxist faith and became a spokesperson for Communist guerrillas. Because Rigoberta was indeed away at boarding school for most of her youth, her detailed accounts of laboring eight months a year on coffee and cotton plantations and organizing a political underground are also probably false.

These and other pertinent facts have now been established by anthropologist David Stoll, a leading academic expert on Guatemala, who interviewed more than 120 Guatemalans, including relatives,

---

[3] *I, Rigoberta Menchu*, op. cit., p. 190

friends, neighbors, former teachers and classmates over a ten-year period for his new biography, *Rigoberta Menchú and the Story of All Poor Guatemalans*.[4] To coincide with the publication of Stoll's book, *The New York Times* sent reporter Larry Rohter to Guatemala to attempt to verify Stoll's findings, which he did.[5]

One of Stoll's salient findings is the way in which Rigoberta distorted the sociology of her family's situation and that of the Mayans in the region of Uspantán. Another is the way she distorted her family biography. Rigoberta had no brother who starved to death, at least none that her own family could remember. The *ladinos* were not a ruling caste in Rigoberta's town or district, in which there were no large estates or *fincas* as she claims. The Menchús, moreover, were not poor in the way Rigoberta describes them. Vicente Menchú had title to 2,753 hectares of land. The 22-year land dispute described by Rigoberta, which is the central event in the book leading to the rebellion and the tragedies that followed, was in fact over a tiny 151-hectare parcel.

Most importantly, Vicente Menchú's "heroic struggle against the landowners who wanted to take our land" was in fact not a dispute with representatives of a European-descended conquistador class of *ladinos* but with his own Mayan relatives, the Tum family, headed by his wife's uncle. Vicente Menchú did not organize a peasant resistance called the Committee for Campesino Unity; he was conservative insofar as he was political at all. His consuming passion was not any social concern but the family feud with his in-laws, who were small landowning peasants like himself. It was his involvement in this feud that caused him to be caught up in the larger political drama that was really irrelevant to his concerns, although it ultimately killed him.

At the end of the Seventies, Cuba's Communist dictator, Fidel Castro, launched a new initiative to sponsor a series of guerrilla

---

[4]*Rigoberta Menchú and the Story of All Poor Guatemalans*, op. cit.
[5]http://partners.nytimes.com/library/books/121598cambodian-memoir.html

offensives in Nicaragua, El Salvador and Guatemala, along lines laid down by Regis Debray and Che Guevara a decade before. The leaders of these movements were generally not indigenous Indians but Hispanics, typically disaffected middle- and upper-class scions of the ruling castes of those countries. They were often the graduates of cadre training-centers in Moscow and Havana, and of terrorist training camps in Lebanon and East Germany. (The leaders of the Salvadoran guerillas even included a Palestinian Communist and Shiite Muslim named Shafik Handal.)

One of these Castroist forces, the Guerrilla Army of the Poor, showed up in Uspantán, the largest township near Rigoberta's village, on April 29, 1979. According to eyewitnesses, they painted everything within reach red, grabbed the tax collector's money and threw it in the streets, broke into the jail, released the prisoners, and chanted "We are defenders of the poor" in the town square for 15 or 20 minutes.[6] None of the guerillas was masked because none of them was local. As strangers, they had no understanding of the Uspantán situation in which virtually all the land disputes were between the Mayan inhabitants themselves. Instead, they perceived things according to the Marxist textbook-version promulgated by Rigoberta and by the Nobel Prize committee, and proceeded to execute two local *ladino* landholders.

Thinking that the guerrillas were now the power in his region, Vicente Menchú cast his fate with them, providing them with a meeting-place and accompanying them on a protest. But the Guatemalan security forces, primed for the hemispheric offensive that Castro had launched, quickly descended on the region with characteristic brutality. They were aided by enraged relatives of the murdered *ladino* peasants seeking revenge on the leftist assassins. The violence this triggered resulted in the deaths of many innocents, including Rigoberta's parents and a second brother, although it is certain that Rigoberta did not witness his death as she falsely claims.

---

[6]*Rigoberta Menchú and the Story of All Poor Guatemalans*, op. cit., p. 43

The most famous incident in Rigoberta's book is the occupation of the Spanish embassy in Guatemala City in January 1980 by
a group of guerrillas and protesting peasants. Vicente Menchú was
the peasant spokesman. The occupation itself was led by the
Robin García Revolutionary Student Front. A witness, interviewed by David Stoll, described how Vicente was primed for his
role:

> They would tell Don Vicente, "Say, 'The people united will never
> be defeated,'" and Don Vicente would say, "The people united
> will never be defeated." They would tell Don Vicente, "Raise
> your left hand when you say it," and he would raise his left
> hand.[7]

When they set out on their trip, the Uspantán peasants who
accompanied the student revolutionaries to the Spanish embassy
had no idea where they were going or what the purpose of the trip
was. Later, David Stoll interviewed a survivor whose husband had
died in the incident. She told him that the journey originated in a
wedding party at the Catholic church in Uspantán. Two days after
the ceremony, the wedding party moved on. "The *señores* said
they were going to the coast, but they arrived at the capital." Once
there, the student revolutionaries proceeded with their plan to
occupy the embassy and take hostages, with the unsuspecting
Mayans ensnared. Although the cause of the ensuing tragedy is in
dispute, David Stoll presents persuasive evidence that a Molotov
cocktail brought by the students ignited and set the embassy on
fire. At least 39 people, including Vicente Menchú, were killed.

As a result of Stoll's research, Nobel laureate Rigoberta
Menchú has been exposed as a Communist agent working for terrorists who were ultimately responsible for the death of her own
family. So rigid is Rigoberta's party loyalty to the Castroist cause
that she refused to denounce the Sandinista dictatorship's genocidal attempt to eliminate Nicaragua's Miskito Indians, despite

---

[7]Ibid., p. 88

billing herself as a champion of indigenous peoples. She even broke with her own translator, Elisabeth Burgos-Debray, over the issue of the Miskitos when Burgos-Debray, along with other prominent French leftists, protested the attacks.

Rigoberta's response to the exposure of her lies has been, on one hand, "no comment," and on the other to add a lie—her denial that she had anything to do with the book that made her famous. David Stoll listened to two hours of the tapes she made for Burgos-Debray, and concluded that the narrative they recorded is identical to the (false) version of the facts in the book itself.

The fictional story of Rigoberta Menchú is a piece of Communist propaganda designed to incite hatred of Europeans, westerners, and the societies they have built, and to build support for Communist and terrorist organizations at war with the democracies of the West. It has become the single most influential social treatise read by American college students as required by their leftist professors. Over 15,000 college theses have been written on Rigoberta Menchú, accepting her lies as gospel, and the Nobel Prize committee has made Rigoberta an international figure and spokesperson for "social justice and peace."

In an editorial responding to the Stoll revelations, the *Los Angeles Times* typically glossed over the enormity of what Rigoberta, the Guatemalan terrorists, the French left, the international community of "human-rights" leftists, the Nobel Prize committee, and the tenured radicals who dominate Latin American studies in American universities have wrought. The *Times* did recognize that something had gone amiss: "After the initial lies, the international apparatus of human-rights activism, journalism, and academia pitched in to exaggerate the dire condition of the peasants when a simple recounting of the truth would have been enough."

But would it? If the simple truth were enough to make her points, Rigoberta's lies would have been unnecessary. If there had been any truth in the myth itself, the Guatemalan guerrillas would not have been wiped out in two or three years. The fact is that there was no social ground for the armed insurrection that Castro and his agents tried to force on Guatemala's poor, any more than there had been for Guevara's suicidal effort in Bolivia years before. Ultimately, the source of the violence and ensuing misery that Rigoberta Menchú describes in her destructive little book is the left itself, and the leftist intelligentsia in particular. Too bad it hasn't the decency to acknowledge this, and to leave the Third World alone.

12

The Secret Power of the Leftist Faith

L et's begin by acknowledging the obvious: I am the last person Christopher Hitchens wants to see defending him in his current imbroglio with White House henchman and ex-friend Sidney Blumenthal. Christopher and I were once political comrades, though we were never quite proximate enough to become friends. But for nearly two decades we have been squaring off on opposite sides of the political barricades; and I know that Christopher's detractors will inevitably use my support of him to confirm that he has lost his political bearings and gone over to the other side. For that reason, let me add that I do not believe Christopher is about to have second thoughts, or to join Peter Collier and myself as critics of the movement to which he has dedicated his life. On the contrary, as everything Christopher has put on the public record in the last year attests, his contempt for Clinton and his decision to expose Clinton's servant as a liar and knave spring from his deep passion for the left and for the values it claims to hold dear.[1]

In one of his *Vanity Fair* dispatches, Christopher accused the commander-in-chief of cynically and mendaciously deploying the armed forces of the greatest superpower on earth to strike at three

---

March 1, 1999; http://archive.frontpagemag.com/Printable.aspx?ArtId= 24276; http://www.salon.com/1999/03/01/nc_01horo/
[1]Christopher never did leave the left. I have written a biographical essay on Christopher, including his last year, which addresses this issue. Cf. "The Two Christophers, Or the Importance of Second Thoughts" in *Radicals: Portraits of a Destructive Passion*, Regnery, 2012

impoverished countries, with no clear military objective in mind. Using the most advanced weaponry the world had ever seen, Clinton launched missiles into the Sudan, Afghanistan and Iraq for only one tangible political purpose: as Christopher puts it, to "distract attention from his filthy lunge at a beret-wearing cupcake [Monica Lewinsky]."[2]

Christopher's claims that Clinton's military actions were criminal and impeachable are surely correct. Clinton's Republican prosecutors, it seems, were right about the character issue, and failed only to show how this mattered to policy issues the public cares deeply about. Instead, they got themselves entangled in legalistic disputes about perjury and constitutional impeachment bars, and lost the electorate along the way. In making his own strong case against Clinton, Christopher has underscored how Republicans botched the process by focusing on criminality that flowed from minor abuses of power, like the sexual harassment of Paula Jones and its Lewinsky subtext, while ignoring a major abuse that involved corrupting the office of commander-in-chief, damaging the nation's security and killing innocents abroad.

Reading Christopher's indictment stirred unexpected feelings of nostalgia in me for the left I had once been part of. Not the actual left that I came to know and reject, but the left of my youthful idealism, when I thought our mission was to be the nation's "conscience," to speak truth to power in the name of what was just. This, as is perfectly evident from what he has written, was Christopher's own mission in exposing Blumenthal as the willing agent of a corrupt regime and its reckless commander-in-chief.[3] In carrying out this mission, Christopher was forced to engage the

---

[2]Christopher Hitchens, "Most Dangerous Presidency: Weapons of Mass Distraction," *FrontPage Magazine*, March 22, 1999, http://archive.frontpagemag.com/readArticle.aspx?ARTID=24223. To be fair, Clinton may well have believed that the pharmaceutical factory in the Sudan was making chemical or biological weapons.
[3]Christopher Hitchens, "The Truth About Sid: What Really Happened," *FrontPage Magazine*, February 16, 1999, http://archive.frontpagemag.com/readArticle.aspx?ARTID=24222

Lewinsky matter when Blumenthal solicited his aid in smearing the credibility of the key witness to the president's bad faith.

It is difficult to believe that a borderline sociopath like Clinton could stop at the water's edge of illicit sex in the Oval Office, or that he is innocent of other serious accusations against him that Starr and the Republicans have been unable to prove. In fact, the same signature behavior is apparent throughout his administration, aptly captured in the title of Christopher's forthcoming book about the Clintons, "No One Left to Lie To." The presidential pathology is manifest not only in his reckless private dalliances (the betrayal of family and office), but also in his strategy of political "triangulation" (the betrayal of allies and friends), and in his fire-sale of the Lincoln bedroom and advanced military technology to adversarial powers (the betrayal of country). Christopher is quite right to strike at the agent of the king, although the king is ultimately to blame.

Given the transparent morality of Christopher's anti-Clinton crusade, it is all the more revealing that so many of his comrades on the left, who ought to share these concerns, have chosen instead to turn on him so viciously. In a savage display of comradely venom, they have publicly shunned him, seeking to cut him off socially from his own community. One after another, they have rushed into print to tell the world at large how repelled they are by a man whom only yesterday they still called "friend," and whom they no longer wish to know.

Leading this pack was Christopher's longtime colleague at *The Nation*, Alexander Cockburn, who denounced him as a "Judas" and a "snitch." Cockburn was joined by a second colleague at *The Nation*, Katha Pollitt, who anathematized Christopher as a throwback to McCarthy-era informers: "Let's say the Communist Party was bad and wrong ... Why help the repressive powers of the state? Let the government do its own dirty work."[4] Pollitt was joined by

---

[4]https://groups.google.com/forum/?fromgroups#!topic/alt.true-crime/lRJ VPacDouA

Todd Gitlin, a 30-year comrade of Christopher's who warned anyone who cared to listen that Hitchens was a social "poison" in the
same toxic league as Clinton prosecutor Ken Starr and Clinton
accuser Linda Tripp; and that Christopher would no longer be welcome at Gitlin's door.

Could one imagine a similar ritual performed by journalists of
the right? Bob Novak, say, flanked by Pat Buchanan and William F.
Buckley, Jr., proclaiming anathemas on Bill Safire because the
columnist had called for the jailing of Ollie North during the Iran-
Contra hearings? Not even North himself felt the need to
announce such a public divorce. When was the last time any conservative figure, let alone a gathering of conservative figures,
stepped forward to end a private friendship publicly over a political
disagreement, and declare the offender a pariah?

The curses rained on Christopher's head are part of a ritual that
has become familiar over generations of the left, in which dissidents are excommunicated and consigned to various Siberias for
their political deviance. It is a phenomenon normal to religious
cults, where purity of heart is maintained through avoiding contact with the unclean. To have caused the left to invoke so drastic
a measure, Christopher had evidently violated a fundamental principle of its faith. But what was it?

In fact, there seem to be at least two charges concerning
Christopher's transgression. On the one hand, he has been accused
of "snitching" on a political ally; on the other, he is said to have
betrayed a friend. These are not obviously identical. Nor is it obvious that the left, as a matter of principle, is generally outraged by
either. Daniel Ellsberg, to take one example, is a radical snitch
who betrayed not only his political allies but his own government.
Yet Ellsberg is a hero to the left. David Brock, who also kissed and
told, is hardly *persona non grata* among leftists. The left's standards for snitching on itself are entirely different from its standards for those who snitch on its enemies.

Christopher's editor at *The Nation*, Victor Navasky, has written
a whole volume about the McCarthy era called *Naming Names* on

the premise that the act of snitching is worse than the crimes revealed because it involves personal betrayal. On the other hand, the bond of comradeship, of loyalty, of belonging, is exactly the bond that every organized-crime syndicate exploits to establish and maintain its regime. There is an immediate reminder of this connection in the Paul Robeson centennial that progressives are observing this year. In a variety of cultural and political events to be held across the nation, the left will celebrate the life and achievement of one of its great heroes on the hundredth anniversary of his birth. Robeson, however, is a man who also betrayed his friend the Yiddish poet Itzhak Pfeffer, not to mention thousands of other Soviet Jews, who were under a death-sentence imposed by Robeson's own hero, Joseph Stalin.[5] In refusing to help them, despite Pfeffer's personal plea to him to do so, Robeson was acting under a code of silence that prevented Communists like him from "snitching" on the crimes their comrades committed. They justified their silence in the name of the progressive cause, allowing the murderers among them to destroy not only millions of innocent lives but their socialist dream as well.

Next month the Motion Picture Academy will honor Elia Kazan, a theater legend who has been blacklisted for nearly half a century by the Hollywood left. He, too, has been called a Judas by leftist members of the Academy who are protesting his award. Kazan's sin was to testify before a congressional committee about his fellow Communists who were also loyal supporters of Stalin's monstrous regime, and who conducted their own blacklist of anti-Stalinists in the entertainment community. Kazan's most celebrated film, *On the Waterfront*, scripted by another disillusioned Communist, Budd Schulberg, depicts a longshoreman who testifies to a congressional committee that is investigating organized crime, specifically a mob that controls his own union and terrorizes its membership. It is a thinly-veiled commentary on Kazan's and Schulberg's experiences in the left. "Snitching" is how the progressive

---

[5]Louis Rapoport, *Stalin's War Against the Jews: The Doctors' Plot and the Soviet Solution*, Free Press, 1990

mob regards the act of speaking truth to power, when the power is its own. The mafia calls its code of silence *omertà*, and the penalty for speaking against the mob is death. The left's penalty for defection when it does not exercise state power is excommunication from its community of saints. This is a kind of death, too.

In my own case, when I decided to leave the left, I avoided informing on friends or even exposing them. My first political statements opposing the left were made a decade after I had ceased to be an active participant in its cause, when the battles I had participated in were over. But this did not make an iota of difference to my former comrades once I made my views public. I was denounced as a "renegade," just as though I had become an informer, and was subjected to the same kind of shunning and betrayal that Christopher is experiencing now. With only a handful of exceptions, all the friends I had made in the first 40 years of my life turned their backs on me when my politics changed.

This tainting and ostracism of sinners is the secret power of the leftist faith. It is what keeps the faithful in line. The spectacle of what happens to a heretic like Christopher when he challenges the party code is a warning to others not to try it. This is why Alger Hiss kept his silence to the end, and why, even 30 and 50 years after the fact, the memoirs of leftists are so evasive when it comes to telling the hard political and personal truths about who they were and what they did. To tell a threatening truth is to risk vanishing in the progressive communities where you have staked your life. Christopher's crime is not the betrayal of friendship. It is the betrayal of the progressive party line, the only bond the left takes seriously.

This is far from obvious to those who have never been insiders. Writing in *The Wall Street Journal*, the otherwise perceptive Roger Kimball described what has happened to Christopher under the following caption: "Leftists Sacrifice Truth on the Altar of Friendship."[6] But this presumes either that they were closer friends of

---

[6]Roger Kimball, "Leftists Sacrifice Truth on the Altar of Friendship," *Wall Street Journal*, February 22, 1999

Blumenthal's than of Christopher's, or that friendship means more to them than politics. None of the denouncers of Christopher claimed a closer friendship with Blumenthal as a reason for their choice. Moreover, there is not the slightest reason to suppose that these leftists would remain friends of Blumenthal's should he, in turn, reveal what he really knows about Clinton's obstructions of justice and the machinations of the White House crew.

To examine an actual betrayal of friendship, one need go no further than Cockburn's *New York Press* column attacking Christopher as a compulsive snitch. Friends can take different political paths and still honor the life that was once between them, the qualities and virtues that made them friends. Alex was once closer to Christopher than Blumenthal ever was. They knew each other longer and their friendship was deeper. Christopher even named his own son "Alex" out of admiration for his friend. But in his column about Christopher's transgression, Alex gratuitously smears Christopher (who is married) as an aggressive closet homosexual, an odorous, ill-mannered and obnoxious drunk, and a pervert who gets a sexual *frisson* out of ratting on his intimates. Not a single member of Christopher's former community, which includes people who have known Christopher as a comrade for 30 years, has stepped forward to defend him from this ugly slander.

What then inspires these *auto-da-fes*? It is the fact that the community of the left is a community of meaning, and is bound by ties that are fundamentally religious. For the non-religious, politics is the art of managing the possible. For the left, it is the path to social and personal redemption. This messianism is the left's political essence. For the left, politics is ultimately not about practical options on which reasonable people may reasonably differ. It is about moral choices that define one as human. It is about taking sides in a war that will decide the future of mankind and about whether principles like "social justice" will prevail. It is about *us* being on the side of the angels, and *them* as the party of the damned. In the act of giving up Sidney Blumenthal to the congressional majority and the special prosecutor, Christopher put power in the hands of the enemies of the people and, worse still, of human decency. He acted as one of *them*.

Katha Pollitt puts it to Christopher this way: "Why should you, who call yourself a socialist, a man of the left, help Henry Hyde and Bob Barr and Trent Lott? If Clinton is evil, are the forces arrayed against him better, with their 100 per cent ratings from the Christian Coalition, and their after-dinner speaking engagements at white-supremacist clubs?"[7] Of course, Katha Pollitt doesn't for a moment think that Clinton is evil. But Christopher's new allies obviously are. Observe how easily she deploys the McCarthy stratagems to taint Christopher's new "friends"—using guilt-by-association, as though the entire Clinton opposition can be implicated in these links (assuming of course that these links to actively white supremacist groups are real, which they are not).

The casting-out of Christopher Hitchens, then, is a necessary ritual to protect the left's myth of itself as a redemptive force. How could Blumenthal, who is one of them, who is loyal to their cause, be connected to something evil, as Christopher suggests? How could *they*? All of Christopher's attackers and all 58 members of the congressional Progressive Caucus who before were opponents of American military power supported the wanton strikes against the Sudan, Afghanistan and Iraq, without batting a proverbial eyelash. Every one of them has found a way to excuse Clinton's abuse of "disposable" women like Paula Jones, Kathleen Willey and Monica Lewinsky. The last thing they want to do now is confront Blumenthal's collusion in a campaign to destroy one of Clinton's female nuisances because she became a political threat. After all, they *want* the reprobate in power. In blurting out the truth, Christopher has slammed the left up against its hypocrisies and threatened to unmask its sanctimonious pretensions. This is the threat which the anathema on Christopher is designed to repel.

---

[7]https://groups.google.com/forum/?fromgroups#!topic/alt.true-crime/lRJ VPacDouA

Here is my own message for the condemned man: You and I, Christopher, will continue our disagreements on many important things, and perhaps most things. But I take my hat off to you for what you have done: for your dedicated pursuit of the truth, and for your courage in standing up under fire. The comrades who have left you are incapable of such acts.

13

Mercy for a Terrorist?

W ho in America today could be associated with a gang that carried out an execution-style murder of a prominent public official and the murder of a pregnant woman during a bank hold-up, and then, when finally arrested, be championed as an "idealist" by church officials, Democratic Party legislators, columnists and local activist groups? The answer: a progressive activist who remains faithful to her leftist beliefs.

Twenty-five years ago, Kathleen Soliah went underground as a fugitive. She was wanted by police as a suspect in the planting of pipe bombs under two randomly-selected police cars that would have killed the occupants had they not failed to explode. During this and other episodes, Soliah was a member of the Symbionese Liberation Army, a group led by ex-convict Donald DeFreeze in the early 1970s, whose defining slogan was "Death to the fascist insect that preys on the life of the people." After DeFreeze and five other SLA members were killed in a shootout with police in Los Angeles, Soliah led a rally for the "victims" in Berkeley's Ho Chi Minh Park, claiming that the six outlaws were "viciously attacked and murdered by 500 pigs in L.A." Soliah singled out her best friend Angela Atwood, one of the dead SLA members, saying: "I know she lived happy and she died happy. And in that sense, I'm so very proud of her."[1]

August 2, 1999; http://www.salon.com/1999/08/02/soliah/

[1]"The Life and Times of Sara Jane Olson," Chuck Haga, *Minneapolis Star-Tribune*, June 27, 1999, http://www.startribune.com/local/16894551. html?refer=y

Soliah was finally apprehended in St. Paul, Minnesota on June 16, where she was living under the pseudonym Sara Jane Olson with her doctor husband, Fred G. Peterson. Soliah has subsequently been released on $1 million bail raised within a week by 250 sympathizers and friends. The *Minneapolis Star-Tribune* described the attitude of the liberal community in St. Paul after learning of her past in these terms: "In the days since her June 16 arrest, Olson [Soliah] has been almost canonized: reader of newspapers for the blind, volunteer among victims of torture, organizer of soup kitchens."[2] The office manager of the Minnehaha United Methodist Church, where she is a member of the congregation, called on its members to build a "contingent of support." Twenty of them were said to have been in court in California on the day she was arraigned.

Soliah's brother-in-law, Michael Bortin, was a Berkeley radical and with his wife, Josephine, was also an SLA member. Recently, Bortin attempted to explain to the press the relationship between the radical gangster Soliah and the St. Paul housewife "Sara Jane Olson," who was such an upstanding member of the progressive community: "There's not this dichotomy between what Kathy was and what she is now. She was doing the same things in the early '70s." Bortin claimed that it was the assassinations of the Kennedys and Martin Luther King, Jr., the presidency of Richard Nixon and the war in Vietnam that changed their attitudes to make them SLA members. "We lost our faith in the country, in due process. In law and justice."[3]

Back then, I was one of the editors of *Ramparts,* the largest publication of the New Left. Like Bortin and Soliah, I would have described myself as a "revolutionary" who had "lost faith in my country." But along with many other leftists at the time (and unlike Bortin and Soliah), I hadn't lost my mind or sense of decency as well. I wrote an editorial for *Ramparts* condemning the

[2]Ibid.
[3]Ibid.

SLA as a criminal organization. It was the first editorial I wrote that I didn't sign. I was concerned enough that the SLA might come and kill me. The SLA had announced itself to the world on November 6, 1973, in a terrible deed that has gone all but unmentioned in the current reportage on Soliah's case. Without warning, three of its "soldiers" ambushed and gunned down the first African-American superintendent of schools in Oakland. Dr. Marcus Foster had no warning when he was met with a hail of bullets in a parking lot behind the Oakland School District office. The bullets had been tipped with cyanide, just so he would have no chance to survive the attack. His crime, according to the SLA's "official death warrant," was that he followed a school-board directive to issue I.D. cards to students, to protect them from drug dealers and gang members wandering onto their campuses intending to do them harm.

The Foster killing revolted me, as it did many, but not all, members of the radical community. Thus *Ramparts* received many letters including one from Yippee leader Stew Albert, who accused us of "giving a green light" to the police to hunt down and "murder" the SLA warriors. Leonard Weinglass, the lawyer for Tom Hayden, Abbie Hoffman and the Chicago Seven and now counsel for Black Panther and cop-killer Mumia Abu Jamal, represented the families of the dead SLA members who sought monetary restitution from the city of Los Angeles for denying justice to their offspring. In my view, however, justice had been done. If anything, the SLA killers hadn't been punished enough.

In fairness to Soliah, it is not clear that she was aware of the SLA's intentions before the murder of Marcus Foster, although she certainly embraced them afterwards. According to Patty Hearst, who was kidnapped by the SLA and then converted to their political agenda, Soliah participated in a 1975 bank robbery the SLA committed in a Sacramento suburb. An innocent bystander, Myrna Lee Opshal, who was pregnant and had come to the bank to deposit church funds, was accidentally shot and killed by SLA member Emily Harris. Later, Harris dismissed the killing to her comrades by saying the victim was "a pig," explaining, "She was married to a doctor." Ironically, Soliah herself is married to a doctor.

These were the deeds, and this was the mentality of the gang to which Kathleen Soliah dedicated her radical political life. Now she is once again being defended by progressives, who blame the Vietnam War and Richard Nixon for the evils they have committed. If Kathleen Soliah's crimes are excused by Nixon's, why would not Nixon's crimes be excused by those his Communist enemies committed?

The radical fantasy that turned the Soliahs into paranoid conspirators is very much alive today in the rhetoric of the left, which is unrelenting in its insane picture of America as a repressive, racist, sexist, imperialist power. It is kept alive in part by the radical rewriting of the history of the '60s, in which "noble idealists" like Soliah declared war on government "fascists" and were, whatever they did, hapless victims of the greater evil of their adversaries. There is a whole library of memoirs and histories by aging New Leftists and "progressive" academics dealing with the rebellions of the 1960s, but hardly a page in any of them has the basic decency or honesty to say, "Yes, we supported these leftist murderers and those spies and agents for an evil empire." I'd like to hear even one of these advocates of "justice" acknowledge that "we greatly exaggerated the evils of this system and underestimated its decencies and virtues and we're sorry." I'd like to hear that from Soliah and her apologists. I'd like to hear them pay a moment's tribute to Marcus Foster and to Myrna Opshal, and to the brave policemen and FBI agents who risked their lives to protect other Americans, including progressives, from the harm they intended. I'd like to hear them say, just once, "I'm sorry."

14

Three Political Romancers

It's been a bad year for prevaricators of the political left. First, Nobel laureate and Guatemalan terrorist Rigoberta Menchú was unveiled by fellow leftist David Stoll as a self-fabricating poseur. Then feminist icon and self-proclaimed suburban housewife Betty Friedan was unmasked (again by a political comrade) as a longtime propagandist for the Stalinist left and a political fibber.[1] Now it's Modern Language Association president and PLO apologist Edward Said's turn to have his inventions uncovered and be exposed as a cunning purveyor of biographical fiction.

These creative dissemblers did not idly conceive their deceptive constructions of self, in which case they would have been mere literary curiosities. Instead, each of them crafted their phony biographies to serve a radical cause. They thus form part of a continuum with what Leon Trotsky once termed the "Stalin school of falsification,"[2] in which historical data are tortured in the interests of a politically useful "truth."

Rigoberta Menchú presented herself as a poor, uneducated Mayan peasant, whose family had been deprived of its land by a *ladino* ruling class, which was descended from the European conquerors of her people. Rigoberta's story told how her family was

September 27, 1999, http://archive.frontpagemag.com/Printable.aspx? ArtId=24314; http://www. salon.com/1999/09/27/said_3/
[1] See "Feminist Icon Debunked" in Volume 5 of this series, *Culture Wars.*
[2] "The Stalin School of Falsification," Leon Trotsky, translated by Max Shachtman in 1937 for Pioneer Publishers, http://www.marxists.org/ archive/trotsky/1937/ssf/

destroyed by their oppressors for peacefully attempting to regain their land. According to Rigoberta, hers was not an individual story but "the story of all poor Guatemalans." In her telling, her autobiography became a political parable with the power to persuade morally decent readers of the justice of the terrorist movement whose spokesperson she had become, and whose strategy was to foment violent confrontations in the Guatemalan countryside to bring Marxists to power.

Every salient element of Rigoberta's parable was based on a demonstrable lie. She was not poor and not uneducated. Her family was not dispossessed by a *ladino* ruling class; its land dispute was with other Mayans—in fact, with members of her family's own clan. And the violence they suffered was not unprovoked, but resulted from the violent confrontations initiated by the terrorists whose pawn she had become.

Betty Friedan presented herself in *The Feminine Mystique*—the book that launched modern feminism—as a suburban housewife who had never given a thought to "the woman question" until she attended a Smith College reunion, which revealed to her the dissatisfaction of her well-educated female classmates, unable to balance traditional roles with modern careers. There were many views Friedan could have taken of the data she subsequently collected. In America an unparalleled technological revolution was unfolding, among whose consequences were the liberation of women from household chores, from death-threatening diseases associated with childbirth and sex, and from the tyranny of their reproductive cycles. All this provided them with options for entry into workplaces and professions where few women had previously ventured. The sheer suddenness of this transformation would have provoked anxiety and dysfunction in any group. Friedan chose to view the malaise in political terms—not as the ambiguities of an epic transition already in progress, but as the consequence of a male conspiracy to oppress females and confine them to traditional roles. In Friedan's radical melodrama, middle-class marriage became a "comfortable concentration camp,"[3] and men's protective attitudes towards women became the oppressive stance of a master race.

It has recently been revealed that Betty Friedan was not candid about the facts of her life and the sources of her radical views. She was hardly a suburban housewife when she wrote those words, but a 25-year veteran of professional journalism in the Communist left, where she had been thoroughly indoctrinated in the politics of "the woman question" *before* attending her class reunion, and specifically in the idea that women were "oppressed." The actual facts of Friedan's life—that she was a professional female ideologue; that her husband, far from forcing her into traditional roles, supported her full-time writing and research; that she had a maid and lived in a Hudson River mansion, attending very little to household chores—were inconvenient to the victim *persona* and radical theory she was determined to promote. So she suppressed them.

Like Rigoberta Menchú and Betty Friedan, Edward Said is a post-modern Marxist uninterested in the concrete realities of individual lives and what they actually imply. For 30 years he has presented himself as a Palestinian Everyman in autobiographical writings and published interviews, and even in a film for the BBC. In all of these he has shaped his personal story as a holograph of the criminal dispossession that he claims Jews have committed against his people. To be sure, Said was a wealthy Everyman, a member of the monied Palestinian and cultural elite. But that very fact served to emphasize the dispossessions of home and homeland that the poorest Palestinians felt. Thus, reviewing one of Said's many books on this subject, the novelist Salman Rushdie observed that by writing about his "internal struggle: the anguish of living with displacement, with exile, ... [Said] enables us to feel the pain of his people."

According to the biography Said constructed and then retailed for 30 years, he was born in 1935 in Jerusalem and grew up in a house located at 10 Brenner Street in the Talbiyeh district until he and his

---

[3]*The Feminine Mystique,* Betty Friedan, Dell, 1964, ch. 12

family were "dispossessed by the city's Jewish occupiers, when Israel became a state in 1948." In Said's own words: "I was born in Jerusalem and spent most of my formative years there and, after 1948, when my entire family became refugees, in Egypt."[4] Said's political uses of the memories surrounding the house at 10 Brenner Street are further on display in a speech he gave last year at Birzeit University on the West Bank: "The house from which my family departed in 1948—was displaced—was also the house in which the great Jewish philosopher Martin Buber lived for a while, and Buber of course was a great apostle of coexistence between Arabs and Jews, but he didn't mind living in an Arab house whose inhabitants had been displaced." In other words, even Martin Buber—the most prominent Jewish critic of a specifically Jewish state, who had proposed instead a bi-national solution which would create a Palestinian state that was both Jewish and Arab—didn't mind benefiting from the dispossession of the Arabs. Such hypocrites, these Jews.

Except that it was Said's aunt and uncle—not his parents—who actually owned the 10 Brenner Street house and who evicted Buber, not the other way around. The eviction took place in 1942. Buber had been living there as a refugee from Nazi Germany, which he had left with his wife and two teenage granddaughters in 1938. The fact that the Bubers would have been exterminated had they not been able to find refuge in Jerusalem apparently meant nothing to the Saids when it came to terminating their lease, nor to Edward in weighing the Jewish presence in a country that—as has now been revealed—was never his home.

This salient fact and others have now been retrieved from Said's false memory by a Jewish scholar and lawyer named Justus Weiner, who spent three years researching the historical record.[5]

---

[4]"Between Worlds: Edward Said Makes Sense of His Life," *London Review of Books*, May 7, 1998
[5]"'My Beautiful Old House' and other Fabrications by Edward Said," Justus Reid Weiner, *Commentary*, September 1999; http://www.commentarymagazine.com/article/%e2%80%9cmy-beautiful-old-house%e2%80%9d-and-other-fabrications-by-edward-said/

What he discovered speaks volumes about Said's integrity and his respect for historical truth. In 1917, the Balfour Declaration offered the Jews a national home in the British Mandate in Palestine. It is an event that, in Said's telling, marks the beginning of the criminal dispossession of his family and people. In that year, however, the Saids were not residents of Palestine. They were living halfway across the world, in Boston, where they had landed in 1911 and where Edward's father had become an American citizen. This was not untypical of the Palestinian elite, which by most historical accounts had no strong sense of national identity, let alone nationalist grievance, until 30 years later, after the establishment of the Jewish state. The Palestine Liberation Organization itself was not created until 1964, 16 years after the birth of Israel. Indeed, when the Saids left America in 1926, it was not to emigrate to a "homeland" in Palestine but to Cairo, where they established a prosperous business. Not once in the ensuing 20 years before the establishment of the Jewish state did the Saids make a move to resettle in the land called Palestine. Egypt was their home. The myth Said has so artfully fabricated plays well on liberal guilt-strings but wreaks havoc with the historical facts. The U.N. partitioned Palestine in 1947, leaving well-defined sectors for both Arabs and Jews. But the Palestinian Arabs rejected the partition. A coalition of the surrounding Arab states then attacked the Jews with the stated objective of driving them into the sea.

Edward Said is a revanchist who opposes the current Oslo peace process and final status negotiations. Politically, he is farther to the left of Arafat than Benjamin Netanyahu is to the right of Shimon Peres. What his fabrications seek to accomplish is the presentation of Palestinian extremism as moderation—better yet, a simple reflex of human pride. Having been caught in his fictional web, Said has taken steps to revise his recently published autobiography, *Out of Place,* to make it accord more closely with the revealed facts. But the new version is itself a form of deception, since the text does not mention the false memory he has promoted for the last 30 years, or attempt to reconcile his differing versions.

Far from conceding that an apology is in order, Said has retained the pose of self-righteous victim. When Weiner's article exposing him appeared, Said replied with a shrill attack in the Arab press under the headline: "Defamation, Zionist Style." From its opening sentence, Said's reply reflects the wretchedly low standards of its author's polemical style: "Given the approach of the final status negotiations between Israel and the Palestinians, it seems worthwhile to record here the lengths to which right-wing Zionists will go to further their claims on all of Palestine against those of the country's native Palestinian inhabitants who were dispossessed as an entire nation in 1948."[6]

The argument could hardly be more disingenuous. Said opposes the current peace negotiations, which he regards as a "sellout," while Weiner does not even mention them. Said's reference to dispossession is typically loaded, ignoring as it does the primary fact that the Palestinians were the aggressors, that *their* agenda was to achieve an ethnic cleansing of the region while the Jews' was not, and that the terrible consequences of their aggression were felt on both sides. For while it is true that hundreds of thousands of Arabs native to the region left or were driven out, it is also true that hundreds of thousands of Jews left or were driven out of Arab countries and eastern Jerusalem and the Old City, the holiest place for Jews, and the West Bank—Judea and Samaria—the historic homeland of the Jews. Reasonable people might conclude that this fateful episode encompassed two ethnic tragedies. But not Edward Said.

Nor is he contrite about the personal details he has falsified. Taking the same tack as Rigoberta Menchú, who claimed that her fabrications were a Mayan cultural tradition—conflating many people's biographies with her own—Said tries to hide behind the Arab understanding of "family" as an extended clan. "[Weiner]

---

[6]*Defamation, Zionist-style,* Edward Said, *Al-Ahram Weekly,* Issue No. 444, August 26, 1999—September 1, 1999, http://weekly.ahram.org.eg/1999/444/op2.htm

does not realize ... that the family house was in fact a family house in the Arab sense, which meant our families were one in ownership. ... I have never claimed to have been made a refugee, but rather that my extended family, all of it—uncles, cousins, aunts, grandparents—in fact was. By the spring of 1948, not a single relative of mine was left in Palestine, ethnically cleansed by Zionist forces."[7]

But this is also false. The names of Said's parents were not on the deed to the "family house" at 10 Brenner Street. Moreover, just last March, in an interview with an Arab paper, Said lamented: "I feel even more depressed when I remember my beautiful old house surrounded by pine and orange trees in Al-Talbiyeh in east [actually western] Jerusalem which has been turned into a Christian embassy." No cultural ambiguities here. It is *my* house. Of course, as an American and a linguist, Said would know very well the meaning his audience would attribute to the words he has used in 30 years of promoting his political lie.

We are presented, then, with three major figures of 20th-century leftwing movements caught in the fabrication not only of their personal histories but of history itself. Are their attempted constructions of reality mere coincidence, or is there a deeper lesson to be learned from these episodes? Over and over again, the vision of the left has failed in this century not because the ideas behind it weren't noble or seductive, but because in practice they did not work. The vision of the left is by nature a romance of good and evil, of liberators and oppressors. Does the sustaining of such a Manichaean vision require the flattening of a reality that is so much more complex, and the reshaping of its narrative truth? Is the vision itself so at odds with the real world that it necessitates this lying, that it requires a fiction to sustain its romance? More practical and prosaic minds will conclude that it does.

---

[7]Ibid.

15

Ordeal by Slander

Winston Churchill once remarked that there was nothing more exhilarating than to be shot at without result. Perhaps that is one of the reasons he was a conservative, since being one guaranteed he would be shot at a lot. Recently I dodged a political bullet when columnist Jack White smeared me as a "racist" in *Time* magazine.[1] It was only a week ago that I was able to pinch flesh and confirm that I had survived. A favorable review of my new book on race, *Hating Whitey and Other Progressive Causes*, had appeared in *Time*, calling it "Indignant Sanity."[2] It served as a pass to allow me back into *Time*'s version of decent society. But I was hardly able to enjoy my resurrection before opening *The New York Times Sunday Magazine* to see myself smeared again as part of a conservative group allegedly on a mission to rehabilitate Joe McCarthy.[3]

In the liberal political culture, after the epithet "racist," the term "McCarthyite" is probably the label most calculated to inflict mortal wounds. I wasn't really surprised that a partisan

---

December 7, 1999, http://archive.frontpagemag.com/Printable.aspx?ArtId= 24346; http://www.salon.com/1999/12/06/weisberg/

[1] See the articles "Letter to Walter Isaacson," "Walk in My Shoes," "I Need Your Help" and "Franken-Style Smears from David Brock's Noise Machine" in Volume VI of this series, *Progressive Racism*.

[2] http://www.time.com/time/magazine/article/0,9171,34358,00.html; the review was a concession by *Time* that its columnist had indeed stepped over the line.

[3] Jacob Weisberg, *The Rehabilitation of Joe McCarthy*, *The New York Times Sunday Magazine*, November 28, 1999

institution of the left like *The New York Times* would be the vehicle for such a hit. Indeed, when writer Jacob Weisberg interviewed me for the piece, I already could guess what was coming. Weisberg subsequently became the editor of Slate, the largest online magazine, and a division of *The Washington Post.* His malicious article was almost a carbon copy of a piece by Joshua Micah Marshall that had appeared a year earlier in *The American Prospect.* That screed was called "Exhuming McCarthy" and it slandered the same small group—Ronald Radosh, Harvey Klehr, John Haynes, Allen Weinstein and myself—labeling us the "New McCarthyites." Like Weisberg's piece, it failed to provide a shred of evidence to back up the charge.

The ostensible subject of both articles was a controversy surrounding the efforts of a few conservative scholars to bring to light new documentary evidence of domestic Communist spying that had surfaced with the opening of the Soviet archives and the recent release of the Venona transcripts. John Haynes and Harvey Klehr were the authors of a series of groundbreaking studies in this field published by the Yale University Press; Radosh had co-written the definitive books on the Rosenberg and Amerasia spy cases, and was known to be writing a study of the Spanish Civil War based on the new sources; Weinstein was the author of the definitive book on Alger Hiss's guilt and had published *The Haunted Wood,* a voluminous text on domestic Communist spies.[4] Arthur Herman, a fifth conservative added by Weisberg to Marshall's targets, had recently published *Joe McCarthy: Reexamining the Life and Legacy of America's Most Hated Senator,* which also took advantage of the new Soviet sources.[5]

And I? I am not now, nor have I ever claimed to be, a scholar in the area of Soviet agents and Cold War spying. I have never written anything about spy cases. I have never read the Venona transcripts

---

[4]*The Haunted Wood: Soviet Espionage in America—The Stalin Era,* Allen Weinstein and Alexander Vassiliev, Random House, 1998
[5]Arthur Herman, *Joseph McCarthy: Reexamining the Life and Legacy of America's Most Hated Senator,* Free Press, 1999

and do not intend to visit the Soviet archives. What am I doing in this piece? I asked myself this question and had even put it to Weisberg when he called me for the interview. His answer then was hesitant and vague in a way that aroused my suspicions. He said that the article he was writing was not merely about the controversy. When the article appeared, it was obvious that Weisberg had lied to me and that his decision to include me was not so that he could discuss other issues but so that he could conflate the academic scholars with comments I had made and smear them. I have a reputation as a tough moral critic of the left, and have made it a point to answer attacks from that quarter in the same uncompromising language as the attacks themselves. This polemical in-your-face style lends itself to distortion by the unscrupulous and offered Weisberg an opportunity to garner the "gotcha" quotes he was seeking. In this, too, he was following Marshall's *American Prospect* piece. In preparing his article, Marshall hadn't read enough of my actual work to come up with a clinching quote, but he presented me nonetheless as "the prime example" of someone who "excoriate[s] the entire progressive tradition for the misdeeds of the extreme left." Weisberg repeated this canard: "Having despised liberals from the left, Horowitz came to hate them just as violently from the right."

In other words, I was included as the straw man that would validate both authors' cases against the scholars they wished to discredit. Odd, is it not, that two men who claim to be horrified at attempts to conflate the innocent with the guilty should lump together as their targets three non-ideological scholars (Haynes, Klehr, and Weinstein), a social democrat (Radosh), a traditional conservative (Herman), and a second-thoughts conservative like myself in order to tar everyone concerned, and then accuse those who were smeared of rehabilitating McCarthyism!

Weisberg's portrait of what he alleges to be my liberal phobia may puzzle many readers of *Salon*, the leftwing magazine I currently write for. Gripped by such demons, why would I want to write columns for a magazine run by liberals and leftists, and why would I defend them (as I occasionally have) from attacks I considered inaccurate by the right? Surely this is strange behavior for an ideologue possessed by indiscriminate hatred of all things left. Why would I write a defense of Christopher Hitchens, a proud tiger of the progressive tradition, when he got what a radical presumably deserves: betrayal by his leftist friends for telling tales out of school?[6] Why would I publicly call Jerry Falwell a "conservative jackass," as I did when he described the Teletubbies TV program as a homosexual plot?[7]

The accounts by Weisberg and Marshall of the controversy over Soviet documents are not merely an offense to the facts but an inversion of the truth—an attempt to condemn the entire tradition of conservative anti-Communism for the misdeeds of an unscrupulous fellow named Joe McCarthy. Although Weisberg and Marshall strain to pretend otherwise, the cause of the current controversy is the archive of indisputable facts brought to light by the Soviet collapse. These facts inconveniently vindicate the old anti-Communist right; they discredit the liberals who defended Alger Hiss and Soviet agents like him, and progressives who provided excuses and denials along the way. The agenda of progressives like Weisberg and Marshall is to make the best of what is for them a bad situation. Since their brand of progressivism has portrayed McCarthy and his conservative allies as far bigger domestic villains than the Communists themselves, it is now implicated in betrayals and atrocities that can no longer be denied.

To manage their defense, the authors' first task is to dispose of the specter that the facts have conjured—the internal threat of a subversive left. This threat was posed by the Stalinists of the early Cold War period, by their genetic heirs, the anti-Amerikkka left-

---

[6]David Horowitz, "Defending Christopher," *FrontPage Magazine*, March 01, 1999, http://archive.frontpagemag.com/readArticle.aspx?ARTID=24276

[7]David Horowitz, "Extremists at Michigan State University," *FrontPage Magazine*, February 25, 2002, http://archive.frontpagemag.com/readArticle.aspx?ARTID=21319

ists of the Vietnam era, and lastly by their politically-correct successors in the Clinton years. Today, the minions of this left dominate the liberal-arts faculties of the nation's elite universities and
thus shape the historiography of the Cold War itself. Haynes and
Klehr have written a book about them called *In Denial.* The Weis-
berg-Marshall strategy is first to belittle the importance of this
left, which they dismiss as "powerless" and "irrelevant," though it
is far from either, and thus to discredit its critics as alarmists.

As it happens, and as they deliberately ignore, all of the individuals Marshall and Weisberg have targeted are on record as sharp
critics of McCarthy and McCarthyism, specifically his demagoguery and recklessness with the facts, his contempt for the legal
process, and his unscrupulous attacks on (a few) innocent or half-
guilty individuals. Each member of this group, including myself,
has also taken care to credit those leftists who were anti-
Communists with their actual achievements in the battles against
domestic totalitarians and not to confuse them with the pro-
Communist factions of the progressive cause.

Weisberg also overstates the achievements of liberal Cold Warriors. In his telling, anti-Communist liberals like Arthur
Schlesinger and Reinhold Niebuhr represent "the one group that
basically got Communism right." But if this is the case, Weisberg
doesn't explain why the pursuit of domestic spies like Hiss, and
Communist agents like Owen Lattimore, was predominantly—if
not exclusively—the work of the anti-Communist right. It was
Nixon who went after Hiss. The Democrats only took on the pro-
Soviet progressives in 1948 when they bolted their party to launch
the Wallace campaign. Then, as now, it was the right that was the
consistent and perdurable promoter of the anti-Communist cause.

While Weisberg notes that anti-Communist liberals are
strangely silent in the current controversy over the allegiances of
pro-Soviet progressives, he doesn't examine the reason for the
silence. Might it have something to do with liberal politics itself?
Could the off-again-on-again popular front between liberalism and
leftism perhaps explain the paradox? Is there not some truth in the

conservative charge that liberals and leftists share goals and differ only in the means to achieve them? On this provocative question, Weisberg takes the Fifth. Instead of confronting it, he diverts the reader's attention by suggesting that the "real" issues in the controversy are psychological, not political.

"Radosh," he writes, "exemplifies a kind of Whig Fallacy in reverse—viewing the present through the lens of one's own painful past." In Weisberg's reading, it is Radosh's alleged attachment to the melodramas of his youth that explains his refusal "to understand ... the way in which Communism, long irrelevant in American politics, has become not just powerless but absurd."[8] But it is Weisberg's comment that is absurd. The same issue of *The New York Times* which contains his article also features an op-ed piece entitled "The Next Dialectic," by a best-selling liberal author who claims that Marx "foretold the present cyber-age" and that "writing about globalization in *Principles of Communism* in 1847, Engels sounds very 1999."

Weisberg doesn't bother to provide any evidence for the claim that Radosh is suffering from a case of arrested development. Instead, his text shifts quite abruptly to the Horowitz straw man: "Radosh is a mild and temperate critic in comparison with an old friend of his from the New Left, and a fellow red-diaper baby, David Horowitz...." As Weisberg proceeds with his Horowitz file, it is quickly apparent that the sole reason for my appearance in his text is to provide the DNA that will make the prosecution's case. Since I am the only member of the group to have written an autobiography that is both personal and political, my work offers him a chance to prove that a psychological matrix lies at the root of anti-Communism and both defines and discredits his targeted group of scholars: "For those most deeply invested in this universe [of Cold War politics], clinging to anti-Communism is as much a personal

---

[8]"Cold War Without End," Jacob Weisberg, *The New York Times*, November 28, 1999, http://www.nytimes.com/1999/11/28/magazine/ cold-war-without-end.html?pagewanted=all&src=pm

as it is a political phenomenon. What comes through vividly in Horowitz's memoirs is a fierce Oedipal struggle entwined with radicalism. Horowitz wanted to antagonize his Communist father; in later years, when he was ailing, Horowitz would bait him by raising the name of Alexander Solzhenitsyn."[9]

When *The Times'* fact-checker read this final sentence to me, I told her it was such a brazen misrepresentation of what I had written that Weisberg should reconsider including it. But Weisberg couldn't do that without destroying his thesis, so he didn't. Here is the actual passage from *Radical Son* wherein I describe the encounter with my father. The time frame is the mid-Seventies, when I am in my thirties and have begun to have second thoughts about the left: "When our discussions veered into the areas of our political disagreements, I was made to feel the spine of his being. It was as though we were back in the house on 44th Street [20 years before], arguing over the [then more conservative] *Times* again. Yet these new eruptions were quickly muted by my decision not to press them. I would raise the issue of Solzhenitsyn's new book to see that he had not changed. But when the expected response came, I did not push him to the wall, as I once had. He was too weakened, too beaten for that. When he dismissed Solzhenitsyn as a reactionary doing the Americans' work, I let it pass. Sometimes I would pare down my quest until it was a simple demand for respect.... What I wanted was my father's recognition that I, too, had won a few hard truths.... "

In other words, my feelings were exactly the opposite of what Weisberg claimed. Far from wanting to antagonize my father, this passage reveals my pain as a frustrated son who wanted to connect with him in an area that was important to us both, and failed. When the failure was evident, I backed off. But this unsuccessful filial effort to connect with an aging parent did not suit Weisberg's purpose, which was to portray me as irreconcilable, and my supposed antagonism as a neurosis that affected my entire outlook.

---

[9]Ibid.

"This sense of acting out of personal injury," Weisberg continued, "permeates everything Horowitz writes today." Not really.

More distortions follow. "This explains Horowitz's penchant for depicting Clinton Democrats in terms borrowed from the era of high Stalinism.... In the online magazine *Salon,* where he has a column, Horowitz wrote recently, 'It is as though the Rosenbergs had been in the White House, except that the Rosenbergs were little people and naïve.'" What Weisberg doesn't tell his readers is that this quote is lifted from a lengthy three-part series of articles that dealt with an unprecedented breach of national security by the Clinton administration that led to an equally unprecedented theft of America's nuclear-weapons secrets by Communist China. This was not something I made up but was national news at the time.[10] I pointed out that this national-security disaster was the result not only of lax security, which made the theft possible, but the calculated *lifting* of security controls by Clinton that allowed the transfer of vital satellite, missile and computer technologies to the Communist dictatorship.

Readers of my text (but not of Weisberg's article) would know that the reference to the Rosenbergs was not intended in any way to draw a parallel between Clinton's motives and those of the Communists. I did not invoke the Rosenbergs as an explanation of *why* Clinton allowed these breaches to take place, but to indicate the consequences of the loss. When the passage is read in full, it is obvious even to the most obtuse reader that I actually used the analogy to *differentiate* Clinton's actions from the actions of Communists like the Rosenbergs—in other words, exactly the opposite of what Weisberg claimed: "It could even be said in behalf of the Rosenbergs that they did not do it for themselves, but out of loyalty to an ideal, however pathetic and misguided. Bill Clinton has no such loyalties—neither to his family, nor his party, nor his country.... The wounds he has inflicted on this nation, and every

---

[10]See "The Manchurian Presidency," in Volume IX of this series, *Progressives in Power.*

individual within it, with consequences unknown for future generations, cannot be said to have been inflicted for ideological reasons or even out of some perverse dedication to a principle of evil. The destructiveness of Bill Clinton has emerged out of a need that is far more banal—to advance the cause of a self-absorbed and criminal personality." Christopher Hitchens, who described Clinton as a sociopath, could have written that. My judgment may have been harsh but was hardly the product of an unresolved Oedipal conflict with my Communist father.

Weisberg's entire effort is designed to erase the question that provoked the argument in the first place. Whose view of this historical epoch of the Cold War was or is correct? Why are there such powerful voices, including *The New York Times*, that seek to trivialize this debate and treat it as a mere rehash of dead issues, or worse yet, as an attempt to resurrect the disreputable politics of the past? The answers to these questions have obvious implications for one's view of both the progressive-liberal tradition and its conservative rival, and thus are hardly irrelevant to present day American politics as Weisberg claims. Indeed, the claim itself is part of his argument.

Discounting the internal Communist threat in the Roosevelt and early Truman years, and the external threat in the post-Johnson era, has been a hallmark of modern liberalism and its irregular alliance with the fellow traveling and pro-Communist left. The summary moment of this strange bed-fellowship occurred in 1941, when Whittaker Chambers tried to warn President Roosevelt that his close aide Alger Hiss was a Communist and a Soviet spy. When Chambers' warning was conveyed to Roosevelt by Assistant Secretary of State Adolph Berle, Roosevelt laughed and then elevated Hiss to even higher levels of policy and responsibility. Weisberg's *Times* piece follows the party line of this tradition quite faithfully, as has *The Times'* own treatment of the revelations from the Soviet archives. The editors of *The Times* buried the Venona story when it first broke; they have remained skeptical to the bitter end on the question of Hiss's guilt; and they have continued to cast a more than tolerant eye on the anti-American radicals of the Vietnam era.

The liberal temperament reflected in these choices is illustrated by Weisberg's treatment of Owen Lattimore, a figure from this history to whom he makes a passing reference in his text. Owen Lattimore was a famous McCarthy target and, in liberal eyes, a still more famous McCarthy victim. Yet despite all that Venona, the Soviet archives, and the latter-day memoirs of repentant Communists have revealed about Lattimore, Weisberg still describes him simply as "the China hand absurdly named as the Soviets' 'top spy' in the United States."[11] It is true that this McCarthy claim was false; every conservative scholar in Weisberg's crosshairs has emphasized that fact, deploring McCarthy's demagoguery and the damage his reckless accusations did to the legitimate anti-Communist cause. Indeed, no one at the time was more furious with McCarthy for this overreach, and the discredit it brought, than J. Edgar Hoover himself. To this day, Lattimore has never been proven a spy and nowhere appears as one in the Soviet documents thus far released. But the image of wounded innocence that surrounded Lattimore then, and still does to this day as in Weisberg's report, is as false to the reality of both the man and the period as the McCarthy smear itself.

In fact, Lattimore was a devious and self-conscious betrayer of his country and a willing servant of the Soviet cause who worked hand-in-glove with its underground spy apparatus in the United States. As the editor of *Pacific Affairs*, and intimate of Lauchlin Currie (the White House liaison to the Department of State), Owen Lattimore was one of America's most influential China experts during the Roosevelt and Truman administrations, a period which marked the crucial stages of the Communist revolution, whose triumph in 1949 preceded McCarthy's crusade by a mere eight months. We now know that Lauchlin Currie, Lattimore's friend and patron at the White House, *was* a Soviet spy.

---

[11]"Cold War Without End," op. cit.

Lattimore's own pro-Soviet outlook was clearly expressed in a memo he wrote to the executive director of the Institute for Pacific Relations, which published his magazine, *Pacific Affairs,* with this advice: "For the USSR—back their international policy in general, but without using their slogans and above all without giving them or anybody else the impression of subservience."[12]

At Currie's suggestion, Lattimore hired a KGB collaborator named Michael Greenberg as his assistant at *Pacific Affairs,* and then, on his own initiative, Chen Han-shen, a Chinese spy, as his co-editor. Lattimore put his request for the co-editor through the channels of the Comintern. Yet, in the battle with McCarthy, Lattimore was the put-upon hero in the eyes of most liberals and Democrats, with important exceptions like Arthur Schlesinger. One of Weisberg's targets, Arthur Herman, reminds us in his book on McCarthy that Herbert Elliston of *The Baltimore Sun,* Al Friendly of *The Washington Post,* Drew Pearson, I.F. Stone, Eric Sevareid and Martin Agronsky all supported Lattimore. The then liberal *New York Post* editorialized: "All those who believe in freedom in this country are in the debt of Owen Lattimore." The same political forces that supported Lattimore painted McCarthy as the devil incarnate; consequently, his bid to expose Lattimore as a traitor was successfully thwarted by the congressional Democrats.

The release of Soviet documents has allowed us to see that, in the Cold War battles of this era, the anti-Communist forces of the right were correctly concerned about the internal threat to American security (as were those liberals who joined them); that the pro-Soviet left was treacherous and subversive; and that the Democrats, for partisan reasons (covering up the security failures of the Roosevelt and Truman administrations), often harbored and protected the Communists who had infiltrated their ranks.

In obscuring these historical realities, Weisberg and *The Times* are playing a role that has parallels to their counterparts at the

---

[12]The Institute for Pacific Relations was a think-tank financed by the Rockefeller and Carnegie Foundations

time. This includes turning a blind eye to the stranglehold of New Left Marxists and Soviet sympathizers—the intellectual heirs of Owen Lattimore—on the teaching of this history in American universities. The two main professional historians' organizations are headed this year by David Montgomery, an unrepentant former Communist, and Eric Foner, a New Left apologist for the Rosenbergs. Sympathizers of the old Communist left now dominate the writing of the historical record in the academic fields of Soviet studies and domestic Communism.[13] The leading academic authority on the McCarthy period is Ellen Schrecker, a self-acknowledged apologist for American Communism. Schrecker's books do not even bother to come up with new defenses for the Communists' treachery, but rehash the disingenuous arguments the Communists made for themselves at the time. In a comment all too typical of her work, Schrecker explains that American Communists turned to spying not because they were traitors, but because they "did not subscribe to traditional forms of patriotism."

Weisberg treads lightly over the left's hold on the historical record. To treat this reality for what it is would require recognizing that conservative scholars have been pushed to the fringes of their profession by a political juggernaut in the universities far more powerful in suppressing dissenters than McCarthy ever was. To acknowledge this would also mean recognizing the left's current influence in the culture at large. It would mean rehabilitating ex-Communists like Elizabeth Bentley, Louis Budenz and Bella Dodd, honoring conservatives like William F. Buckley, Jr. and institutions like the FBI, for the important roles they played in defending America against the Communist threat. Instead, Weisberg proposes that the story of American Communists themselves be approached "in a less judgmental fashion," because "the Cold War is history now." Clemency for the Communists, hostility towards

---

[13]John Earl Haynes and Harvey Klehr, *In Denial: Historians, Communism and Espionage,* op. cit.

the anti-Communists; in Irving Kristol's memorable formulation, the Cold War has come home.

Despite his pretense of being above the fray, Weisberg is himself a partisan in this Cold War. Just four years ago he wrote a cover story for *New York Magazine* called "The Un-Americans,"[14] a reprise of the McCarthy-era stigma that he applied not to anti-American leftists but to six conservatives: Phil Gramm, Gordon Liddy, Oliver North, Rush Limbaugh, Pat Robertson and Jesse Helms. Their collective thought-crime was to have criticized the federal government; their subversive act was to have used words like "revolution" in connection with Newt Gingrich's Contract with America, and thus, in Weisberg's addled view, to have provided an ideological rationale for the bombing of a federal building in Oklahoma City which killed 168 people.

When Weisberg called to interview me for his *Times* piece, I brought up the article. I told him I didn't trust his ability to treat conservatives fairly. He pretended not to know what I was talking about. He didn't remember if he had written such a story, he said. His memory is short in a lot of areas and the fact that he is on his way to becoming an important arbiter of the national culture has implications for the culture that are troublesome to contemplate.

---

[14]"The Un-Americans," Jacob Weisberg, *New York Magazine*, May 8, 1995

16

A Question for the Millennium

A millennium is too big a concept for the imagination; a thousand years contains 30 generations, a duration that has no flesh-and-blood dimension for the living. Half a millennium ago, Columbus had just landed in the Western hemisphere; half that, and the United States did not exist.

But a hundred years has resonance; it spans the two or three lifetimes we have ourselves have touched. I can trace my grandparents' path back to Moravia and Ukraine, though I can't go farther back than that. My grandparents were married just before the turn of the last century, and their children's lives began with its first years. Brief as this interval is in the overall span of time, three generations are probably enough to understand who we are.

Our century was a stage for the destructive dramas of a secular religious faith called socialism, inspired by dreams of a social redemption that would be achieved by human agency, through the force of politics and the state. In its Communist form, the efforts of this faith devastated whole continents and destroyed a world of human lives. My millennium question is this: Have we learned from these disasters, or will the passions of this faith follow us into the century to come?

In search of an answer, I turned to the pages of *The Nation,* an institution of the left that was an active participant in these tragedies across the entire century, and whose editorial stances at

December 28, 1999, http://archive.frontpagemag.com/Printable.aspx?
ArtId=24357; http://www.salon.com/1999/12/28/millenium/

all defining moments of the Communist project have been brutally refuted by historical events. The editors of *The Nation* supported the Bolshevik coup and the Stalinist collectivization; the infamous purge-trials and the Nazi-Soviet Pact; the Soviet conquest of Eastern Europe and the Maoist *gulag* in China; the Communist conquest of South Vietnam; Pol Pot's genocidal Cambodian campaign; and, of course, Castro's long-lived police state in Cuba. The editors of *The Nation* opposed the Truman Doctrine, the formation of NATO and SEATO, and the efforts of Western military and intelligence organizations generally to contain the expansion of the Soviet empire and to free its captive peoples. Over five decades, *The Nation*'s editors waged a journalistic war against the defenders of freedom in the West, against America's Cold Warrior presidents Truman, Kennedy, Nixon and Reagan, and against their national security policies. At the same time, *The Nation* was the defender of Soviet apologists and advocates, of Soviet spies like Harry Dexter White, Owen Lattimore, John Stewart Service and the Rosenbergs. As recently as this month—the last of the century—its editor was still defending Alger Hiss.

During the unraveling of the Marxist empire, the socialist movement was often fragmented and somewhat demoralized and found its comfort in the shadows of politics. But now it has come into the open and is bolder than ever. At this turn of a century, the socialist left is more influential in America's political and cultural institutions than it has been at any time in the American past. Its adherents reach into the Congress; they are the leaders of America's labor movement and of the principal academic, professional and arts associations, and of the most important media organizations as well.

In this pre-millennial moment the editors of *The Nation* have chosen to run two features appraising the socialist century past and assessing the prospects of a socialist century to come, which provide an answer to my question. In the December 13 issue, there is a long review article called "Exploiting a Tragedy, or *Le Rouge en Noir*" ("The Red in Black"), written by the magazine's longtime

European editor, Daniel Singer, a godson and disciple of the Marxist writer Isaac Deutscher, and also the magazine's resident expert on the subject of the Communist past.[1] The focus of Singer's article is *The Black Book of Communism*, a French treatise that attempts in one massive volume to sum up the human horror of the progressive project to make a better world.[2] According to the book's authors, during the 20th century, between 85 and 100 million human beings were slaughtered in peacetime by Marxists in the effort to realize their impossible dream.[3] The foreword by Martin Malia sensibly suggests: "Any realistic accounting of Communist crime would effectively shut the door on Utopia."

Indeed, that is the minimal lesson one might expect someone to learn from the unbroken record of the socialist utopias of the century just past. But it is exactly the lesson *The Nation*'s feature fervently rejects. Writes Singer: "Our aim—let us not be ashamed to say so—is to revive the belief in collective action and in the possibility of radical transformation in our lives." This passion for social redemption he calls "the Promethean spirit of humankind," a concept employing Marx's own term for the destructive project he launched over 150 years ago. Socialism is dead. Long live socialism.

For Singer and *The Nation*, the unrelieved human horrors and colossal economic failures of the Marxist experiments over the course of a century are not to be regarded as a sobering lesson for those who promoted them, nor a reason to reconsider their

---

[1] Daniel Singer, "Exploiting a Tragedy, or Le Rouge en Noir," *The Nation*, December 13, 1999, http://www.thenation.com/article/exploiting-tragedy-or-le-rouge-en-noir

[2] *The Black Book of Communism: Crimes, Terror, Repression*, Jean-Louis Panné, Andrzej Paczkowski, Karel Bartosek, Jean-Louis Margolin, Nicolas Werth, Stéphane Courtois, Mark Kramer, Jonathan Murphy, Harvard University, 1999

[3] Subsequent estimates of the toll in China increased the figures to well over 100 million; Jung Chang and Jon Halliday, *The Unknown Mao*, 2005; "Mao's Body Count, Communism, and Stupid Ideological Tricks," Cathy Young, *The Y-Files*, December 1, 2005, http://cathyyoung.wordpress.com/2005/12/01/maos-body-count-communism-and-stupid-ideological-tricks/

utopian faith. The history of Communism is just a tragedy of errors that need not be repeated, and is no reason to be discouraged. As far as *The Nation* is concerned, it is the story of "a revolution in a backward country failing to spread and the terrible result then presented to the world as a model." In other words, had there been sufficient Communists in America and Europe to make revolutions, the utopia that Marxists dreamed of would have been realized.

In its next issue, *The Nation* is already promoting the unfolding of this dream. In an editorial called "Street Fight in Seattle," the editors hail the eruption of political violence in the state of Washington as the beacon of a socialist renewal.[4] The protest against the World Trade Organization and the global market is celebrated as "something not seen since the Sixties," when an anti-capitalist left last took its socialist fantasies and nihilist agendas to America's streets. The voices cited in the editorial are themselves familiar. "A week ago no one even knew what the World Trade Organization was," proclaimed former Democratic assemblyman Tom Hayden, one of the most destructive Luddites of the previous generation. "Now these protests have made WTO a household word. And not a very pretty word."

From generation to generation, the rhetoric has not changed. "A corporate-dominated WTO that puts profits before people and property rights before human rights can no longer sustain its current course," comment *The Nation*'s editors. They also quote Gerald McEntee, a government union president and a major power in Democratic politics: "We refuse to be marketized." (How intelligent, how progressive is that?) Quoting the famous words of Carl Oglesby, a Sixties radical, McEntee proclaimed: "We have to name the system, and that system is corporate capitalism."

In short, *The Nation*'s war—and the left's war—is the same war the Communists fought, and is directed against a system that in

---

[4]"Street Fight in Seattle," Marc Cooper, *The Nation*, December 2, 1999, http://www.thenation.com/article/street-fight-seattle

the last 50 years has brought unimagined well-being to hundreds of millions of people previously excluded from all but the barest minimum of the fruits of their labor; a system that remains the only creator of democratic freedoms the world has ever known. *The Nation*'s mantra—"Profits before people and property rights before human rights"—is the same anathema on the market system that originated with Marx and is now resurrected in Seattle. But how is it possible to have lived through the 20th century without understanding that property rights are the basis of any rights that human beings have been able to secure—rights that are not mere paper promise; or that, far from conflicting with human needs, profits are the only practical means that have succeeded in fulfilling them?

Such willful ignorance is not from lack of intelligence. It has a deeper source in human desires that can only be satisfied by religious faith. The socialist dream of achieving a kingdom of heaven on earth is as old as Eden. "You shall be as God," was the serpent's fatal promise to Adam and Eve. You shall create a new world. This is the Promethean dream that Marx identified as his own, and that *The Nation*'s editors are intent to revive. It is the idea of exerting human control over the impersonal structures of the social order, beginning with the economic market and extending to the constitutional order. In desiring this, socialists fail to understand that an economic market which political forces cannot control, and a political process that imposes limits on its designs, are the very disciplines that human beings require in order to be free. Without such restraints and the limits they impose, humanity will quickly descend into the barbarism that the 20th century has made all too familiar. Yet it is precisely these lessons, as we go into the 21st century that *The Nation* and its comrades refuse to learn.

Is there anything really new under the sun concerning the passions that inspire us and the consequences that flow from them? The Homeric epics, the first literary productions of our civilization, were written three millennia ago, yet are inhabited by people whose emotions and aspirations are familiar today. The ideas of

Plato and Aristotle, and the ethics of the religious founders who lived more than two millennia ago, pretty much encompass the ideas, ethics, and religious faiths we see around us today.

Call this continuity "human nature." We are constrained by who we are and what we can learn. What we can learn about ourselves is pretty well set by the real individuals we are connected to, and by whom we are touched. One, two or at most three generations encompass this extended family that lets us know who we are. And so, my millennial question: Have enough of us learned from the Marxist disasters of this century that we are not doomed to repeat them one way or another in the next? Realistically, the answer probably is no.

PART III

Loyalties

I

Spy Stories:
The Wen Ho Lee Cover-Up

BI Director Louis B. Freeh got my attention when he tried to explain why the Justice Department dropped 58 of 59 charges against suspected nuclear spy Wen Ho Lee. "The Department of Justice and the FBI stand by each and every one of the 59 counts in the indictment of Dr. Lee," Freeh told the Senate Judiciary and Select Intelligence committees.[1] "Each of those counts could be proven in December 1999 [when Lee was indicted], and each of them could be proven today." Justice had agreed to a deal of guilt on one count (and a sentence of time served) in order to secure Lee's cooperation in locating the missing files he was accused of stealing from the nation's top nuclear-weapons lab. But the real reason for the cave-in was that the rules of a trial "posed serious obstacles to proving those facts without revealing nuclear secrets in open courts." It was *that* statement that touched me.

For these were the same words, almost verbatim, that a Harvard law professor had used in a conversation with me 28 years ago, when I was editor of the radical magazine *Ramparts*. Not coincidentally, this lawyer was giving me advice on how to get away with violating the same part of the U.S. espionage code that Wen Ho Lee had been accused of breaking. The professor's name was Charles Nesson. I had called Nesson in Los Angeles, where he

---

October 3, 2000, http://archive.frontpagemag.com/Printable.aspx?ArtId=
24332; http://www.salon.com/2000/10/03/lee_8/
[1]*The Associated Press*, September 26, 2000

was serving as part of the defense team for Daniel Ellsberg, a Pentagon official who had copied a classified history of U.S. Vietnam policy (subsequently known as "The Pentagon Papers") and illegally delivered them to *The New York Times*, which then made them public.

I had made the call to one of the leading constitutional law experts in the country because of a story we were about to publish. It had come unsolicited to us from a man who told us his name was "Winslow Peck," which was later exposed as an alias. He had come to the *Ramparts* office with a tale about a then secret U.S. spy agency called the National Security Agency, which was tasked with all U.S. electronic intelligence operations. He himself had been an intelligence operative stationed in Turkey, but had become disaffected because of the Vietnam War. Now he wanted to reveal to the world, including America's enemies, the secrets to which he had been privy.

When we sat down with him, tape recorders running, Winslow Peck told us how the National Security Agency operated and what America's intelligence professionals knew. He gave us the code words that they used to describe their operations. One of our staffers, Bob Fitch, who had served in intelligence in the 82nd Airborne Division during the Cuban Missile Crisis, was so shaken to recognize these official codes that he refused to work on the article. He was that sure he would be sent to jail. Peck told us that he had listened in on the last minute telephone conversation that Soviet premier Alexei Kosygin had with a doomed Russian cosmonaut whose ship was not going to make it back to earth. He told us he had intercepted the communications between the Israeli command center in Tel Aviv and General Moshe Dayan relieving Dayan of his post. He told us that the United States knew the name of every Russian pilot and the destination of every Russian airplane, around the clock.

The crucial secret that Peck was revealing to us (something I did not understand at the time) was that United States intelligence had cracked the codes of the Soviet Union and was able to read its electronic communications. This information would have been among the most guarded of intelligence secrets. By making public to both ally and enemy alike that the United States had broken their codes, our informant was, in fact, alerting the enemy to change them. Thus the information Peck gave us was, or might have been (we had no way of knowing), a major blow to national security in the midst of the Vietnam War.

As New Leftists, my fellow editors and I may have been arrogant and irresponsible, but we were not crazy. We understood that we had skated onto dangerously thin ice, with consequences we could only dimly imagine, and we wanted to know as clearly as possible what consequences we might be facing if we decided to publish the story that Peck had brought us. I was delegated by my fellow editors to put in a call to the Ellsberg defense team to see just what risks we might be taking. That is how I happened to be talking to Harvard law professor Charles Nesson.

After I had outlined the situation, Nesson explained the law. Technically, he said, we would be violating the Espionage Act. But it was a law that had been written in 1918 and in such a way that it applied to classified *papers* removed from government offices, or material copied from government files. The government was able to indict Ellsberg because he had reproduced actual papers. It was important for us in insulating ourselves from possible prosecution, Nesson counseled, "not to acknowledge that any papers existed."[2] If any did exist, he said, destroying them would be "helpful." I cannot help asking myself now whether this same calculation might have been behind Wen Ho Lee's destruction of 310 of the classified computer files which he had illegally removed from the Los Alamos Lab after finding out that the FBI was on his tail.

If we took his advice, Nesson suggested we might get away with publishing the article. To make its case in a court of law, the government would have to establish that we had indeed damaged

---

[2]David Horowitz, *Radical Son: A Generational Odyssey*, Free Press, 1997, p. 200

national security. To do so, it would be necessary to reveal more than the government might want the other side to know. In fact, the legal process would certainly force more information to light than the government would want *anybody* to know. On balance, there was a good chance that we would not be prosecuted.

I am struck by the fact that Nesson's strategy, which columnist William Safire has called "graymail"—daring government prosecutors to go into open court and reveal their hand—is precisely the reasoning that Freeh volunteered to the congressional committee to explain the prosecution's decision not to proceed with its case against Wen Ho Lee. To prove in a court of law that a defendant has endangered national security requires that a prosecution reveal far more information about a nation's security systems than any government may want to reveal. In other words, I had just been given advice by a famous constitutional law professor on how to commit treason and get away with it.

Is Wen Ho Lee guilty? Wen Ho Lee illegally removed 400,000 files from the nation's top nuclear-weapons lab over a period of years when he had repeated contacts with Chinese government scientists, and at a time when the Chinese Communist dictatorship was systematically stealing the secrets of America's most sophisticated nuclear arsenal. Lee's response to the FBI investigation was that of a seemingly guilty man. He destroyed files in his possession and repeatedly tried to break into the lab after his access was denied. Yet Wen Ho Lee has acquired an almost martyr-like status among progressives as a victim of government persecution, and even of "racism." The presiding judge roundly condemned the ineptitude of Lee's prosecution and his "punitive" treatment, in particular the fact that he was held in solitary confinement for months, and threatened by his interrogators with the specter of the Rosenbergs, who were executed for a crime similar to the one of which he was accused. The president himself has apologized for his own Justice Department's handling of the case. And the nation's editorial rooms have resounded with outrage at the entire affair.

Yet the arguments of Wen Ho Lee's supporters are unconvincing. Begin with Clinton's peculiar apology (without explanation) for a prosecution he himself was responsible for. The U.S. attorney who handled the Lee case is Clinton's friend and former college roommate. Within a week of his apology, Clinton was in New Mexico to raise money for the same prosecutor's run for a state office. The argument of some of Lee's supporters, that an anti-Chinese bias was behind an intemperate Justice Department prosecution, is hard to square with the fact that the current deputy attorney general in charge of civil rights is of Chinese descent himself.

Columnist William Safire and others have suggested a more plausible explanation. The zealous pursuit of Lee followed the release of the bipartisan Cox report detailing the theft of America's nuclear arsenal by the Chinese government. Much of this theft took place during Clinton's watch. Moreover, the Clinton administration had been aggressive in lifting security controls on satellite, missile and computer technologies particularly instrumental in developing nuclear-tipped ballistic weaponry. The Clinton administration had then sold those technologies to the Chinese.

The Cox Report came on the heels of congressional investigations by government oversight committees into the unprecedented access given by the Clinton-Gore administration to Chinese military and intelligence officials and their agents, possibly in exchange for illegal contributions to the Democratic National Committee and the Clinton-Gore campaign. Senator Fred Thompson had opened his hearings with the charge, based on CIA testimony, that the Chinese government systematically set out to influence the presidential elections of 1996 that put Clinton and Gore in the White House. More than a hundred witnesses called to testify about these facts took the Fifth Amendment or fled the country. Finally, among the charges leveled at the Clinton-Gore administration was that it routinely authorized electronic surveillance of U.S. citizens—seven hundred wiretaps were approved—but had turned down the FBI's request for a tap on Wen

Ho Lee. In fact, this was virtually the only tap the Clinton Justice Department refused. In sum, the zealous prosecution of Wen Ho Lee, according to this theory, took place only after a period of end-less foot-dragging and dangerous laxity on security issues, followed by the sensational revelations of the Cox Report. At this juncture, Clinton's personal political interest dictated a vigorous effort to establish his vigilance, particularly in relation to security threats from the Chinese. Only when his personal jeopardy was over was he able to resume the posture of minimizing the problem itself.

The support for Wen Ho Lee and the view that he is an inno-cent victim of overzealous government security concerns is a familiar trope in American politics. The same attitude can be seen as a dominant feature of American liberalism regarding the Hiss case over half a century ago, and even the Rosenbergs. Charles Nesson, the professor who counseled me on how to commit trea-son, is still a highly respected law professor at Harvard. In fact, the culture of Harvard is completely comfortable with Nesson, who has never, so far as I know, expressed regret for his subversive advice. At the same time, the political culture of Harvard is com-pletely uncomfortable with someone like myself who has regret-ted his betrayal of country. My case is not an anomaly. The most prominent scholars to have used the newly-opened Soviet archives to establish the guilt of Hiss, the Rosenbergs and other American spies are without exception conservative intellectuals and are shunned outsiders to the university culture. On the other hand, the most prominent scholars of American Communism, in that same culture, are almost without exception apologists for Ameri-can Communism and partisans of the political left. The defining argument of their historical perspective, in fact, is to deny treason-ous activity or treasonous intent on the part of actual Commu-nists in the Forties and Fifties.

These are but two expressions of a phenomenon that is obvious but rarely examined. A large swath of the intelligentsia shaping opinion towards the Wen Ho Lee case is what is a community that is indifferent at best to perceived American national interests, including national security. Since World War II, this community has never been persuaded that America has enemies it does not deserve. The adversary culture can find a moral equivalency between American democracy and virtually any oppressive regime that is not American. I have a vivid memory of the late conductor Leonard Bernstein being interviewed on television during the election of 1988, which was one year before the fall of the Berlin Wall and a time when the Soviet dictatorship was still intact. Bernstein practically spit into a television news camera the following comment: "I infinitely prefer Mr. Gorbachev to Mr. Bush."

The "adversarial" culture assumes that America is so powerful as to be invulnerable to foreign threats. It is typified by the attitude of Energy Secretary Hazel O'Leary's as she announced her declassification of eleven million pages of nuclear information, including the records of all American nuclear tests. According to the Secretary, nuclear secrecy was part of a "bomb building culture"[3] that it was necessary to end. In her view, the so-called bomb building culture could be ended by sharing America's national secrets with everyone, thus "leveling the playing field." This was precisely the attitude that inspired me and the other radical editors at *Ramparts* to divulge the secrets of America's electronic intelligence agency to the world. We viewed it as an effort to level the military playing field, so that America would no longer be the superpower that was able to lord it over everyone else.

In retrospect, the most important lesson of my Sixties encounter with a defector from our own intelligence service was the tolerance, sympathy and even support for treason that can be found in the mainstream liberal culture. Even though we thought of ourselves as radicals, the cultural mainstream we despised was so tolerant, and even supportive of our radical postures, that we were never prosecuted for the crime we had committed. Instead we were afforded the status of heroes for our "journalistic coup" in printing the revelations of "Winslow Peck."

---

[3]*Washington Post*, December 8, 1993

It is obvious to me now that the adversarial attitude that motivated us in the Sixties, and which I have since abandoned, lies
behind the sympathy for Wen Ho Lee and the preposterous belief
that his activities were "innocent." This attitude is typified by an
old comrade of mine, who preceded me at *Ramparts* and who later
became a national correspondent for the *Los Angeles Times*, which
is the very paper that led the attack on the Cox Report and also the
defense of Wen Ho Lee. There is perhaps no more outspoken champion of Lee than Robert Scheer, who has authored more than a
dozen columns on the case, including one filed from Albuquerque
where Lee was indicted and held. Scheer has even called Lee "an
American Dreyfus," after the French Jew who was falsely accused of
treason by anti-Semites in 19th-century France: "In a case that parallels the frame-up of Alfred Dreyfus, a Jewish captain in the French
army a century ago, the U.S. government is hell-bent on destroying
Wen Ho Lee, a naturalized American citizen and former Los Alamos
nuclear weapons scientist.... In both cases, the 'foreignness' of the
suspect was used by officials and the media to stoke fears of betrayal
of the nation's security to a dangerous enemy."[4]

The idea that the administration of Bill Clinton singled out Lee
for ethnic persecution is laughable. The notion that Dreyfus, a
French Jew, and Lee, a Chinese immigrant whose nation of origin
is hostile to the United States, are comparable is simply ludicrous.
Even before taking up Lee's cause, Scheer joined the attacks on the
bipartisan Cox Report, released in the spring of 1999, which documented the theft of designs for America's nuclear arsenal, including the miniaturized W-88 warhead suited for placement on
cruise-type ballistic missiles. Attacking Cox and the Democrats
who supported him as "fear-mongers" and national-security
hysterics, Scheer actually claimed that there were no nuclear

---

[4]Robert Scheer, "What's Left of Case Against Lee? Not Much; Spy scandal:
Instead of admitting it had the wrong man, the government is still chasing the former Los Alamos scientist." *Los Angeles Times*, Metro Section,
December 19, 1999, p. 11; http://articles.latimes.com/1999/dec/14/local/
me-43741

secrets to begin with, so the Chinese couldn't have stolen them. "The dirty secret of the nuclear weapons business is that there are no secrets," Scheer wrote in the *Times* on August 3, 1999, without being checked by his editors. "Nothing has happened since Hiroshima and Nagasaki to render these weapons any more plausibly useful as weapons. A crude nuclear weapon dropped from a propeller-driven plane or carried in a suitcase does the job of terrorizing civilian populations—the only function of nuclear weapons—as effectively as the modernized warheads, whose technology some claim Beijing has stolen."[5]

Scheer's statement exhibits an astounding ignorance of modern nuclear strategy. But this doesn't deter him and he presses on, invoking Energy Secretary Hazel O'Leary's "level playing field" to justify transferring nuclear secrets to the Chinese. Whatever weapons the Chinese Communist dictatorship lacked, Scheer argues, the United States should provide to them, in the interests of peace: "It would be in our national security interest to supply the Chinese with a Trident-class sub that works, as opposed to their lone sub contender that leaks radiation so badly that it isn't operational. And, heresy of heresies, we should give the Chinese some submarine-suitable missiles armed with the miniaturized W-88 warhead that they are supposed to have stolen. That way, even if they thought a nuclear weapon was en route to them, they would not have to instantly respond, being secure in the knowledge that they possessed survivable retaliatory power."[6] This is what passes for informed commentary at the *Los Angeles Times*.

---

[5]Robert Scheer, "China Spy Case Takes Aim at the Wrong Issue; Espionage: Beijing's capability is so primitive that giving it better bombs might make it feel less trigger-happy." Metro Section, *Los Angeles Times*, August 3, 1999, http://articles.latimes.com/1999/aug/03/local/me-62155

[6]Robert Scheer, "China Spy Case Takes Aim at the Wrong Issue; Espionage: Beijing's capability is so primitive that giving it better bombs might make it feel less trigger-happy." Metro Section, *Los Angeles Times*, August 3, 1999, p. 7; http://articles.latimes.com/1999/aug/03/local/me-62155

Where do such bizarre, alienated attitudes come from? As I have already mentioned, Robert Scheer preceded me as editor of *Ramparts*. My co-editors and I had fired him in 1969, less than three years before we published the revelations of national security defector "Winslow Peck." The firing was not political, and after leaving he veered even farther to the left than any of us who remained. While we were divulging the secrets of America's electronic intelligence agency in the pages of *Ramparts*, Scheer was joining the Red Sun Rising Commune and becoming an acolyte of North Korean dictator Kim Il-Sung.

Unlike those of us who have had second thoughts, Scheer has apparently had none. He may have shed some of the beliefs he held in the Sixties and has probably reconsidered some of the actions he took. But he has never regretted the war he and his comrades conducted against the United States, has never acknowledged how wrong he had been, and has never relinquished the ideas that led him down that path in the first place. That is the real national-security problem that the latest turn in the Wen Ho Lee case reveals.

2

The Lawyer Who Came In
from the Cold

C harles Nesson responded as follows to the article I published about Wen Ho Lee: "David Horowitz, in his piece
titled 'Spy Stories,' refers to a telephone conversation he
supposedly had with me in 1972, asserting that I advised him to
commit treason and destroy evidence. I have no recollection of any
telephone conversation with Mr. Horowitz. I do not know Mr.
Horowitz. I have never represented or advised either Ramparts
magazine [sic]. I do not counsel treason. I do not counsel destruction of evidence. I am an Evidence professor who teaches and has
written on the necessity of preserving, not destroying evidence. I
refer you to my casebook, *Green & Nesson, Evidence*, to my article, 'Incentives to Spoliate Evidence in Civil Litigation: The Need
for Vigorous Judicial Action,' 13 Cardozo L. Rev. 793, 793 (1991),
and to any students who have ever taken my class."

My reply to Nesson:

"This is what we call a not-so-subtle evasion. No denial that you
worked on the Ellsberg defense team, for example. And how
would I know that you even did, if you had not responded to my
call to the Ellsberg defense team? 'I do not recall' is not very helpful to you or to anyone else.

"I wrote about our conversation in *Destructive Generation*,
which was published in 1989, and then again in *Radical Son*,

October 6, 2000; http://archive.frontpagemag.com/Printable.aspx?ArtId=
19855

which was published in 1997. I discussed your advice to me on C-Span and on innumerable radio shows. It is difficult to believe that you did not hear the story or that no one ever brought it up to you. Yet you have never contacted my publisher or me in all the years since to complain. Why are you coming forward now with this kind of half-hearted file and shuffle? 'I do not recall,' indeed.

"I am not a law student or a lawyer. I have never attended Harvard. I would never even have come across your name if it weren't for that call. Nor do I have any reason to single you out, since I don't know you and know nothing about you except as a voice on the other end of that phone-line. The only reason I even know your name is that you gave it to me when you came on the phone after I had contacted the Ellsberg defense team and asked for help. Perhaps you gave out this kind of advice so frequently and casually in those days, you cannot now place my call—but I doubt even that.

"I certainly didn't make this up. The conversation is vivid enough in my mind because the future not only of myself but of my wife and four children depended on the advice I sought and got from you. Moreover, others were waiting for my report of what you said. My *Ramparts* co-editor Peter Collier remembers your name, the phone call, and the advice I reported, as clearly as I do. His freedom and his family's future were also on the line. I never claimed that you represented *Ramparts*. I called the Ellsberg defense team and you came on the phone. And you gave me the advice exactly as I described it in my book *Radical Son*. What appalls me about people like you is not only that you provided such counsel, but that you persist in lying about what you did 30 years after the fact. Alger Hiss went to the grave lying; maybe you will too. I'm sorry to be so blunt, but then your lack of candor (with malice) invites a direct response."

Let me add to this exchange, that the incident itself is the most shameful and humiliating thing I ever did. Thousands of New Leftists actively abetted or collaborated with America's enemies during the Sixties and Seventies and Eighties, and committed similar acts. But I am virtually the only one who has admitted what I did and told how it was done. That is the only reason I have subjected myself to the embarrassment of telling this story again.

3

Scheer Lunacy at the
Los Angeles Times

On a hot August day in 1988 I was standing in the New Orleans Convention Center with my longtime writing partner, Peter Collier, when an old comrade unexpectedly crossed our path. Peter and I had been editors of the New Left magazine *Ramparts* in the 1960s. We were in New Orleans for the Republican convention as speechwriters for Bob and Elizabeth Dole, part of our recent odyssey from the ranks of the left to the other side of the political barricades. Suddenly we became aware of the presence of our former boss, Bob Scheer, whom we had not seen in the 20 years since we had overthrown him in a Sixties-style staff rebellion and booted him out of the magazine.

Scheer was covering the convention for the *Los Angeles Times,* whose "national correspondent" he had become. For a beat or two the three of us just stood there, eyeing each other at a distance that might have been 40 paces, each trying to make up his mind whether to engage or not. "Hi, Bob," I finally said, breaking the ice. But Scheer was not up for any reunions. Taking a step towards the exit, he looked over his shoulder almost in the manner of a drive-by and flung in our direction the most crushing retort he could muster. "Deutscher was right," he said, and walked away. It was vintage Scheer; smug, shallow and intellectually lazy.

For Sixties veterans like us, Isaac Deutscher had provided the key to our continuing radical faith. A famed biographer of Trotsky

February 19, 2001, http://archive.frontpagemag.com/Printable.aspx? ArtId=24417; http://www.salon.com/2001/02/20/scheer/

and Stalin, Deutscher had explained the monstrosity socialism had become in a way that made it possible for us to continue on our radical paths. Deutscher described the Soviet Union as still encrusted with the tyranny of Old Russia but transformed by socialist economics into a competitive world power. The scientific logic of socialism, he assured us, would soon transform the tyranny into a modern democratic state. We had a New Left *bon mot* to sum up this Deutscherian vision. The first socialist revolution, we said, would take place in the Soviet Union.

It was this hope that encouraged us to support the Soviet bloc and believe it was still "progressive" despite its totalitarian excrescences; and it was this hope that made us turn our backs on democratic America as reactionary and oppressive. Scheer's parting taunt to Peter and me expressed his belief that the reforms of *glasnost* and *perestroika,* then taking place under Mikhail Gorbachev, would transform the Soviet Union into a modern, democratic socialist state.

To the true believer, Gorbachev's reforms may indeed have looked like the transformation Deutscher had predicted, but the result was obviously anything but. A year after our encounter with Scheer, the Berlin Wall came crashing down and the Soviet empire with it. Its collapse revealed not the economic superpower of Deutscher's imaginings but the pathetic shell of a Third-World backwater, whose gross national product output was less than South Korea's. Contrary to Deutscher's vision, Marx's socialist prescriptions had turned the Soviet Union into an economic desert. In 1989, after 60 years of Five-Year Plans, the average meat intake of a Soviet citizen was less than it had been in 1913 under the Czar. In a landscape devastated by the Marxist ideas that progressives like Scheer continued to embrace, the new era of freedom meant only another round of poverty and despotism, albeit not quite as bad as before. Deutscher could hardly have made a bigger mistake. He was wrong about the economic achievements of the Soviet past, which turned out to be little more than a Potemkin illusion; and he was wrong about the bright prospect of the Soviet future.

Scheer was wrong too, but his retro-Marxism had done nothing to impede his upward climb in the capitalist world he loved to feed off and attack at the same time. While Peter and I were doing our slow-motion disengagement from the totalitarian temptation, Scheer, along with an entire generation of New Left intellectuals, was burrowing into the institutions they had tried to burn down, and busily infiltrating the Sixties into the mainstream culture.

Scheer's path to success was made a lot easier by his marriage to Narda Zacchino, one of the top editors at the *Los Angeles Times*. In 1976, he was made the *Times'* national correspondent, a post he held for 17 years before transitioning to his present role as all-purpose pundit and chief in-house columnist. His journalistic fronting for the Clinton White House earned him a spot on Sidney Blumenthal's email list of media friends. Scheer's power-marriage at the *Times* helped insulate him from critical scrutiny and created an ideal vantage within a profession that had become a left-wing redoubt. Among his many prestigious perks, Scheer was appointed to a visiting professorship on the faculty of the prestigious Annenberg School of Journalism at USC by its dean, Geoffrey Cowan, a former Clinton administration official.

An aggressive sybarite even when I first met him 40 years ago, Scheer had acquired a townhouse, a boat, pals like Barbara Streisand and Warren Beatty, and a first-name familiarity with some of the finest restaurateurs in town, all while he continued his sanctimonious attacks on the ruling class in his columns in the *Times*. Nor had he lost his reputation for intellectual sloth first acquired among subordinate staffers at *Ramparts* who were conscripted to write his copy and his books. In the early Nineties, I had lunch with a city editor at the *Times* who swore he had never seen anyone go so far on so little as Bob Scheer. Two writing consequences flowed from this general life-approach. In 1961, Scheer had published his first book, a celebration of Castro's revolution, co-authored with Maurice Zeitlin. During the next 40 years, Scheer managed to produce little besides a few collections of articles and a pamphlet. Periodic notices did appear in literary gossip-columns, announcing that he had received a six-figure advance to write a book on Gorbachev or the official biography of Jane Fonda. But years passed and the books never came. The second result of this lassitude was a shallowness that characterized everything he did manage to complete.

Scheer's column on the power crisis in California, a story in his own journalistic backyard, will illustrate. By general consensus, the California crisis was triggered by the unexpected convergence of at least four significant factors: (1) a 30 per cent increase in demand for electricity in one of the nation's fastest-growing states; (2) a shortage of power sources due to environmental attitudes that had prevented the state from bringing online a single new power plant in 15 years; (3) an increased dependency on power from other states in which demand was also rising; and (4) a misguided legislative decision to deregulate the industry halfway, allowing utility companies to purchase power at market rates on the supply side of the equation, but maintaining regulatory controls on consumer prices on the demand side. By 2001 the cost of power to California's utilities was more than ten times what they were allowed to charge consumers who, because *their* price was fixed, lacked the incentive to restrict demand. This put the utility companies on the verge of bankruptcy, unable to purchase additional power. Hence the crisis.

To Scheer, such complexity was only a distraction from ideological clarity. This is how he distilled the situation in a December 26 column, mixing metaphors of Santa Claus, Disney and the Land of Oz:

> Capitalism is falling apart.... Yes, Virginia, we do need government regulation ... because the market mechanism left to its own devices inevitably spirals out of control. Recognition of that reality has guided this country to prosperity ever since Franklin D. Roosevelt pulled us out of the Great Depression. But in recent decades, conservative economists and their fat-cat corporate sponsors have led us down the yellow brick road of deregulation. Getting government out of the market would free creativity and

investment, leading us to the Magic Kingdom of Oz, where all would prosper. If anything went wrong, the wizard of Oz—a.k.a. Alan Greenspan—would make it all better.[1]

Like the inscrutable reference to Federal Reserve chief Alan Greenspan, Scheer's sophomoric column never actually got around to the facts. Instead it provided a Cook's tour of the author's anti-corporate prejudices, along with many arcane irrelevancies off the top of the author's head, including the AOL-Time Warner merger and Europe's mad-cow epidemic. Scheer's column concluded with a plea for "passage of the McCain-Feingold campaign finance reform" and "the revival of the consumer movement" to achieve "more, not less, regulation," which was his solution to the problem.

I once asked an editor at the *Times* whether Scheer was, in fact, protected by its editorial powers from being held to the journalistic standards other writers were expected to observe. The editor replied, "Bob Scheer is anointed."

It is this latitude, perhaps, that has made Scheer's capacity for ignorant mischief seemingly boundless, extending even to matters of the nation's security. Over the last two years, Scheer has become the nation's leading defender of suspected atomic spy Wen Ho Lee, whom he has lauded as "an American Dreyfus" and about whom he has written a dozen columns—all proclaiming Lee's innocence, while portraying him as a victim of an anti-Asian conspiracy. Scheer has now been hired as "technical consultant" to an upcoming four-hour whitewash of Lee. The mini-series is to be produced for ABC-TV by long-time leftwing activist Robert Greenwald, whose last feature film, an adoration of Sixties juvenile delinquent Abbie Hoffman, closed almost as quickly as it opened.

As Scheer has been an outspoken anti-American leftist since the onset of the Cold War, his immoderate defense of an accused

---

[1]Robert Scheer, "These Messes Are What Deregulation Gets Us," *The Nation*, January 8, 2001; http://www.thenation.com/article/these-messes-are-what-deregulation-gets-us#

spy was reckless enough to surprise me. After all, every Communist spy identified by the FBI in the half-century since the Cold
War began—the Rosenbergs, Morton Sobell, Joel Barr, Judith
Coplon, William Remington, Alger Hiss—was eventually proven
guilty beyond any reasonable doubt. Every one of those spies had
also been defended as innocent by progressives like Scheer and
Greenwald. Why would Scheer want to expose himself to such
embarrassment again? There were only two possible answers.
Either was that Scheer had not been paying enough attention to
realize his exposure, or the culture had shifted so far to the left
that he knew there was no risk of that happening.

The immediate context of the Wen Ho Lee case had been set by a
report released in May 1999 by the so-called Cox Committee on the
theft of nuclear secrets during the Clinton administration. The
report, approved by a bipartisan committee, had concluded: "The
espionage inquiry found Beijing has stolen U.S. design data for nearly
all elements needed for a major nuclear attack on the U.S., such as
advanced warheads, missiles and guidance systems." Scheer's journalistic response to these disturbing facts proved to be no different
than his approach to the California power crisis: begin and end with
an ideological premise; in between, stuff the column with half-baked
information, unfounded accusation and irrelevant asides. On May
11, Scheer responded to the findings of the bipartisan committee on
the theft of nuclear secrets with the following column:

Our Secrets Are of No Use to Them
by Robert Scheer

Let's as those Apple computer ads implore, think different. There
are no nuclear weapons secrets or, indeed, nuclear "weapons" for
China to have stolen.[2]

Scheer did not actually try to substantiate the claim that the
United States had no nuclear-weapons secrets, leaving it to float in

---

[2]Robert Scheer, "Our Secrets Are of No Use to Them," *Los Angeles
Times*, May 11, 1999; http://articles.latimes.com/1999/may/11/local/
me-35987

the ether. But he did make a stab at the idea that there are *no* nuclear weapons: "Nuclear bombs are not actually weapons because, in today's world, they cannot be employed to win battles but can serve only as instruments of mass terror." (Think about that one for a moment.) The statement—and the entire column— showed an ignorance of deterrence theory astounding for a man whose personal website boasts that "from 1976 to 1993, he served as a national correspondent for the *Los Angeles Times,* where he wrote articles on such diverse topics as the Soviet Union, arms control, national politics and the military." A good thesis for a graduate student at the USC Annenberg School for Communication and Journalism where Scheer teaches might be to find out what the *Times* editors, other than Scheer's wife, could have been thinking when they appointed him to his position.

Having asserted that there were no nuclear secrets to steal, Scheer found it relatively easy to reach the conclusion that Los Alamos scientist Wen Ho Lee was innocent of the suspicions the FBI had focused on him—notwithstanding the fact that he had removed thousands of pages of classified files from the Los Alamos nuclear weapons lab, in and of itself a violation of the Espionage Act.

Drawing on years of training in the left, Scheer went on the offensive, identifying Lee as the hapless target of a racial witch-hunt. Two months later, on August 3, Scheer wrote his first Wen Ho Lee column, which began with the following subtlety: "The 'Chinaman' did it. The diabolical Asian has long been a staple of American racism, and it's not surprising that the folks attempting to whip up a new red espionage scare would focus on Wen Ho Lee."[3]

In making these bizarre accusations, Scheer was obviously aware that any such witch-hunt against Lee would have to have

---

[3]"China Spy Case Takes Aim at the Wrong Issue," Robert Scheer, *Los Angeles Times,* August 3, 1999, http://articles.latimes.com/1999/aug/03/local/me-62155

been orchestrated by Lee's prosecutors: Attorney General Janet Reno, FBI director Louis Freeh and the local U.S. attorney on the case, who happened to be a former college roommate and close political friend of Bill Clinton himself. To make the persecution of Lee seamless, there would also have to be collusion on the part of acting deputy attorney general for civil rights, Bill Lann Lee—himself an American of Chinese lineage and a hyper-sensitive critic of racial profiling.

All this did not cause Scheer a moment's pause in making his accusations. Instead he just plucked a different culprit out of his journalistic hat, actually two: the Republican head of the bipartisan nuclear-secrets committee and the chief media rival to his own paper. "Facts evidently don't matter to those in Congress, led by Rep. Christopher Cox (R-Newport Beach), and in the media, where the august *New York Times* has acted as head cheerleader for those sounding the alarm of a Chinese nuclear threat." The following day Congressman Cox responded. In a letter to the *Times*, he pointed out that the name Wen Ho Lee had actually not appeared in his Committee's report, and that "neither I nor any member of the Select Committee had even heard of Wen Ho Lee when we completed our report in January." Cox further pointed out that when Energy Secretary Bill Richardson actually fired Lee, calling him a man who had "massively violated our security system," Cox had issued a widely-publicized statement criticizing the media's spotlight on Lee, saying that it was wrong without proof "to juxtapose him with some of the most serious crimes that have ever been committed against our military secrets."

The fact that the man whom Scheer falsely accused of persecuting Lee had actually defended his right to be presumed innocent did not prevent Scheer, in a column the following month, from repeating the slander.[4] "It's time to pronounce the Chinese

---

[4]Robert Scheer, "Time to Say Farewell to Spy Scandal; It was a nice diversion from more mundane worries like global competition, but there was nothing to it to begin with," Metro Section, *Los Angeles Times*, September 14, 1999, p. 7; http://articles.latimes.com/1999/sep/14/local/me-9893

nuclear weapons spy story a hoax," he repeated. Turning to the alleged witch-hunt of Lee, he said its rationale was provided by an investigation "led by an outraged Cox, who represents the more right-wing fringes of Southern California, eager to find a new evil empire as justification of a military buildup, once the staple of that region's economy."

In prose even more inept than usual, Scheer had managed to start a witch-hunt of his own, tarring Cox, a respected congressional leader, as a member of the farthest-right fringe. Scheer's September 14 column, which was called "Time to Say Farewell to Spy Scandal," provoked a joint rebuttal from Cox and the ranking Democrat on the committee, Norm Dicks, a liberal from Washington: "[Robert Scheer's] column asserted four main 'facts,'" their letter asserted; "each of them is false."[5]

Five days before Scheer's column appeared, the National Intelligence Estimate, representing the consensus of the entire U.S. intelligence community, had been released. The estimate stated that China was ready to test a longer-range intercontinental missile (one of the secrets that had been passed to the Chinese) which would be targeted primarily against the United States. This missile technology had been shared with Kim Il-Sung's loony police-state in North Korea. The letter also stated that the missile would be fitted with "smaller nuclear warheads—in part influenced by U.S. technology gained through espionage." It was the design for the W-88 warhead, small enough to fit a missile that Wen Ho Lee was suspected of stealing.

In the midst of Scheer's false claims and accusations, he got a break. On September 13, 2000, the government announced that it was dropping 58 of the 59 charges against Lee. President Clinton even volunteered an apology, as though some kind of injustice had been done. This didn't prevent him, however, from flying to New

---

[5]Rep. Christopher Cox (R) and Rep. Norm Dicks (D), "Chinese Spy Scandal," *Los Angeles Times*, September 20, 1999; http://articles.latimes.com/1999/sep/20/local/me-12216

Mexico the very next week to raise campaign money for Lee's prosecutor. *The New York Times* also apologized. Janet Reno and Louis Freeh did not. Freeh told a congressional committee: "The Department of Justice and the FBI stand by each and every one of the 59 counts in the indictment of Dr. Lee. Each of those counts could be proved in December 1999 [when Lee was formally indicted], and each of them could be proven today."

I wrote a column about Freeh's statement for *Salon* recalling an episode that had taken place when Peter and I were running *Ramparts*, after we had fired Scheer, in the early Seventies.[6] We were planning to publish an article by a defector from an American spy program and thus to break the same Espionage Act that Wen Ho Lee had violated in removing secret files from the Los Alamos Lab. In my column, I recalled how I had been advised by Charles Nesson, then as now a left-wing law professor at Harvard, on how to get away with the crime. Nesson advised us—with a cynicism I will never forget—that, since we lived in a democracy, in order to prosecute us for treason the government would have to prove in open court that we had damaged national security. In other words, it would have to reveal to the court and to our country's enemies far more than it would be willing to reveal. Hence, if we had the nerve to do it, we would most likely get away with what we were planning, which was to print national secrets in the pages of our magazine. I was sure that it was just this cynicism—using the privileges of America's democracy to attack her—that lay behind the calculations of Wen Ho Lee's defense lawyers.

Because I was convinced that Scheer's motivation in defending Lee and the Chinese Communists was a bedrock of conviction that had not changed in 40 years, I put in the following sentence: "While we were divulging the secrets of America's electronic intelligence agency in the pages of *Ramparts*, Scheer was joining the Red Sun Rising Commune [in Berkeley] and becoming an

---

[6]"Wen Ho Lee's Reckless Defenders" http://www.salon.com/2000/10/03/lee_8/, or see chapter 1 above.

4

Guru of the Anti-American Left

Without question, the most devious, dishonest and, in this hour of his nation's grave crisis, treacherous intellect in America belongs to MIT professor Noam Chomsky. On the 150 campuses that staged "teach-ins" and rallies against America's right to defend herself after 9/11; on the streets of Genoa and Seattle, where "anti-globalist" radicals have attacked the symbols of free markets and world trade; among the demonstrators at Vieques, who wish to deny our military its training grounds in Puerto Rico; and wherever young people manifest an otherwise incomprehensible rage against their country, the inspirer of their loathing and the instructor of their hate is more often than not this man.

There are many who ask how it is possible that our most privileged and educated youth should come to despise their own nation—a free, open, democratic society—and to do so with such ferocious passion. They ask how it is possible for American youth even to consider lending comfort and aid to the Osama bin Ladens and Saddam Husseins. A full answer would involve a search of the deep structures of the human psyche, but the short answer is to be found in the speeches and writings of an embittered academic and his intellectual supporters. For 40 years, Noam Chomsky has

---

This article was originally printed in two parts. The first was on September 26, 2001; http://archive.frontpagemag.com/Printable.aspx?ArtId= 24447; http://www.salon.com/2001/09/26/treason_2/. The second was on October 10, 2001, http://archive.frontpagemag.com/Printable.aspx?ArtId= 24449; http://www.salon.com/2001/10/08/chomsky_2/

turned out book after book, pamphlet after pamphlet and speech
after speech with one message, and one message alone: America is
the Great Satan, the fount of evil in this world.

In Chomsky's demented universe, America is responsible not
only for its own bad deeds but for the bad deeds of others, including those of the terrorists who struck the World Trade Center and
the Pentagon. In this attitude, he is the medium for all those who
now search the ruins of Manhattan not for the victims of the
attack but for the "root causes" of the catastrophe that befell
them. A recent pamphlet of Chomsky's, *What Uncle Sam Really
Wants,* has already sold 160,000 copies but represents only a tiny
sample of his output.[1] His venomous message is spread on tapes
and CDs as well as on the campus lecture-circuit; he is promoted
at rock concerts by superstar bands such as Pearl Jam, Rage
Against the Machine and U-2, whose lead singer Bono called
Chomsky a "rebel without a pause." He is the icon of Hollywood
stars like Matt Damon, whose character in the Academy Award-
winning film *Good Will Hunting* invokes Chomsky as the go-to
authority for political wisdom.

According to the *Chicago Tribune,* Noam Chomsky is "the
most often cited living author. Among intellectual luminaries of
all eras, Chomsky placed eighth, just behind Plato and Sigmund
Freud."[2] On the Web, there are more chat-room references to
Noam Chomsky than to Vice President Dick Cheney and ten
times as many as there are to Democratic congressional leaders
Richard Gephardt and Tom Daschle. This is because Chomsky is
also the political mentor to the academic left, the legions of Sixties
radicals who have entrenched themselves in American universities to indoctrinate students in their anti-American creeds. *The
New York Times* has called Chomsky "arguably the most important intellectual alive," and the pop-music magazine *Rolling*

---

[1]Noam Chomsky, *What Uncle Sam Really Wants,* Odonian Press, 1992
(interviews with David Barsamian)
[2]"Strong Words," Ron Grossman, *Chicago Tribune,* January 1, 1993

Stone, which otherwise hardly acknowledges the realm of the mind, has him as "one of the most respected and influential intellectuals in the world."[3]

In fact, Chomsky's influence is best understood not as that of an intellectual figure but as the leader of a religious cult, an ayatollah of anti-American hate. This cultic resonance is not unnoticed by his followers themselves. His most important devotee, David Barsamian, is an obscure public-radio producer on KGNU in Boulder, Colorado, who has created a library of "Chomskyana" on tape from interviews he conducted with the master and converted into pamphlets and books. In the introduction to one such offering, Barsamian describes Chomsky's power over his disciples in these words: "Although decidedly secular, he is for many of us our rabbi, our preacher, our *rinpoche,* our pundit, our *imam,* our *sensei.*"[4]

The theology that Chomsky preaches is Manichean, with America as its evil principle. For Chomsky, no other nation's evil, however great, can exceed America's, while America is also the cause of evil in others. This is Chomsky's key to the mystery of the attackers of September 11: *The devil made them do it.* In every one of the 150 shameful demonstrations that took place on America's campuses on September 20, these were the twin themes of those who agitated to prevent America from taking up arms in her self-defense: America is responsible for the "root causes" of this criminal attack; even if the attack was heinous, America has done worse to others.

Chomsky's response to Osama bin Laden's calculated strike on buildings containing 50,000 innocent human beings was to eclipse it with an even greater atrocity he was confident he could attribute

---

[3]Noam Chomsky, op. cit.

[4]Noam Chomsky, *Propaganda and the Public Mind,* Interviews by David Barsamian, Cambridge, 2001, p. x. In the endpapers *The New York Times* is quoted praising Chomsky as "an exploder of received truths." *The Guardian* (London): "One of the radical heroes of our age ... A towering intellect..." The *Times Literary Supplement:* "Chomsky's work ... has some of the qualities of Revelations, the Old Testament prophets and Blake."

to former president Bill Clinton. This infamous September 12 statement "On the Bombings" began:

> The terrorist attacks were major atrocities. In scale they may not reach the level of many others, for example, Clinton's bombing of the Sudan with no credible pretext, destroying half its pharmaceutical supplies and killing unknown numbers of people (no one knows, because the US blocked an inquiry at the UN and no one cares to pursue it).[5]

Chomsky's opening reference to the attacks serves as a kind of rhetorical throat-clearing so that he can get to the real culprit, which is us. It is a message that says: "Look away from the injury that has been done to you, and contemplate the injuries you have done to *them.*"

In point of fact—and just for the record—however ill-conceived Bill Clinton's decision to launch a missile into the Sudan, it was not remotely comparable to the World Trade Center massacre. It was, in its very design, precisely the opposite, a defensive response that attempted to minimize casualties. Clinton's missile was launched in reaction to the blowing-up of two of our African embassies, the murder of hundreds of innocent people and the injury to thousands, mostly African civilians. It was designed to prevent the loss of innocent life. The missile was fired at night, so that no one would be in the building when it was hit. The target was selected because the best information available indicated it was not a pharmaceutical factory, but a factory producing biological weapons. Chomsky's use of this incident to diminish the monstrosity of the terrorist attack is a typical expression of an instinctive mendacity along with the anti-American dementia that infuses everything he writes and says.

This same animus warps the historical perspective he offered to his disciples in an interview conducted a few days after the

---

[5]Noam Chomsky, "A Quick Reaction," *Counterpunch*, September 12, 2001, http://www.counterpunch.org/2001/09/12/a-quick-reaction/

World Trade Center's destruction. It was intended to present America as the devil incarnate and to incite others to follow the *jihadists'* example. It was the first time America itself—or as Chomsky put it the "national territory"—had been attacked since the War of 1812. "During these years the US annihilated the indigenous population (millions of people), conquered half of Mexico, intervened violently in the surrounding region, conquered Hawaii and the Philippines (killing hundreds of thousands of Filipinos), and in the past half century particularly, extended its resort to force throughout much of the world. The number of victims is colossal. For the first time, the guns have been directed the other way. That is a dramatic change."[6] Direct the guns the other way. Listening to Chomsky, you can almost feel the justice of Osama bin Laden's strike.

If you were one of the hundreds of thousands of young people who had been exposed to Chomsky's propaganda, and the equally noxious teachings of his academic disciples, you too would be able to extend your outrage against America into the present. According to Chomsky, in the first battle of the postwar conflict with the Soviet Empire, "the United States was picking up where the Nazis had left off." According to Chomsky, during the Cold War, American operations behind the Iron Curtain included "a 'secret army' under US-Nazi auspices that sought to provide agents and military supplies to armies that had been established by Hitler and which were still operating inside the Soviet Union and Eastern Europe through the early 1950s." According to Chomsky, in Latin America during the Cold War, U.S. support for legitimate governments against Communist subversion led to U.S. complicity, under John F. Kennedy and Lyndon Johnson, in "the methods of Heinrich Himmler's extermination squads." According to Chomsky, there is "a close correlation worldwide between torture and U.S. aid."

---

[6]Interview by Svetlana Vukovic & Svetlana Lukic, *B92*, September 19, 2001; http://www.chomsky.info/interviews/20010919.htm; http://www.b92.net/intervju/eng/2001/0919-chomsky.phtml

According to Chomsky, America "invaded" Vietnam to slaughter its people, and even after America left in 1975, under Jimmy Carter and Ronald Reagan, "the major policy goal of the US has been to maximize repression and suffering in the countries that were devastated by our violence. The degree of the cruelty is quite astonishing."[7] According to Chomsky, "the pretext for Washington's terrorist wars [i.e., in Nicaragua, El Salvador, Chile, Guatemala, Iraq, etc.] was self-defense, the standard official justification for just about any monstrous act, even the Nazi Holocaust."[8]

In sum, according to Chomsky, "legally speaking, there's a very solid case for impeaching every American president since the Second World War. They've all been either outright war criminals or involved in serious war crimes."[9] In light of such atrocities, what decent, caring human being would not want to see America and its war criminals brought to justice?

What America *really* wants, according to Chomsky, is to steal from the poor and give to the rich.[10] America's crusade against Communism was actually a crusade "to protect our doctrine that the rich should plunder the poor."[11] That is why America launched a new crusade against terrorism after the end of the Cold War: "Of course, the end of the Cold War brings its problems too. Notably, the technique for controlling the domestic population has had to shift.... New enemies have to be invented. It becomes hard to disguise the fact that the real enemy has always been 'the poor who seek to plunder the rich'—in particular, Third-World

---

[7]Noam Chomsky, *What Uncle Sam Really Wants*, Odonian Press, 1992, pp. 8, 18, 29, 31, 32, 56–58

[8]Chomsky, *Profit Over People*, 1999, p. 102

[9]Noam Chomsky, *What Uncle Sam Really Wants*, Odonian Press, 1992, p. 32

[10]Chomsky has set up a smokescreen to the effect that he is an anarcho-socialist in the vein of Pannekoek, Mattick, or Kropotkin. But since he has spent his intellectual life making excuses for and defending Stalinist regimes and now Islamic fascist networks, only the terminally credulous will take these protestations seriously.

[11]Ibid. p. 79

miscreants who seek to break out of the service role."[12] According to Chomsky, America is afraid of the success of Third World countries and does not want them to succeed on their own. Those who threaten to succeed—like the Marxist governments of North Vietnam, Nicaragua and Grenada—America regards as viruses. According to Chomsky, during the Cold War, "except for a few madmen and nitwits, none feared [Communist] conquest—they were afraid of a positive example of successful development. What do you do when you have a virus? First you destroy it, then you inoculate potential victims, so that the disease does not spread. That's basically the US strategy in the Third World."[13] No wonder they want to bomb us.

Schooled in these big lies, taught to see America as greed incarnate and a political twin of the Third Reich, why wouldn't young people—with no historical memory—come to believe that the danger ahead lies in Washington rather than Baghdad or Kabul? It would be easy to demonstrate how on every page of every book and in every statement that Chomsky has written the facts are twisted, the political context is distorted, often inverted, and the historical record systematically traduced. Every piece of evidence, every analysis is subordinated to the overweening purpose of Chomsky's lifework, which is to justify an *idée fixe* —his pathological hatred of his own country. To expose his method in detail would take volumes but there really is no need because every Chomsky argument exists to serve this end, a fact transparent in each offensive and preposterous claim he makes.

The attacks of September 11 presented a political problem for American leftists, who knew better than to celebrate the event even though it was the realization of their desires. The destroyed buildings were the very symbols of the American empire with which they are at war. In a memoir published on the eve of the attack, Sixties terrorist Bill Ayers recorded his joy at striking one

[12]Ibid., p. 82
[13]Ibid., pp. 56–7

of the targets years before: "Everything was absolutely ideal on the day I bombed the Pentagon. The sky was blue. The birds were singing. And the bastards were finally going to get what was coming to them."[14] In the wake of September 11, Ayers, now a "Distinguished Professor of Early Childhood Education" at the University of Illinois, had to backtrack feverishly and explain that these revealing sentiments did not mean what they obviously did. Now feigning to be "filled with horror and grief" over 9/11, Ayers refashioned his terrorist years as a struggle with "the intricate relationships between social justice, commitment and resistance."[15]

Chomsky is so much Ayers' superior at prevarication that he works the same denial into his account of the World Trade Center bombing itself. Consider first the fact that the Trade Center is the very symbol of American capitalism and "globalization" that Chomsky and his radical comrades despise. It is a synecdoche of "Wall Street," its twin towers filled with bankers, brokers, international traders and corporate lawyers—the hated men and women of the ruling class. It is the palace of the Great Satan, the object of Chomsky's lifelong righteous wrath. But Chomsky is too clever and too cowardly to admit it. He knows that in the hour of the nation's grief this is a third rail to be avoided, so he just rewrites the text: "The primary victims, as usual, were working people: janitors, secretaries, firemen, etc. It is likely to be a crushing blow to Palestinians and other poor and oppressed people."[16]

Chomsky's message to his disciples—the young on our college campuses, the radicals in our streets, the moles in our government offices—is also a message of action. To those susceptible to his words of hate, Chomsky has this instruction: "The people of the Third World need our sympathetic understanding and, much more than that, they need our help. We can provide them with a margin of survival by internal disruption in the United States. Whether

---

[14]Bill Ayers, *Fugitive Days*, 2001, p. 256
[15]Statement on the publisher's website, http://www.beacon.org
[16]Noam Chomsky, "A Quick Reaction," *Counterpunch*, September 12, 2001, http://www.counterpunch.org/2001/09/12/a-quick-reaction/

they can succeed against the kind of brutality we impose on them depends in large part on what happens here."[17] This is the voice of the fifth-column left. Disruption in this country is what the terrorists want, what the terrorists need, and what the followers of Noam Chomsky will want to give them. Of course, Chomsky himself, a Cambridge millionaire, is too important to the struggle to take such risks personally; his role is to incite others.

In President Bush's address to Congress just after the attacks, he reminded Americans: "We have seen their kind before. They are the heirs of all the murderous ideologies of the 20th century. By sacrificing human life to serve their radical visions, by abandoning every value except the will to power, they follow in the path of fascism, Nazism and totalitarianism. And they will follow that path all the way to where it ends in history's unmarked grave of discarded lies." The president was talking about the terrorists and their sponsors abroad. But he might just as well have been talking about their fifth-column allies at home.

One of the typical illusions of the Chomsky cult is the belief that its guru is not the unbalanced dervish of anti-American loathing he appears to be to everyone else, but an analytic giant whose dicta flow from painstaking and scientific inquiries into the facts. "The only reason Noam Chomsky is an international political force unto himself," writes a typically fervid acolyte, "is that he actually spends considerable time researching, analyzing, corroborating, deconstructing, and impassionately [sic] explaining world affairs." This conviction is almost as delusional as Chomsky's view of the world itself. It would be more accurate to say of the Chomsky *oeuvre*—lifting a famous line from the late Mary McCarthy—that everything he has written is a lie, including the "and's" and the "the's."

A lot of facts do appear in Chomsky's texts, or—more precisely—appear to appear in his texts. On closer examination, every

---

[17]Noam Chomsky, *What Uncle Sam Really Wants*, Odonian Press, 1992, p. 100

one of them has been ripped out of any meaningful historical context and then distorted with such cynicism that the result has about as much in common with the truth as *Harry Potter's Muggles' Guide to Magic*. In Chomsky's narrative, for example, the bipolar world of the Cold War appears as a world with only one pole. In Chomsky's world, the Soviet empire hardly exists; not a single American action is seen as a response to a Soviet initiative or conquest; and the Cold War is thus "analyzed" as though it had only one side, which makes the United States the aggressor in every case. In the real world, the Cold War was about America's effort to organize a democratic coalition against an expansionist empire that conquered and enslaved more than a billion people. The war ended at the precise moment that the empire gave up, and the walls that had kept its subjects locked in came tumbling down.

Chomsky's method would lead to writing a history of the Second World War without mentioning Hitler or noticing that the actions of the Axis powers so much as influenced its events. Actually, in Chomsky's malevolent hands, matters get even worse. If one were to follow Chomsky, one would cite every problematic act committed by any party in the coalition attempting to stop Hitler, and attribute it to a calculated policy of the United States. One would then put together a report-card of these crimes and present it as the historical record. This record—consisting of the worst acts the allies could be accused of, and the most dishonorable motives they may be said to have acted upon—would then constitute the data from which America's portrait would be drawn. The result would be the great demon of Chomsky's deranged fantasies.

What Uncle Sam Really Wants begins with Chomsky's description of America as having "benefited enormously" from the Second World War in contrast to its "industrial rivals"—skipping over the 420,000 lives America lost, its generous Marshall Plan to aid those same rivals or, for that matter, its victory over Nazi Germany and the Axis powers. In Chomsky's portrait, America in

1945 emerges as a wealthy power that profited from others' misery and now seeks world domination. "The people who determine American policy were carefully planning how to shape the postwar world," he asserts without evidence; "American planners—from those in the State Department to those on the Council on Foreign Relations (one major channel by which business leaders influence foreign policy)—agreed that the dominance of the United States had to be maintained."[18]

Chomsky never names the actual people who agreed that American policy should be world dominance, or how they achieved unanimity in deciding to transform a famously isolationist country into a global power.[19] For Chomsky, America has no internal politics that matter. Thus Chomsky does not bother to acknowledge or attempt to explain the powerful strain of that isolationism, specifically in the Republican Party—the party of Wall Street and the Council on Foreign Relations businessmen who he claims determine policy. Above all, he does not explain why—if world domination was really America's goal in 1945—Washington disbanded its wartime armies overnight and brought them home.

Between 1945 and 1946, America demobilized the 1.6 million troops it had stationed in Europe, a fact immediately at odds with a desire for world dominance. By contrast, when the war ended, the Soviet Union maintained its two-million-man army in place in the countries of Eastern Europe, whose governments it had already begun to undermine and replace. It was the Soviet absorption of the formerly independent states of Eastern Europe in the years between 1945 and 1948 that triggered America's subsequent rearmament, the creation of NATO and the overseas spread of American power. These developments were designed to contain an expansionist Soviet empire and prevent a repetition of the appeasement that had led to World War II.

---

[18]Ibid. pp. 7–8

[19]What he does is to select quotes from isolated individuals and government documents that can be made to appear as though they lend credibility to his malicious distortions.

These facts never appear in Chomsky's text. There is no excuse for the omission, other than that Chomsky wants this history to be something other than it was. The Cold War, the formation of the postwar Western alliances and the mobilizing of Western forces was brought about by the Soviet conquest of Eastern Europe. That is why the Cold War ended as soon as the Iron Curtain fell and the states of Eastern Europe were free to pursue their independent paths. It was to accomplish this great liberation of several hundred million people, and not any quest for world domination, that explains American Cold War policy, not Chomsky's fantasy of a Wall Street cabal.

Having begun his account of the postwar period with an utterly false picture of the historical forces at work, Chomsky is ready to conduct a campaign of malicious slander against the democracy which has provided him with a privileged existence: "In 1949, US espionage in Eastern Europe had been turned over to a network run by Reinhard Gehlen, who had headed Nazi military intelligence on the Eastern Front. This network was one part of the US-Nazi alliance...."[20] Let's pause for a moment over this display of the Chomsky method. We have jumped—or rather Chomsky has jumped us—from 1945 to 1949, skipping over the little matter of the Soviet Union's conquest of Eastern Europe. Instead of these matters, the reader is confronted with what appears to be a shocking fact about Reinhard Gehlen, which is quickly inflated into a big lie—a "US-Nazi alliance." There was no such alliance; the United States *used* Gehlen, not the other way around. The U.S did not turn over its intelligence network to anyone.

In 1949, all of Eastern Europe was occupied by the Red Army—a state of affairs that continued until the end of the Cold War. All the regimes in Eastern Europe were police-states, and the two million Soviet troops were in an aggressive posture threatening the democratic states of Western Europe with invasion and occupation. In these circumstances, which Chomsky does not mention,

[20]Chomsky, op. cit. p. 8 (the second page of Chomsky's text)

the use of a German intelligence network with experience and assets in Eastern Europe and the Soviet Union was a reasonable measure to defend the democracies of the West.[21] This episode was no Nazi taint on America but a necessary part of America's Cold War effort in the defense of democracy. With the help of the Gehlen network, the United States kept Soviet expansion in check, and eventually liberated hundreds of millions of captive peoples in Eastern Europe from the horrors of Soviet regime.

Chomsky recounts this history as though the United States had not defeated Hitler but had joined him instead. According to Chomsky, America's real postwar agenda was establishing a Nazi world order—with business interests at the top and the "working classes and the poor" at the bottom. Therefore, "the major thing that stood in the way of this was the anti-fascist resistance, so we suppressed it all over the world, often installing fascists and Nazi collaborators in its place."[22] Claims like these give conspiracy theories a bad name.

It would be tedious to run through all of Chomsky's distortions. One will suffice. In 1947, a civil war in Greece became the first Cold War test of America's resolve to prevent the spread of the Soviet empire. Chomsky presents the conflict as a struggle between the "anti-Nazi resistance" and U.S.-backed interests. In Chomsky's version, these interests were "US investors and local businessmen" and "the beneficiaries [of U.S. policies] included Nazi collaborators, while the primary victims were the workers and the peasants...."[23] But the leaders of the anti-Communist forces in Greece were not Nazis, and what Chomsky calls the "anti-Nazi resistance" was in fact the Soviet-backed Communist Party and its fellow travelers. What Chomsky leaves out of his account are the proximity of the Red Army to Greece, the intention of the Greek Communists to establish a Soviet police state,

---

[21]Ibid. p. 8
[22]Ibid. p. 14
[23]Ibid. p. 16

and the fact that their defeat paved the way for an unprecedented economic development benefiting all classes and the eventual establishment of a political democracy, which soon brought democratic socialists to power.

Of the countries in which Chomsky's "anti-fascists" were victorious, not a single one ever established a democracy or produced any significant betterment in the economic conditions of the great mass of its inhabitants. This puts a somewhat different color on every detail of what happened in Greece and what the United States did there. The only point of view from which Chomsky's version of this history makes sense is that of the Kremlin, whose propaganda points have merely been updated by the MIT professor.

A key chapter of *What Uncle Sam Really Wants* is called "The Threat of a Good Example." In it, Chomsky offers his explanation for America's diabolical behavior in Third World countries: "What the US-run contra forces did in Nicaragua, or what our terrorist proxies do in El Salvador or Guatemala, isn't only ordinary killing. A major element is brutal, sadistic torture—beating infants against rocks, hanging women by their feet with their breasts cut off and the skin of their face peeled back so that they'll bleed to death, chopping people's heads off and putting them on stakes."[24] There are no citations in Chomsky's text to support the claim that these atrocities took place, or that the United States directed them, or that the United States was in any meaningful way responsible for them. But according to Chomsky, "US-run" forces and "our terrorist proxies" do this sort of thing routinely and everywhere: "No country is exempt from this treatment, no matter how unimportant."[25]

According to Chomsky, U.S. business is the evil hand behind all these policies, even when there is no direct business interest at stake. "As far as American business is concerned, Nicaragua could disappear and nobody would notice. The same is true of El Salvador. But both have been subjected to murderous assaults by the

---

[24]Ibid. pp. 21–22
[25]Ibid. p. 22

U.S., at a cost of hundreds of thousands of lives and many billions of dollars."[26] Chomsky explains the paradox: "There is a reason for that. The weaker and poorer a country is, the more dangerous it is *as an example* [italics in original].[27] If a tiny, poor country like Grenada can succeed in bringing about a better life for its people, some other place that has more resources will ask, 'why not us?' "[28]

In other words, what Uncle Sam really wants is to control the world. This control means absolute misery for all the peoples that come under Uncle Sam's sway, which means the U.S. must prevent all the poor people in the world from realizing that there are better ways to develop than with U.S. investments. Chomsky gives the example of Grenada: "Grenada has a hundred thousand people who produce a little nutmeg, and you could hardly find it on a map. But when Grenada began to undergo a mild social revolution, Washington quickly moved to destroy the threat."[29] This is his entire commentary on the U.S. intervention in Grenada. It is his proof that the goal of U.S. policy is to prevent "the threat of a good example."

Actually, something quite different took place in Grenada. In 1979 an internal coup established a Marxist dictatorship complete with a Soviet-style "politburo" (its official designation). This was a tense period in the Cold War. In the same year, the Soviet Union invaded Afghanistan, and Communist insurgencies armed by Cuba were spreading through Central America. Before long, Cuban military personnel began to appear in Grenada and build a new airport capable of accommodating Soviet bombers. Tensions over the uncompleted airport developed between Washington and the Grenadian dictatorship.

While this was taking place, there was another internal coup. It was led by the Marxist "Minister of Defense" who assassinated

---

[26]Ibid. p. 23
[27]Ibid.
[28]Ibid.
[29]Ibid. p. 22

the Marxist dictator and half his politburo, including the pregnant Minister of Education. The new dictator put the entire population of the island, including U.S. citizens resident there, under house arrest. It was at this juncture that the Reagan administration sent in the Marines to protect U.S. citizens, stop the construction of the military airport and restore democracy to the island. The U.S. did this at the request of four governments of Caribbean countries who feared a Communist military presence in their neighborhood. A public opinion poll taken after the invasion showed that 85 percent of the citizens of Grenada welcomed the intervention and America's help in restoring their freedom.

There was no "threat of a good example" in Grenada and there are none anywhere in the world of progressive social experiments. There is not a single Marxist country that has ever provided a "good example" in the sense of making its economy better or its people freer. Chomsky is in denial about this most basic fact of 20th-century history: Socialism doesn't work. Korea is an obvious example. Fifty years ago, in one of the early battles of the Cold War, the United States military prevented Communist North Korea from conquering the anti-Communist South. Today Communist North Korea is independent of the United States and one of the poorest countries in the world. A million of its citizens have starved in the last few years, while its Marxist dictator has feverishly invested his country's scarce capital in an intercontinental ballistic missile program. So much for the good example.

South Korea is defended by 50,000 U.S. troops stationed along the border to prevent another Communist attack. For 50 years, U.S. businesses and investors have operated freely in South Korea. The results are interesting. In 1950, South Korea, with a per capita income of $250, was as poor as Cuba and Vietnam. Today it is an industrial power and its per-capita income is more than twenty *times* greater than it was before it became an investment region of the United States. South Korea is not yet a full-fledged democracy, but it does have elections and more than one party and a press that provides its readers with information from the outside world. This is quite different from North Korea, whose citizens have no access to information that their dictator does not approve. Unlike the citizens of the south, North Koreans are not free to leave their *gulag* state. It is pretty clear which side in these battles fears the threat of a good example.

Communism was an expansive system that ruined nations and enslaved their citizens but Chomsky dismisses America's fear of Communism as a mere cover for its own diabolical practices. He explains the Vietnam War this way: "The real fear was that if the people of Indochina achieved independence and justice, the people of Thailand would emulate it, and if that worked, they'd try it in Malaya, and pretty soon Indonesia would pursue an independent path, and by then a significant area [of America's empire] would have been lost."[30] This is a Marxist version of the domino theory. But Vietnam has pursued an independent path for 25 years and it is still one of the poorest nations in the world, while its people live in a primitive Marxist police state.

After its defeat in Vietnam, the United States withdrew its military forces from the entire Indochinese peninsula. The result was that Cambodia was overrun by the Khmer Rouge, the very Communist forces that Noam Chomsky, the North Vietnamese and the entire American left had supported until then. The Khmer Rouge proceeded to kill two million Cambodians who, in their view, stood in the way of the progressive good example they intended to create. Chomsky earned himself a bad reputation by first denying and then minimizing the Cambodian genocide until the facts made denial impossible. Now, of course, he blames the Communist genocide on the United States.[31] Chomsky also blames the United States and the ravages of the Vietnam War for the fact that Vietnam is still poor, and not a "good example": "Our basic goal—the crucial one, the one that really counted—was to destroy the virus [of independent development], and we did

[30]Ibid. pp. 23–4
[31]Ibid. p. 59

achieve that. Vietnam is a basket case, and the U.S. is doing what it can to keep it that way."[32]

This is a typical Chomsky falsehood, and a standard Chomsky excuse for every malfeasance of socialist regimes—*the devil made them do it*. Japan and Germany were pulverized during the Second World War, and were occupied by the United States. But they had capitalist, free-market economies, and quickly restored their economic prowess in the years that followed. The difference is that the victorious Vietnamese Communists were Marxists, and Marxism is a crackpot theory that doesn't work. *Every* Marxist state has been an economic basket case.

Take another example. Cuba has not been bombed and has not suffered a war, but it is poorer today than it was more than 40 years ago when Castro took power. In 1959, Cuba was the second-richest country in Latin America. Now it is the third-poorest, just above Haiti and Belize. Naturally, Chomsky and his followers claim that the U.S. economic boycott is responsible. *The devil made them do it*. But the rest of the world trades with Cuba. Cuba not only trades with all of Latin America and Europe but receives aid from the latter. Moreover, in the 1970s and 1980s, the Soviet Union gave Cuba the equivalent of three Marshall Plans in economic subsidies and assistance, tens of billions of dollars. Cuba is a fertile island with a tropical climate. It is poor because it has followed Chomsky's examples, not America's. It is poor *because* it is socialist, Marxist and Communist. It is poor because, in Cuba, America lost the Cold War.

It is the Communist-Chomsky illusion that there is a way to prosperity other than that of the capitalist market. This illusion is what produces the poverty of states like Cuba, North Korea and Vietnam. The illusion that socialism promises a better future is also the cause of the Chomsky cult. It is the messianic hope that creates the progressive left. Insofar as it is believed, the choice appears to the believers as a battle between good and evil.

---

[32]Ibid. pp. 59–60

Opponents of socialism, Marxism and Communism personify worldly evil. They are the party of Satan, and their leader America is the Great Satan.

What Uncle Sam Really Wants is an explication of this world-view, with Chomsky as its prophet. His great service to the progressive faith is to deny the history of the last hundred years, which is the history of progressive atrocity and failure. In the 20th century, progressives in power have killed more than 100 million people in the attempt to realize their impossible dream. But as far as Noam Chomsky is concerned, these catastrophes never happened. "I don't much like the terms left and right," Chomsky writes in a screed called *The Common Good*. "What's called the left includes Leninism [i.e., Communism], which I consider ultra-right in many respects.... Leninism has nothing to do with the values of the left—in fact, it's radically opposed to them."[33]

You have to pinch yourself when reading sentences like that. The purpose of such Humpty-Dumpty mutilations of language is perfectly clear, however. It is to preserve the faith. Lenin is dead. Long live Leninism. The Communist catastrophes can have "nothing to do with the values of the left" because if they did, the left would have to answer for its deeds and confront its moral and intellectual bankruptcy. Progressives would have to face the reality that they killed 100 million people for nothing, for an idea that didn't work.

The real threat of a good example is the threat of America, which has lifted more people out of poverty, within its borders and all over the world, than all the socialists and progressives put together. To neutralize *this* threat, it is necessary to kill the American idea. This is, in fact, Noam Chomsky's mission in life.

---

[33]Noam Chomsky, *The Common Good*, Odonian Press, 1998

5

Port Huron and the War on Terror

Forty years ago I wrote the first book about the New Left, which included a kind of manifesto of what it intended.[1] In the same year, a much more famous document appeared: "The Port Huron Statement,"[2] which was the founding manifesto of Students for A Democratic Society.[3] This was an organization that began by agitating for "participatory democracy" and became the new left's largest organization. A bare seven years later, SDS was calling for war against "Amerikkka" and spawning the "Weather Underground," America's first terrorist cult.

Tom Hayden, one of the two principal authors of the Port Huron Statement, was also one of the loudest voices calling for that "war of liberation" in Amerikkka, and formed his own little guerrilla army to achieve that goal. Not surprisingly, Hayden does not care to remember or explain this political devolution, even though it was accurately predicted at the time by dissenters from the Port Huron Statement, notably the late Irving Howe. Even in 1962, Howe understood that Hayden and his comrades were totalitarians in the making. Now, Hayden and co-author Dick Flacks have written a feature story for the August 5 issue of *The Nation*, "The Port Huron Statement at 40,"[4] in which they celebrate its

July 23, 2002, http://www.salon.com/2002/07/29/port_huron/
[1]*Student*, 1962, ebook version, 2011
[2]http://coursesa.matrix.msu.edu/~hst306/documents/huron.html
[3]http://www.sds-1960s.org/documents.htm
[4]"The Port Huron Statement at 40," Tom Hayden and Dick Flacks, *The Nation*, August 5, 2002, http://www.thenation.com/article/port-huron-statement-40

longevity and influence as though the seeds of malevolence they sowed (and the rest of the nation reaped) were something to be proud of.

The picture the two activists paint—rosy by even the most generous standards—is made possible by a selective forgetting of the kind Milan Kundera has drawn attention to in his writings on the totalitarian delusion. Thus Hayden describes himself in those early days as "a Midwestern populist by nature, rebelling apolitically against the boring hypocrisy of suburban life—until the Southern black student sit-in movement showed him that a committed life was possible." This is the purest eyewash, which any reasonable reader can detect by asking how this description squares with the fact that Hayden found himself in the leadership of a socialist organization and surrounded by Marxists, like his co-author Dick Flacks, who were self-consciously working to revive a revolutionary movement that had been tainted by Stalinism. The key battle at Port Huron, which is not even addressed in the Hayden-Flacks nostalgia piece, was whether to include members of the Communist Party in the coalition that would become SDS.

At Port Huron, Hayden went head to head over this issue with Irving Howe's ideological ally, Michael Harrington, who was representing SDS's parent organization, the League for Industrial Democracy. The Hayden-Flacks account presents the debate this way: "While the draft Port Huron Statement included a strong denunciation of the Soviet Union, it wasn't enough for LID leaders like Michael Harrington. They wanted absolute clarity, for example, that the United States was blameless for the nuclear arms race.... In truth, they seemed threatened by the independence of the new wave of student activism...."[5]

Criticizing abuses of power in the Soviet Union was easy for leftists in 1962. Nikita Khrushchev, the head of the Soviet Communist Party, had already denounced Stalin's crimes and one-man

---

[5]http://faculty.txwes.edu/csmeller/human-prospect/ProData09/03WW2 CulMatrix/Weather/SDS/SDS.htm

rule six years earlier. What Howe and Harrington actually felt threatened by was the lack of absolute clarity on the part of Hayden and his friends in condemning Communist totalitarianism, in distancing themselves from supporters of Communism in the United States and in making clear which side they were on in the Cold War, the great moral struggle of the time.

To be fair, Hayden and Flacks do quote a critic or two, one of whom happens to be me. "The former radical David Horowitz reads the [Port Huron] statement as encoding a 'self-conscious effort to rescue the Communist project from its Soviet fate.'" This is a phrase from my autobiography *Radical Son*, a book in which I recall that those of us who created the New Left were trying to throw out the Stalinist bathwater but not the socialist baby. *Radical Son* is in part an account of how the continuing commitment to a socialist agenda and the unwillingness to be identified with the anti-Communist cause led to the New Left's embrace of totalitarian causes, in particular the wars of Ho Chi Minh and Pol Pot. Tom Hayden is one of the few New Leftists who ever gave a moment's thought to the millions of peasants in Southeast Asia he helped to slaughter by backing the Communists in their wars. Unfortunately, Hayden's moment of clarity in his memoir *Reunion* was half-hearted and brief, and he seems to have forgotten it altogether.

Reading Hayden and Flacks, one would never know that these issues even exist. In their account, the New Left was born not out of the collapse of the Old Left but out of a generalized apathy of the Fifties generation and its alleged obliviousness to the possibility that any social problems might exist. Thus, "on some campuses, professors and students were questioning the Cold War arms race"—as though others had failed to notice it or were too dense to give any thought. "There were stirrings on the fringe, too, where students were listening to Bob Dylan and rock and roll. SDS represented the first defections from the mainstream."[6]

---

[6]http://www.participatory-democracy.org/porthuron.php

In fact, SDS didn't represent defections from anything, nor were its members "mainstream." Defections from the mainstream took place later, as a result of the military draft, when college students who were reluctant to risk their lives in war came scurrying into its ranks. In 1962, SDS was a collection of red-diaper babies and political fellow travelers trying to revive a left whose collusion with Communism had brought it into disrepute and decimated its ranks. That is why they veiled their language (and apparently their memories). The pivotal concept of the manifesto they adopted, for example, and the idea that Hayden and Flacks are most eager to celebrate, is called "participatory democracy" and not "Soviet democracy," which is where the concept originated and what it was an attempt to reproduce. Changing the words was a way of gaining freedom from the stigma:

> Participatory democracy sought to expand the sphere of public decisions from the mere election of representatives to the deeper role of "bringing people out of isolation and into community" in decentralized forms of decision-making. The same democratic humanism was applied to the economy in calls for "incentives worthier than money," and for work to be "self-directed, not manipulated."[7]

Whom do Hayden and Flacks think they're fooling with this description at this late date? Anyone familiar with the history of the left will recognize these ideas as quintessential communist doctrines. Indeed, what economy do the authors have in mind that would be based on "incentives worthier than money"—Cuba, North Korea? "Workers' Councils" to the anarchists, "Soviets" to the Russians—these are other names for "participatory democracy," but the idea is the same: the political enforcement of an equality of condition, the destruction of due process and all hierarchies—

---

[7]"The Port Huron Statement at 40," Tom Hayden and Dick Flacks, *The Nation*, August 5, 2002, http://www.thenation.com/article/port-huron-statement-40

professional, scientific, meritocratic, traditional—all in the name of "social justice," which is itself another name for totalitarian rule. For how can "social justice"—a political concept—be achieved except through the control of everyone in the social contract? The never-changing leftist idea of social justice is that the state should act as if it were God, arranging a perfectly ordered world that conforms to its own prejudices.

> It was no wonder, then, that the [Port Huron] statement was inspired by participatory democracy. Participation is what we were denied, and what we hungered for. Without it, there was no dignity. Parents and professors lectured us, administrators ordered us, draft boards conscripted us, the whole system channeled us, all to please authority and take our place in line.[8]

What must it be like to have lived as long as Hayden and Flacks and to have learned so little, including the virtue of gratitude? Still no appreciation for all that parents and professors and authority brought them. Leftists like Hayden and Flacks remind me of the punch-line to one of those jokes told on the edge of puberty: "I want what I want when I want it!" All the self-absorbed and destructive egotism of adolescents. So it is hardly coincidental that this aging pair of unreconstructed communists should have no wiser view of the challenges we face as a nation 40 years later. Or that they should take pleasure in continuing to encourage the most destructive elements in our culture—the hate-America, corporation-phobic gremlins of the newest left. "There is a new movement astir in the world, against the inherent violence of globalization, corporate rule and fundamentalism, that reminds us strongly of the early 1960s.... The war on terrorism has revived the Cold War framework. An escalating national security state attempts to rivet our attention and invest our resources on fighting an elusive, undefined enemy for years to come, at the inevitable price of our civil liberties and continued neglect of social justice.

---

[8]Ibid.

To challenge the framework of the war on terrorism, to demand a search for real peace with justice, is as difficult today as challenging the Cold War was at Port Huron."

Here is a noteworthy confession. The difficulty for Hayden, Flacks and the New Left about "challenging the Cold War" was that they were challenging a war—America's war—on behalf of human freedom. One and a half billion people liberated from the chains of the Soviet imperialism testify to that. What is difficult for Hayden, Flacks and the newest left about challenging the war on terror is the same. It is the fact that their country's battle is right and yet they hate it, and for that very reason. What is interesting is that Hayden, Flacks and the editors of *The Nation* would be so forthright in declaring their intention to weaken and undermine America's war against terror, and to use "civil liberties" and "social justice" as the instruments for accomplishing it. Let us hope the American people are taking note.

6

The Destructive Romance
of the Intellectuals

The British novelist Martin Amis has written a book about the utopian delusion and Soviet Communism called *Koba the Dread*. It is about the romance of western intellectuals with a fantasy whose real-world incarnation has already killed at least 40 million citizens of the Soviet Union and more than 100 million people worldwide. The crime committed by these victims of the progressive dream was their refusal to go along with the claims of "social justice" and the requirements of instituting a socialist state. This is what Martin Amis says about the adventure of creating the Soviet Union: "The dictatorship of the proletariat was a lie; Union was a lie, and Soviet was a lie, and Socialist was a lie, and Republics was a lie. Comrade was a lie. The revolution was a lie."

Question: How many western progressive intellectuals embraced and spread these lies and colluded in the enslavement, death, and generalized misery of hundreds of millions of socialist citizens? This is Martin Amis's answer: "The overwhelming majority of intellectuals everywhere."

To make the point perfectly clear: every intellectual magazine that today calls itself "progressive," including *The Progressive, The Nation, Social Text, October, Zmagazine,* and *The Village Voice,* plus tens of thousands of professors in American universities, including the intellectual pioneers, models and instructors in

July 29, 2002, http://archive.frontpagemag.com/Printable.aspx?ArtId= 23452

virtually every Women's Studies, Black Studies, Chicano Studies, American Studies, Post-Colonial and Cultural Studies program, the heads of the American Historical Association, the Organization of American Historians and the Modern Language Association—were either apostles of this lie in its own time, or are apostles today of the same utopian idea, along with the same anti-capitalist, anti-American social analyses and the same anti-Western, anti-American historical narratives that produced the lies and their attendant atrocities.

Amis's book asks another question: Why are even those left-wing intellectuals who managed to understand all along that these were lies—or who have come to realize that they are lies—still comfortable in thinking of those who supported them as "progressives" and, worse, as "comrades?" In his book, Amis addresses this question to his best friend Christopher Hitchens: "Comrade Hitchens! There is probably not much in these pages that you don't already know. You already know, in that case, that Bolshevism presents a record of baseness and inanity that exhausts all dictionaries; indeed, heaven stops the nose at it. So it is still obscure to me why you wouldn't want to put more distance between yourself and these events than you do, with your reverence for Lenin and your un-regretted discipleship of Trotsky. These two men did not just precede Stalin. They created a fully functioning police state for his later use."

Amis recalls an evening spent at London's Conway Hall listening to Hitchens recall his leftist past: "At one point, reminiscing, Christopher said that he knew this building well, having spent many an evening in it with many 'an old comrade.' The audience responded as Christopher knew it would ... with affectionate laughter.... Why? If Christopher had referred to his many evenings with many 'an old blackshirt,' the audience would have...."

---

[1]July 28, 2002, http://www.nytimes.com/2002/07/28/books/a-million-deaths-is-not-just-a-statistic.html?pagewanted=all&src=pm

Amis's book was cogently reviewed by socialist writer Paul Berman in the Sunday *New York Times,* under the title, "A Million Deaths Is Not Just a Statistic."[1] While generally supporting Amis's commentaries, Berman attempted to diminish the seriousness of his most unsettling question by characterizing Hitchens's Trotskyism as "more of an eccentricity than anything else." This was Berman's way of diminishing the complicity of progressives, like himself, in what happened to an idea and a movement to which they are still attached (the movement being "progressive" and the idea "anti-anti- Communism"). To regard Hitchens's Trotskyism as an eccentric tic is patronizing, and not a judgment to be taken seriously. Hitchens is a witty thinker but usually not a frivolous one.

A mark of the seriousness of Hitchens' Trotskyism is his authorship of the introduction to *The Prophet Armed,* a forthcoming reprint of the first volume of Isaac Deutscher's trilogy of Trotsky's life. The book is scheduled to be released under the imprint of Verso, the New Left publishing house. Isaac Deutscher was my friend and mentor, so I write the following with heartfelt regret. He was a brilliant thinker and literary stylist, but his life's work, including his masterpiece on Trotsky, is finally a monument to the intellectual bankruptcy of Marxism itself. When all is said and done, the Trotsky biography must be seen as the sad waste of a remarkable talent. The intellectual framework of Deutscher's portrait of Trotsky, including the standard by which its hero's thoughts and deeds are measured, has been utterly falsified by the historical events that took place after the author's death in 1967.

In particular, the failure of Gorbachev's reforms in the Soviet Union and the collapse of what proved to be the hollow shell of the Soviet empire brutally refute the essence of all that Deutscher wrote about them. Deutscher believed that socialism was an economically sound system that had enabled Stalinists to build an advanced industrial base in Russia, though they overlaid it with a repellent political superstructure. Deutscher was convinced—and this was his hallmark contribution to Marxism—that the advanced socialist economic base would eventually create an advanced democracy as well. Trotsky's own theories were premised on this expectation. Instead, the opposite proved to be the case. The advanced economic base was another socialist lie, and the introduction of democracy destroyed the system itself. What then is left of intellectual Marxism but the atrocities it produced?

Deutscher, Lenin, Trotsky and Marx all staked their claims on the belief that socialism would produce abundance and freedom. A horrifying history has shown irrefutably that it doesn't. Socialism is really a theory of economic theft, and what it produces is poverty. Socialist systems are unable to foster the technological development necessary to sustain a modern economy. And they are fundamentally incompatible with human liberty. None of these four revolutionaries still admired by the left had a clue as to the critical importance of private property in making political liberty possible. None of them understood the necessity of a capitalist economy to technological progress and economic wellbeing. In the last half of the 20th century, vast masses of humanity—hundreds of millions in fact—were lifted out of subsistence poverty in those countries that protected and supported private property and free markets. This liberation by capitalist economics of poor working people so they are able to achieve lives of relative dignity and modest luxury represents a revolution unprecedented in the 5,000-year history of mankind.

Despite Christopher Hitchens' fluid and interesting new politics, he has been unable to shed many of the illusions of his progressive comrades. These are manifest in his continuing nostalgia for the Allende regime in Chile, whose elements are laid out in the lead article of the latest issue of the *London Review of Books*. Here is how Hitchens describes the aftermath of the coup that toppled the socialist Allende and established the capitalist dictatorship of Augusto Pinochet: "Much more significant in the long run were the policy intellectuals ... who wanted to revive the free market doctrines of Hayek and Friedman. The paradox in their case was obvious: it might take a very strong state to impose those libertarian values. Milton Friedman himself, and others of the so-called 'Chicago School' of political economy, had been engaged by the Pinochet regime as advisers. In 1976, Allende's former comrade Orlando Letelier, by then living in exile in Washington, wrote an extraordinary essay for *The Nation* entitled 'The Chicago Boys in Chile.' I remember getting the *New Statesman* to reprint it. It laid out the principle of the 'free economy/strong state' equation: 'shock treatment' number one being the application of electrodes to the recalcitrant, and 'shock treatment' number two being the withdrawal of public subsidy for the unfit or the inefficient. A few months after publishing the article, Orlando Letelier was torn to pieces by a car bomb in rush-hour Washington traffic, just a few blocks from where I am writing these words."[2]

Before responding, let me first observe that these are not the reflections of a man whose leftism is mere "eccentricity." Second, allow me to acknowledge that Christopher lost friends in this conflict and that I respect the passions of his brief, if not the analysis that accompanies it. In Hitchens' Chilean equation, now reflected nearly 30 years later, free-market economics still equals torture and dictatorship, which is pretty much the end of the story for him. But of course it was not the end of the story. What followed, and what flowed directly from the Pinochet dictatorship, including the above-referenced policy advice from Chicago, is pretty interesting, as well as being obviously important in evaluating what is at stake in these conflicts. Allende was a Castro leftist. He even brought the Cuban dictator to Cuba for a month-long political campaign to promote support for his Chilean revolution (and antagonism towards the United States). Allende had been elected by less than half the popular vote and thus was not in a strong position to advance the radical social and economic agendas he did. While something of a socialist "moderate" himself, he had forged a coalition with the Communist left. Hitchens even quotes

---

[2]"11 September 1973," *London Review of Books*, July 11, 2002

an elegy for the Allende regime by the notorious Stalinist Pablo Neruda, who was a respected member of Allende's political family.

What does Hitchens think would have happened if Allende had succeeded in carrying out his radical programs? The historic record on Marxist regimes is pretty clear. Allende's programs would have brought even greater poverty to Chile, along with brutal repression. But Allende never got the chance to institute a Castro regime in Chile because his inflammatory measures and political alliances quickly provoked a counterrevolution, which was supported (if not instigated as Hitchens would have it) by the United States. This was the famous coup of September 11, 1973 which overthrew the elected government and brought to power the Pinochet junta. It was, as Hitchens has written, a ruthless and cold-hearted military regime; but it was no more ruthless or cold-hearted, and probably a lot less so, than the "dictatorship of the proletariat" run by Allende's friend and hero in Cuba.

This does not make Pinochet's crimes acceptable. The murder of innocents should not be justified, whether the left or the right commits the crimes. What Hitchens and his comrades leave out of the story is that the dictator Pinochet managed to make the capitalist economic system work in Chile, albeit by these regrettable means. Unlike the sadistic Castro, however, who is now the longest-surviving dictator in the world, Pinochet eventually agreed to a popular referendum on his rule. He lost the vote but in doing so actually won a greater plurality than had his victim Allende in winning the presidency.

Pinochet's referendum ended his rule and restored political democracy to Chile. Today Chile is a political democracy, unlike any of the Marxist states on which Allende attempted to model his own. Equally important, Pinochet's Chicago advisers have been proven right. Today Chileans enjoy one of the highest per-capita incomes in all Latin America. For the last decade, Chile has been Latin America's fastest-growing economy, raising more and more Chileans out of poverty and into the middle class. Unlike socialism, free markets work.

This is really the bottom line separating the intellectual apologists and nostalgists for socialism and those of us who have had second thoughts and no longer think of the left as "comrades." What defines the politics of leftwing intellectuals like Hitchens and Berman is that they still nourish an enthusiasm for the utopian chimera. Whatever their misgivings, their blood still warms when they hear the word "revolution," and entertain visions of a world put right. We second- thoughters beg to differ. Our attention is focused not on a historical romance but on the practical consequences of progressive futures. Above all, we are impressed by the fact that the counterrevolution in the long run produces more compassionate results. For the proletariat, conservative free-market solutions are actually best.

7

Guilt of the Son

L ast week frontpagemag.com posted an "Open Letter to the Rosenberg Son" by Ronald Radosh.[1] It was written in response to the newly-published memoir *An Execution in the Family* by Robert Meeropol, the younger of the Rosenbergs' two orphaned sons (who have kept the name of their adoptive parents). Among the adverse reactions to Radosh's article was an email from Harold Meyerson, editor of *The American Prospect,* Bill Moyers's publication for the Democratic Party's socialist caucus.[2] In his "Open Letter" Radosh had said:

> In the end the truth remains that your parents were traitors who betrayed their country and their sons for an illusion. They acted with courage, but for a cause that was corrupt. By recognizing this you would restore their humanity, and perhaps heal the wound you obviously still feel. Instead, you have chosen to continue the charade, pretending that their cause was noble and that they were heroes of an American "resistance." To *what*?

This challenge was apparently too much for Meyerson, who wrote to Radosh:

June 23, 2003, http://archive.frontpagemag.com/Printable.aspx?ArtId= 17577

[1] "An Open Letter to the Rosenberg Son," Ronald Radosh, *FrontPage Magazine,* June 19, 2003, http://archive.frontpagemag.com/readArticle.aspx? ARTID=17639

[2] Meyerson later became a regular columnist at *The Washington Post,* without changing his leftist views.

Ron, I can't even begin to fathom the callousness of your letter. If you had this argument with anyone else but Robert, it would be fine, and I know your take on the Rosenbergs is the right one. But to hector their son this way, publicly, really is industrial-strength insensitivity. How would you like it if I wrote an open letter to your son hectoring him to publicly acknowledge that his father is an insensitive jerk? An assertion I fear, that is as hard to deny as the Rosenbergs' guilt.

But is Radosh's response really insensitive? The Rosenberg sons are the ones who have chosen to make the whitewash of their parents' crime a political cause, and Robert's book is but its latest expression. In his private life Robert Meeropol appears to be a nice man. I met him 30-odd years ago and it was immediately apparent that he was a shy, gentle person, not comfortable even with the public aspect of the small political event the brothers had organized and I attended. When the event got underway, his brother Michael did all or most of the speaking, laying out his conviction that their parents had been framed by a vindictive government which no one could respect.

When the question-period was over, and people were milling around, I approached Robert to ask him a question that was on my mind. His diffidence caused me to be a little tentative in framing my words. At the time I was having "second thoughts" about my own progressive commitments, and I knew in my heart that what his parents and mine had done in devoting their lives to the Communist Party and the Soviet Union was wrong, terribly wrong. Approaching the subject gingerly, I asked him whether he could entertain the possibility that his parents were in fact guilty of spying for the Soviet Union. I found it an especially affecting and appealing moment when he said that he could.

I have retained a soft spot for Robert Meeropol ever since, and was particularly eager to read his memoir. Unlike his brother, Robert did not seem ideologically hardened. He genuinely appeared to have a private side that he was anxious to protect. In my own memoir I had wrestled with the issue of an individual life that becomes enmeshed in political abstractions like his, and I was curious to see what he had to say. As I turned the opening pages of the book, I was not disappointed. In his text, Meeropol emerges as a sensitive and self-conscious individual, concerned to preserve his anonymity and protect his own life from the forces bearing down on it from all sides. As a young parent, he was preoccupied with family, in particular with providing his young children the stability and shelter that were traumatically lacking in his own. He writes disarmingly about his insecurities, his lack of physical and moral courage, his inability to find himself or to establish an adult life. He and his wife seem to have lived for an exceptionally long time as college students, both literally—extending their schooling into their thirties, teaching courses half-heartedly while working on the Rosenberg case—and metaphorically, finding jobs that were in one way or another related to their progressive political community and its agitations. About finally obtaining a law degree, he comments: "I was a bit concerned that at thirty-seven I was still trying to figure out what I was going to do when I grew up."[3]

At first the answer is estate planning, which has obvious and poignant resonances for himself, and aptly expresses his lifelong quest for healing. But he cannot find a "leftwing estate-planning firm"[4] and turns to business law instead. When his apprenticeship is complete and the firm gives him adult responsibilities, they prove too much for his fragile psychology. The pressures of making decisions and "closing deals" soon overwhelm him, and he has a nervous breakdown. Surviving on doses of Xanax in the daytime and Halcyon at night, he eventually decides to leave the law firm. Even an opponent of his politics like myself would agree that only a flinty heart would flush this troubled soul from its hiding place to attack him for his parents' deeds.

---

[3]Robert Meeropol, *An Execution in the Family: One Son's Journey*, St. Martin's, 2003, p. 168
[4]Ibid.

This is the partial truth on which Meyerson makes his case. But it is also a small truth. This is because more than 30 years ago, before he entered law school, Robert Meeropol made a crucial decision to abandon the anonymity provided by his new name and turn his private life into a public cause. In 1974, he and his brother Michael published a book, *We Are Your Sons*, proclaiming their parents' innocence. Emerging for the first time as public figures, they threw their energies—as organizers, fundraisers and spokesmen—into the National Committee to Re-Open the Rosenberg Case. This effort and its offshoots have—by Robert's own account—been the main activity of both their lives ever since.

Their crusade—and that is the only way to characterize it—is not confined, moreover, to the question of their parents' innocence. A man's effort to prove his own parents innocent of a crime they did not commit, and for which they were executed, could almost be seen as a private matter. He might have to make himself a public figure to do it, but the quest itself can still be understood in individual terms. In fact, this is one of the complaints of Robert's book—that his quest to prove his parents innocent has often been discounted by others, reporters in particular, as the understandable quest of an orphaned son. But this is not Robert's quest, or at least not what his quest has become. Over the years, incontrovertible evidence has appeared, including material from the Soviet archives, confirming his parents' guilt. In a revealing confession of the political nature of what began as his campaign to exonerate them, Robert writes:

> I used to hope that when we finally got to the bottom of what really happened in my parents' case, the facts would show their unequivocal innocence. I no longer feel that way. Now I'd rather my parents had been conscious political actors than innocent victims.[5]

---

[5]Ibid., p. 262

What Robert can only mean by this is that he wishes his parents had committed the crime they were charged with because it was a "crime" only in the eyes of their persecutors. Robert Meeropol is not a defender of his parents' legal innocence but of their Communist cause. The real crime is American capitalism; the cause they served as Soviet agents, the socialist future, is just. The entire enterprise of the Meeropol brothers, the art-shows and memorials and literary and film productions they have sponsored, are efforts to establish their parents as political martyrs for the progressive cause.

Appearing on stage as featured "performers" at the recent 50th-anniversary "celebration" of their parents' death, the Meeropols included the son of Mumia Abu Jamal, the Panther radical convicted of the cold-blooded murder of a Philadelphia policeman. Robert Meeropol finds an unproblematic parallel in his own parents' trial and martyrdom to Mumia's. Robert's description of this affinity and of his support for Mumia is more than interesting. "Like my parents before him, Mumia was not the typical death-row inmate, because regardless of what he had done, his most dangerous crime was his articulate resistance to the dominant forces of our society."[6]

In other words, it doesn't really matter whether Mumia Abu Jamal emptied his gun into the prone body of 26-year-old police officer Daniel Faulkner, any more than it matters whether Robert's parents actually stole the plans for American jet fighters or the trigger of the atomic bomb, as they were accused of having done. What matters is their "resistance to the dominant forces of our society." What matters is that they were self-declared enemies of the United States and its ruling class. This resistance makes them "progressives," servants of a worthy cause, and therefore above America's capitalist morality and law. *An Execution in the Family* is finally the story of a son's discovery that he is his parents' child.

---

[6]Ibid., p. 229

While still a college student and long before becoming a lawyer, Robert joined Springfield's junior chamber of commerce "in preparation for my proposed urban anthropology dissertation about the impact of businessmen's decision-making networks on public policy."[7] Writing about this in his memoir, Robert asks himself the following questions: "Where did my recurring desire to burrow into the bowel of American business come from? Was there something about what happened to my parents that made me want to spy on my enemy and learn his tricks?"[8] The question he does *not* ask himself is: why was business his enemy? Robert Meeropol's enmity towards business was not the result of anything business had done to his parents or him, but was a reflection of the Communist culture he grew up in. It evokes an irony he is unable to appreciate: it was his parents' irrational belief that American business was their enemy that made them Communists, and caused them to become involved in the conspiracies that brought about their deaths. To explore this avenue of reflection would invite possibilities too daunting—that his parents sacrificed their lives on the altar of a political prejudice and in the service of a superstitious faith. It is Communism that killed his parents.

Robert Meeropol found his true vocation when he created the Rosenberg Fund for Children, which he serves as executive director and which has become his life's work. But it is not really a fund for "children." It is not even a fund for children whose parents are the victims of miscarriages of justice. This would connect it to a personal tragedy and the healing of personal wounds, but at this juncture in his life Robert has lost all touch with what the personal might actually be. Instead, the Rosenberg Fund for Children is a self-described support-group for the children of "political prisoners." This is his own description of how he came to create the Fund: "I was startled to learn how many children today were vulnerable to the same kind of nightmares I endured after my parents'

---

[7]Ibid., p. 172
[8]Ibid.

arrest. I learned that our country held over more than [sic] one hundred political prisoners (Black Panthers, American Indian Movement members, Puerto Rican Nationalists, and white revolutionaries like the Ohio Seven).["][9]

The first beneficiaries of the Fund were the children of "the Ohio Seven," a group of activists who had formed a "revolutionary" cell and were "convicted of carrying out bombings against multinational corporations that invested in apartheid South Africa during the late 1970s and early 1980s, and of robbing banks to support their clandestine lifestyle." Meeropol is no more interested in the innocence or guilt of these individuals than he is in his parents' or Mumia Abu Jamal's. What makes these prisoners "political" is that they committed their crimes in the name of a leftist cause. Another group of early beneficiaries were the children of members of the Communist Workers' Party, a Stalinist sect whose leaders had intruded themselves into the community of Greensboro, North Carolina to urge people to "Kill the Klan" and were chanting "Death to the Klan" in a public square when they were fired upon by Klansmen and killed. To present themselves as innocent victims and make their cause support-worthy, the survivors of this absurdist tragedy have called the episode "the Greensboro Massacre."

By the time he created the Fund, Robert Meeropol was in his forties and had become an un-self-reflecting member of the neo-communist left, at war with America and actively supporting its radical enemies. But Meeropol was really a communist all his life, never having left the community of his parents. Only his diffidence and fears prevented him earlier from publicly linking his parents' causes and his own. The couple who adopted him were diehard Stalinists, unaffected by the Khrushchev revelations in 1956 that Stalin had indeed committed the monstrous crimes that conservatives and other anti-Communists had claimed. These revelations caused the majority of American Communists to leave

[9]Ibid., p. 192

their party and many to abandon their Communist faith, but not the Meeropols.

By his own account, Robert "had never felt so isolated"[10] as he did during the Cuban Missile Crisis of 1962, when the nation teetered on the brink of nuclear war. His feelings of isolation were due to the fact that he identified with Communist Russia and Cuba, rather than with his own country under attack. Robert was already steeped in the Communist worldview and was devoted to his boyhood idol, the dictator Fidel Castro: "[In school] we were supposed to underline the passages [in the newspapers] we felt were most important and discuss them during the current events period of the school week. Although I still had some difficulty reading, and was embarrassed at how poorly I read aloud, for the entire school year I read, cut out, and underlined every article about Fidel and the Cuban revolution published in *The New York Times*. I taped each clipping into a scrapbook that soon bulged and had pieces of articles protruding from it at all angles. In Fidel I found my contemporary hero."[11]

Events periodically shattered the coalitions of the Communist left, the invasion of Czechoslovakia and the Communist genocide in Cambodia among them. But Robert Meeropol's political faith never wavered. In the 1980s he and his wife became organizers of a chapter of the Committee in Solidarity with the People of El Salvador, an organization set up in the United States by Cuban intelligence to aid the Communist guerrillas in Central America. "The United States funded and equipped the contras' terrorist campaign to overthrow the Sandinista government in Nicaragua,"[12] writes Meeropol, parroting Communist propaganda. Nowhere does he stop to consider that the Nicaraguan dictatorship was modeled on Castro's and armed by the Soviet police-state; or that when the international community imposed elections on the Sandinista

[10]Ibid., p. 59
[11]Ibid., p. 41
[12]Ibid., p. 169

dictators, the *contra*-supported candidate won in a popular land-slide. Indeed, there is not a hint of serious reflection in this entire book on the failures and crimes of the movement to which the son of Julius and Ethel Rosenberg has become wedded.

This is most striking in Meeropol's failure even to mention the epoch-making events of 1989–1991: the fall of the Berlin Wall, the liberation of Eastern Europe and the collapse of Communist system. For here was revealed the bankruptcy of everything his parents had worked and died for. It was all a monumental lie. Yet the implosion of the fantasy his parents had served, the revelation that tens of millions of innocents had been killed, the exposure of socialism's economic bankruptcy—none of it makes an appearance in Meeropol's memoir or evidently has an impact on his thinking at all. Such is the religious character of his progressive faith.

Along with his parents' discredited beliefs, Robert Meeropol has acquired their selective blindness and hypocrisy as well. Of course it matters to him whether the Rosenbergs were innocent or not, despite his statement to the contrary. They chose to die rather than admit they had lied because they put the cause of communism before their children. They chose to orphan their sons rather than confess their guilt and live. If they were in fact guilty, then they were guilty of betraying not only their country and their countrymen but their sons as well.

This is a corruption endemic to a political faith. If the ends are justified in the eyes of the believers, then the means don't matter. Individual lives count for nothing; the cause is all. But if the cause is all, why care about the Rosenbergs themselves, about whether they are innocent or not? All that really matters is their role as political symbols. In abandoning his concern over his parents' innocence or guilt, Robert Meeropol's own conscience has been extinguished. In betraying his original mission to establish their innocence, he has betrayed himself.

Even his attitude to the death-penalty as such reveals this political corruption. Early in his memoir he confesses to a very human desire for revenge. In high school he fantasizes the victory of a Communist revolution in the United States and wishes to be the hanging judge who sentences his parents' executioners to death. But after undertaking his mission to exonerate them and studying their case, he has second thoughts. Because he is still willing to entertain the possibility of his parents' guilt, he is forced to weigh the actual evidence. The record impresses him with the risks of human error. "Almost all of us accept that humans are imperfect beings. We make mistakes. Sooner or later all the safeguards in a human-built system will fail. It is unrealistic, therefore, to expect a mistake-proof justice system. A large majority of people will readily agree that capital punishment allows no room for error. It is, therefore, inevitable that mistakes will be made and innocent people will be executed. Once someone has been executed you can't say 'Oops' and take it back."[13]

This reasoning makes him an opponent of capital punishment. He is passionate about it, referring to President Bush as "Governor Death," because Bush enforced the law in Texas. But this passion has a sharp limit. It applies only to the capitalist enemy. Robert Meeropol is silent about the many executions ordered by his hero Fidel Castro, including the recent capture, trial and execution, all within a week, of three black Cubans, whose crime was not stealing atomic secrets but trying to escape from Fidel's island-prison. Like every other personal, private, and moral insight in Robert Meeropol's book, this one is subordinated to the political cause.

What began as a Rosenberg son's failed effort to rehabilitate his parents' memory has become a successful quest to re-inhabit their lives and resuscitate their myths. By casting his lot with the community of the left, he has hermetically sealed not only his own life but his family's within the circle of the progressive illusion. In doing so he has ensured for them and himself the reproduction of his parents' political world, along with its "mistakes" and crimes.

---

[13]Ibid., p. 234

Despite the record of its epic cruelties, this neo-communist left is still a force to be reckoned with. It has been reconstructed by narratives like this one—through books, movies, plays, and the memories of like-minded comrades. Already in 1974, when the Rosenberg sons' first volume appeared, the support for their parents' martyrdom was impressive. ABC Television aired a dramatization that, in Meeropol's words, "left the impression that something was dreadfully wrong with my parents' trial and execution."[14] This was followed by a PBS broadcast of "The Unquiet Death of Julius and Ethel Rosenberg," which also supported the Meeropols' cause. And even though the opening of the Soviet archives and the release of the Venona decrypts between Soviet intelligence officers and their American agents has put to rest the possibility of the Rosenbergs' innocence, the praise for Robert Meeropol's new book follows this receptive pattern. The notice in *Publishers Weekly* is illustrative: "The Rosenbergs were executed for a crime the government knew they did not commit. Their sons have battled valiantly to clear their names and to lead productive lives, and Meeropol's captivating memoir deserves a spot on American history bookshelves."[15]

In 1997, a documentary filmmaker interviewed Robert's children. "My daughters reported that the interviewer seemed surprised when they told her that being a granddaughter of the Rosenbergs was more boon than burden. Their pride in their heritage placed them within an international community of support.... Understanding the choices made by both their grandparents and their parents helped form their worldview and gave them a clear sense of right and wrong."[16]

This is the secret of the left's longevity, its ability to withstand the discrediting of its idea, to ignore the millions of its victims, and thus to renew itself in the next generation. It is the creation of

---

[14]Ibid., p. 127
[15]http://www.publishersweekly.com/978-0-312-30636-6
[16]*An Execution in the Family: One Son's Journey*, op. cit. p. 121

a culture, a historical narrative, and of a living community that perpetuates its myths and sustains its progressive faith. In 2003, the Rosenberg grandchildren can take pride in their heritage at being the heirs of Communists and spies, and receive encouragement and praise from "an international community of support."

Early in his memoir, Robert Meeropol offers this insight about himself: "I often put myself in others' shoes. This sense of understanding what others felt led me to sympathize with those who were picked on."[17] It's a nice sentiment. But there is not a single sentence in this book, or act in Robert Meeropol's life, that suggests he ever stepped into the shoes of those whom his parents betrayed and helped the Soviets to kill, or whom he himself demonized and "picked on"—nor that he ever extended sympathy or a helping hand to any of them. His memoir is the story of a man whose adult life began as an effort to rehabilitate his parents for a crime he believed they did not commit, and ended as a crusade to justify the crimes they did commit. In writing this book, Robert Rosenberg Meeropol has made himself complicit in those crimes and a worthy subject for judgment himself.

---

[17]Ibid., p. 3

8

The Trouble with Treason

I have always admired Ann Coulter's satiric skewering of liberal pieties and her bravery under fire. Not many conservatives can fight back with as much verve and venom as she can, and if politics is war conducted by other means, Ann is someone I definitely want on my side.

I began running Coulter columns on frontpagemag.com shortly after she came up with her most notorious line urging America to put *jihadists* to the sword and convert them to Christianity. Liberals were horrified; I was not. I thought to myself, this is a perfect send-up of what our Islamo-fascist enemies believe—that as infidels we should be put to the sword or converted to Islam. I regarded Coulter's philippic as a Swiftian commentary on progressive illusions of extending a multicultural outreach to people who want to rip out our hearts. Another reason I have enjoyed Ann's attacks on so-called liberals is that they have been richly deserved. No one wields the verbal knife more ruthlessly than pundits on the left like *Salon*'s Joe Conason, to cite but one example. I have been the subject of many below-the-belt Conason attacks, and if people like Joe were outraged by Ann, I could rest confident that justice had been done.

But now, to my dismay, I find myself unable to find such satisfaction in Conason's reaction to Ann's new book *Treason,* or in the responses of other liberals like *The Washington Post*'s Richard

July 8, 2003, http://archive.frontpagemag.com/Printable.aspx?ArtId=17332

Cohen (who has also directed nasty attacks at me). It is distressing when someone you admire gives credibility to the opposition's attacks. But that, unfortunately, is what *Treason* has managed to accomplish. Here is how it opens: "Liberals have a preternatural gift for striking a position on the side of treason. You could be talking about *Scrabble* and they would instantly leap to the anti-American position. Everyone says liberals love America, too. No they don't. Whenever the nation is under attack, from within or without, liberals side with the enemy. This is their essence."

As polemical satire this passage works, and there is enough evidence to sustain it. But what if is not satire? Is it the case that liberals like Harry Truman, Lyndon Johnson and John F. Kennedy sided with the enemy? Of course not. They were *anti*-Communists, hated by the left as "Cold War liberals." And they were not alone. There were many liberals—Scoop Jackson and Jeane Kirkpatrick among them—who were just as worthy defenders of America and prosecutors of the anti-Communist cause. Until 1963, Ronald Reagan was a pro-Kennedy, anti-Communist, Cold War liberal. In Coulter's book, Democrats (whom she conflates with liberals) come under blistering attack for their perfidious role in the so-called "McCarthy era." A lot of what she says about Democrats is true, but nearly half the members of McCarthy's own Senate Subcommittee on Governmental Operations were Democrats (as were members of the later-demonized House Committee on Un-American Activities). Bobby Kennedy was a McCarthy staff lawyer. Not all Democrats were liberals and not all liberals sided with the enemy. In 1968, Tom Hayden, a radical supporter and servant of the Communist cause in Vietnam, organized a riot at the Democratic Party convention in order to destroy the presidential candidacy of Hubert Humphrey. The reason? Humphrey was an anti-Communist, pro-Vietnam War liberal. Later, however, Hayden was invited to the White House and given a Medal of Freedom by Jimmy Carter, sort of making Ann's case.

But by failing to draw a clear line between satirical hyperbole and historical analysis—by refusing to credit the laudable role played by patriotic, anti-Communist liberals like Harry Truman,

John F. Kennedy and Hubert Humphrey—Coulter compromises her case and undermines her attempt to correct a record that desperately needs correction.[1]

Liberals have—just as she charges—distorted postwar history to protect the guilty. Franklin Roosevelt did laugh off the information that one of his top aides, Alger Hiss, was a Soviet agent and did, despite the warning, *elevate* Hiss to be his one of his chief advisers at Yalta and at the founding conference of the UN. Democrats *did* allow the Communists to penetrate their party and their administrations in the 1930s and 1940s. The Truman administration *did* dismiss Republican charges of Communist influence as partisan politics and *was* lackadaisical before 1947 in taking the internal Communist threat seriously. But in 1947 that changed. Truman instituted a comprehensive loyalty program to ferret out Communist influence in government. It was the Truman administration that prosecuted Alger Hiss and the Rosenbergs. In fact, some of the decisive battles of this era took place *inside* liberalism. It was Walter Reuther, a socialist, who purged the Communists from the CIO; and it was Truman's anti-Communist loyalty oath that provoked the Communists into leaving the Democratic Party and forming the Progressive Party to oppose his re-election in 1948.

By ignoring these complexities or dismissing them, Coulter makes her case seem indefensible even when it is not. It is true, as Coulter maintains, that the accusation of "McCarthyism" has been and still is used as a cover for treachery by the political left. To pick a contemporary example she does not mention: leftwing groups like the ACLU, the American Association of University Professors and the National Lawyers Guild are currently defending the terrorist Sami al-Arian as a victim of "McCarthyism."[2]

---

[1]A more reliable attempt at this is Arthur Herman, *Joe McCarthy: Reexamining the Life and Legacy of America's Most Hated Senator*, Free Press, 1999.

[2]Ronald Radosh, "The Case of Sami Al-Arian," *FrontPage Magazine*, February 08, 2002, http://archive.frontpagemag.com/readArticle.aspx?ARTID=24023; http://www.discoverthenetworks.org/Articles/Sami%20Al%20Arian%20and%20the%20PAnti-Patriot.htm

Al-Arian is one of three founders of the terrorist organization Palestine Islamic Jihad and is responsible for the murders of more than 100 innocent people. No one familiar with the facts can doubt this. But the left has chosen to defend al-Arian by putting John Ashcroft and the Justice Department on trial instead. The anti-McCarthy left did provide aid and comfort to the enemy and its agents inside the United States, and is still doing so.

It is a shame that Coulter mars her case with some claims that cannot be sustained. In making McCarthy the center of her history, ironically, she has fallen into the very liberal trap she warns about. It is the left that wants McCarthy to be the center of (and in effect to define) the postwar era so that it can use his recklessness to discredit the anti-Communist cause. In fact, as Coulter herself points out, McCarthy began his anti-Communist crusade *after* the decisive anti-Communist battles of 1947 and 1948, surfacing only in 1950 with the onset of the Korean War. By then, even Henry Wallace, the Progressive Party's presidential candidate, knew he had been duped. This is why McCarthy did not unearth any Communists in government. They had all been previously identified by the FBI, whose agents despised McCarthy for damaging their efforts.

On the other hand, there are many perceptions in this book that are memorable. It was only in reading Coulter's text that I realized what a fraud the hero of all anti-McCarthy histories, Joseph Welch was, and how his moment of glory in "exposing" McCarthy was a hypocritical sham. Coulter reminds us that one of McCarthy's great sins, according to liberals, was to have identified Owen Lattimore as Stalin's chief agent in America. This was indeed false. But Lattimore was a supporter of Stalin's and Mao's political agendas, an ally of Soviet agent and State Department official Lauchlin Currie, and a willing tool of Soviet policies. Having been identified as such, Lattimore was also hired by Harvard. Liberals are indignant that McCarthy exaggerated. But, as Coulter writes, "liberals' threshold for outrage dropped when it came to McCarthy. In fact, McCarthy's rhetoric was mild by the standards of his time. In President Truman's 1948 campaign, he railed, 'If anybody in this country is friendly to the Communists it is the Republicans.'"

The fact that Lattimore behaved like a Soviet agent is somewhat different from McCarthy's claim that he was the *chief* Soviet agent. Coulter doesn't explain how McCarthy's misidentification of Lattimore served the anti-Communist cause. In fact, it did just the opposite. But Coulter wants us to think of McCarthy as the anti-Communist hero of the era: "In his brief fiery ride across the landscape, Joe McCarthy bought America another thirty years." The very opposite has been argued by many anti-Communists, whom Coulter brusquely dismisses: "Lost amid all the mandatory condemnations of Joe McCarthy's name—he gave anti-Communism a bad name, did a disservice to the cause, was an unnecessary distraction—the little detail about his being right always seems to get lost. McCarthy's fundamental thesis was absolutely correct: The Democratic Party had fallen to the allures of totalitarianism." But if Coulter is correct, why did the totalitarians abandon the Democratic Party *en masse* in 1948 to support the presidential campaign of Henry Wallace? McCarthy exploited the anti-Communist sentiment that was already the popular wisdom of the time. By giving flesh to the fears of open-ended witch-hunts he allowed the left to regroup, and in 1972 to return to the Democratic Party fold.

Many of the inaccurate generalizations of *Treason* are indeed the hyperbole of Coulterian satire, but crucial ones are not. I realized this when I saw Ann defending her claims on Chris Matthews's *Hardball:*

> **Chris Matthews:** What do you mean by the cover of this book?
> **Ann Coulter:** What I mean is that the Democratic Party, as an entity, has become functionally treasonable, including what you're talking about, turning over documents to the enemy....
> **Chris Matthews:** Well, should they be prosecuted?
> **Ann Coulter:** I wish it were that easy a problem, but that trivializes the point of my book, which is not that there are just a

few dozen traitors out there. It is that the entire party cannot
root for America.

Chris Matthews: Well, let's talk about the leaders of the Democratic Party over the years. Was Jack Kennedy a traitor? Was he
guilty of treason?

Ann Coulter: He was not as strong a president as a Republican
would have been. But I'm referring, as I say again, I'm referring
to a party that is functionally treasonable. . . .

Chris Matthews: Was Jack Kennedy a traitor?

Ann Coulter: No, he was not a traitor.

Chris Matthews: Was he guilty of treason?

Ann Coulter: His heart was in the right place but he was surrounded by bad policymakers and he harm[ed] the country and
its national security.

This exchange made me extremely uncomfortable. When
somebody as smart and gutsy as Ann Coulter equivocates over so
direct a question—*Was Jack Kennedy guilty of treason?*—you
know (and she knows) that something is wrong with the position
she is defending. Equally disturbing was Coulter's use of the
phrase "functionally treasonable," in the phrase "[the Democratic
Party] has become functionally treasonable." This is problematic
on several counts. In the first place, "treasonable" is not a word
but seems to suggest "capable of treason," which is different from
being actually *treasonous.* That distinction is important. "Functionally treasonable" is also disturbingly reminiscent of the old
Stalinist term "objectively fascist." This was how people who
swore their loyalty to the cause were condemned (often to death) if
they deviated from the party line. Stalinists defined all dissent as
"objectively" treacherous. This is not a path that conservatives
should follow. When intent and individuality are separated from
actions in a political context, we are entering a totalitarian realm
where Ann Coulter does not really want to be.

Why is she equivocating about Jack Kennedy, anyway? Kennedy
was not only *not* a traitor, he was not even a weak anti-Communist,
as she claims. He was arguably stronger than Eisenhower or Nixon

in prosecuting the Cold War. His politics were those of Ronald Reagan, who was one of his supporters. He was a militant anti-Communist and a military hawk, authorizing the largest defense buildup in peacetime history. What can she mean when she says that Kennedy was "surrounded by bad policymakers," i.e., policymakers who were presumably liberals and therefore harmed the country and its national security? Kennedy was surrounded by *Republican* policymakers. His secretaries at State, Defense and Treasury—the three key foreign-policy posts—were all Republicans. He launched his administration by declaring that America would pay any price to defend the cause of freedom. He tried to overthrow Castro by force. It's true that he lost his nerve and bungled the invasion, but Dwight Eisenhower failed the Hungarians in 1956, while Nixon and Kissinger betrayed the Vietnamese in the infamous truce of 1973. In 1961, Kennedy stood the Russians down in Berlin—risking nuclear war to do so—and a year later he again risked nuclear war to force the removal of Soviet missiles in Cuba. He put 16,000 troops into Vietnam rather than abandon that country to the Communists. Why would Ann equivocate on the question of his loyalty, or commitment to the anti-Communist cause?

It is important for conservatives to make distinctions between those on the left who were (and are) traitors or self-conceived enemies of the United States, those who were (and are) the fellow travelers of enemies of the United States, and those who are neither traitors, nor enemies, nor friends and protectors of enemies, but are American patriots who disagree with conservatives over policy issues. It is important, first, because it is just, and also because it is a condition of democracy. Citizens will disagree over many issues. In order for the democratic process to survive, all parties should refrain from attempts to delegitimize those who disagree with them, provided they have reasonable concerns and dissents. If every Democrat is a traitor, if "the entire party cannot root for America," we are left with a one-party system.

The final reason for making these distinctions is that this charge—that no Democrat, apparently including Jack Kennedy, can root for America—is obviously absurd, and if conservatives do not recognize that it is absurd, nobody is going to listen to them. That is why Conason and Cohen are cackling rather than yelping. That is why Conason doesn't even think he has to answer her claims, only list them:

> "Whether they are defending the Soviet Union or bleating for Saddam Hussein, liberals are always against America," according to [Coulter's] demonology. "They are either traitors or idiots, and on the matter of America's self-preservation, the difference is irrelevant. Fifty years of treason hasn't slowed them down." And: "Liberals relentlessly attack their country, but we can't call them traitors, which they manifestly are, because that would be 'McCarthyism,' which never existed." (Never existed? Her idol gave his 1952 book that very word as its title.)[3]

Fortunately, Conason's bad faith is also showing in this passage, which underscores why a defense of the anti-Communism of the "McCarthy era" (but not McCarthy) is in order. Of course McCarthy titled his own book "McCarthyism." Liberals had made the term an issue. Is Conason really suggesting that McCarthy's book is a defense of the liberal caricature of himself? Does Conason really think that the tactics of guilt by association and prosecution by committee—the hallmarks of "McCarthyism"—are exclusively the vehicles of anti-Communists and not weapons of choice for liberals themselves?

If liberals abhor "McCarthyism," why are they such worshippers of Hillary Clinton, the unrepentant author of the most infamous McCarthyite smear since the senator's censure fifty years ago? In fact, liberals like Joe Conason were eager abettors of her lie that a "vast rightwing conspiracy"[4] invented her husband's affair with Monica Lewinsky in order to destroy his liberal good works.

---

[3]"Has She No Shame?," Joe Conason, *Salon,* July 4, 2003, http://www.salon.com/2003/07/04/treason_4/
[4]"First Lady Launches Counterattack," David Maraniss, *Washington Post,* January 28, 1998

Liberals like Conason regularly engage in "McCarthyite" smears and "guilt-by-association," gleefully linking political opponents (myself for example) to those they have already demonized, like Richard Mellon Scaife, the alleged kingpin of the alleged vast rightwing conspiracy. Where was the liberal opposition to prosecutions by congressional committee when Col. Oliver North and other patriots were in the dock? Who on the left objected when Senator Inouye, Democratic chair of the Iran-Contra investigating committee, in true McCarthy fashion, used his immunity from libel torts to condemn North as a "traitor" before a national television audience and in a setting where North had none of the protections of a court proceeding? The only difference between the Iran-Contra victims of Senator Inouye and the Communists who were pilloried by Joe McCarthy was that the Iran-Contra witnesses were patriots and the Communists called before McCarthy's committee were not.

If so many liberals and Democrats had not provided cover for Communists and Soviet spies like Alger Hiss and Harry Dexter White, there would have been no "McCarthy era"—no wave of loyalty oaths and no congressional investigations. Derelictions like Roosevelt's created a heightened anxiety over security issues when the public realized that there *was* an enemy within who had thoroughly penetrated the Democratic Party and was indeed controlled by the Kremlin. The refusal of Democratic leaders to take the threat as seriously as they should have *created* the demand for investigations and made the exploits of demagogues like McCarthy inevitable.

The problem with Coulter's book is that she is not willing to concede that McCarthy was, in fact, demagogic, or that his recklessness injured the anti-Communist cause. Ronald Radosh, Harvey Klehr and John Haynes have distinguished themselves as historians by documenting the Communist menace that many liberals discounted at the time and still discount today. But they have also documented the irresponsible antics of McCarthy, which undermined the anti-Communist cause. Coulter dismisses such conservative criticisms as caving to the liberals. She is wrong. But the fact that she is wrong should not obscure the way in which she is right in the larger argument about whether McCarthy and McCarthyism have been used by those on the left to cover their own indefensible tracks.

Here is a way to assess the merits of that argument: a quick Google search will show that there are two periods in American history that have become known as eras of "Red Scares"—the so-called McCarthy period and the period of the Palmer Raids, when anarchist radicals were rounded up in the 1920s as subversives and terrorists. The first "Red Scare" provides a good yardstick for judging the one under review because it is free of the presence of the controversial senator and his antagonists, yet involves parallel claims that an anti-radical hysteria led to an assault on civil liberties and the persecution of individuals for their political beliefs. In fact, the Palmer Raids were triggered by a massive domestic campaign of terror conducted by anarchist organizations, which involved a hundred mail bombs and an attempt to blow up the Attorney General of the United States (Mitchell Palmer) along with banker J.P. Morgan and others. One anarchist bombing killed 40 people—the biggest terrorist atrocity in American history until then. Another plot to poison 200 members of the Archdiocese of Chicago who were attending a dinner party failed when the guests merely became sick.

Given these facts, it would be more reasonable to designate the Red Scare of the Twenties as the Era of the Red Threat. The same is true of the McCarthy episode. Neither are so designated because the institutions that make the cultural record—the academic history profession and the highbrow media—are dominated by the political left which is protecting its own, and which regularly deploys the charge of "witch-hunt" to silence its critics. That is also why *The New York Times,* one of Coulter's justly favorite targets, has spent so much newsprint promoting contemporary terrorists like Kathy Boudin, Bill Ayers and Bernardine Dohrn, and why it has equivocated over the guilt of Alger Hiss and played down the significance of the Venona decrypts from the Soviet archives. The McCarthy era has been written into college and high school curriculums and even government history standards as a time of witch-hunts instead of a time of fifth-column treasons for the same reason. Coulter is right to emphasize this.

The opening of the Soviet archives and the release of the Venona decrypts have established beyond any reasonable doubt that McCarthy's so-called victims, with few exceptions (James Wechsler would be one), were people who either served the intelligence agencies of the biggest mass-murderer in history or supported the despotic empire he built, or were fellow travelers of the same. The remedy for preventing any injustices that may have occurred through the hearings of McCarthy's subcommittee and the House Committee on Un-American Activities would be to close congressional hearings to the public. But no one to my knowledge, liberal or otherwise, has proposed this.

Today, liberals are busy whipping up hysteria about a government threat to civil liberties in regard to terrorist suspects incarcerated at Guantanamo. Here is Coulter's take: "[After 9/11, liberals] wailed about 'McCarthyism' and claimed to be 'very very concerned'—not about terrorist attacks on America but about 'civil liberties.' Liberals' idea for fighting domestic terrorism was to hold folk-song rallies with Muslims. When they aren't complaining about alleged threats to civil liberties, they are complaining about us. Two days after the [9/11] attack, novelist Norman Mailer, whose last successful novel was written fifty-four years ago, said the crumpled World Trade Center was 'more beautiful than the building was,' and America was 'the most hated nation on earth.' As Mailer saw it, the terrorist attack was retaliation for the Happy Meal: 'We come in and we insist on establishing enclaves of our food there, like McDonald's.'" *Touché.*

There are many genuine patriots who are concerned about the balance between liberty and security. William Safire is one from the Republican side; Nat Hentoff is one from the left. Making such discriminations is important, and to the extent that she hasn't made them, Ann Coulter opens herself to the criticisms that have been leveled against her. But in the long run, this fault pales in comparison to the one that emphasizes the wrong problem or promotes America's enemies as America's victims, which is what her liberal antagonists have done.

9

The Left on Trial

Radical attorney Lynne Stewart is a progressive icon. A protégée of the late William Kunstler and Ramsey Clark, a member of the National Lawyers Guild and the Center for Constitutional Rights, Stewart is a hero of the "legal left" under whose professional code radical attorneys select clients whom they regard as the victims of an oppressive system, the persecuted champions of just causes. Attacking the United States qualifies as one of those causes. Stewart is the former attorney for the "Blind Sheik," Omar Abdul Rahman, who was convicted of masterminding the first World Trade Center bombing, and plotting to blow up the Lincoln and Holland tunnels during rush hour, which could have killed 100,000 people. Currently she is on trial as a terrorist herself for aiding the sheik in carrying out his terrorist agendas in the Middle East.

Stewart is being defended by Michael Tigar, a celebrated Washington attorney whom I knew as a radical in Berkeley at the beginning of the Sixties. He was also the counsel for Terry Nichols, the convicted second bomber in the attack on the Oklahoma City Federal Building in 1995. Tigar is a progressive icon, the author of books on *Law and the Rise of Capitalism* and *Persuasion: The Litigator's Art*. Michael Tigar's idea of persuasion is captured in *The New York Times'* account of the Stewart trial: "While the government regarded Mr. Abdel Rahman as a dangerous terrorist, Mr.

January 10, 2005, http://archive.frontpagemag.com/Printable.aspx?ArtId=9981

Tigar said, to Mrs. Stewart he was an 'old man' held in conditions of cruel isolation, in a federal prison in Rochester, Minnesota. Mr. Tigar compared the sheik to Nelson Mandela and Menahem Begin who were treated as terrorists at one time in their careers."[1]

The left itself is on trial in the Stewart case. The idea Tigar is attempting to sell the jury—that his client regards Abdel Rahman simply as an old man cruelly isolated—is laughable. Lynne Stewart is on record *approving* "directed violence," which—as she explained to *The New York Times* —"would be violence directed at the institutions which perpetuate capitalism, racism and sexism."[2] The World Trade Center, for instance. Lynne Stewart has specifically endorsed the Muslim *jihadists* who destroyed it: "They are basically forces of national liberation," she told the Marxist magazine *Monthly Review*. "My own sense is that, were the Islamists to be empowered, there would be movements within their own countries ... to liberate."[3] At the National Lawyers Guild annual convention last year she attacked her own country as having "a poisonous government that spreads its venom to the body politic in all corners of the globe," and raised a glass to her heroes: "Ho and Mao and Lenin, Fidel . . ." and of course Che Guevara, whom she quoted: "At the risk of seeming ridiculous, let me say that the true revolutionary is guided by a great feeling of love."[4] Hate would be more accurate.

Radical lawyer Ron Kuby, another Kunstler protégé, described to a *New York Times* reporter Stewart's "passionate ... identification" with the Blind Sheik, and confessed that movement lawyers like himself are "cowards ... [who] live vicariously through their

---

[1]Julia Preston, "Defense Assails Terror Case Against Sheik's Lawyer," *New York Times*, January 5, 2005.

[2]Joseph P. Fried, "In Muslim Cleric's Trial, a Radical Defender; Left-Leaning Lawyer and Revolutionary Sympathizer Comes Back in the Limelight," *New York Times*, June 28, 1995.

[3]*Monthly Review*, November 25, 2002.

[4]Speech to the National Lawyers Guild Convention, Minneapolis, Minnesota, October 26, 2003, p. 2, http://www.lynnestewart.org/LynneStewartNLGMN.pdf

clients. 'Movement' lawyers, especially, identify with the people they represent."[5] That is precisely the problem, for Lynne Stewart, for Michael Tigar and for the left itself.

That left is now in full attack-mode against its own democratic government in a time of war. It identifies as victims and even "liberators" the Islamic terrorists who want to destroy us. Michael Moore has said it in so many words: "The Iraqis who have risen up against the occupation are not 'insurgents' or 'terrorists' or 'The Enemy.' They are the REVOLUTION, the Minutemen, and their numbers will grow—and they will win. Get it, Mr. Bush?"[6] And on the leftwing website CommonDreams.org, former SDS radical and Democratic California senator Tom Hayden has even laid out a plan to defeat his own country: "The anti-war movement can force the Bush administration to leave Iraq by denying it the funding, troops, and alliances necessary to its strategy for dominance."[7]

This is not a loyal opposition. It is no longer the voice of a progressive future that previously would have opposed the misogyny, thuggery and depravity of regimes like Saddam Hussein's or movements like Sheik Omar Abdel Rahman's Islamic Group. Whatever the outcome of the Stewart trial, the trial of the left she is a part of, will continue, and the verdict is increasingly bleak.[8]

[5]George Packer, "Terrorist Lawyer," *New York Times*, September 23, 2002
[6]Michael Moore, "Heads Up ... from Michael Moore," April 14, 2004, http://www.michaelmoore.com/words/mikes-letter/heads-up-from-michael-moore
[7]"How to End the Iraq War," Tom Hayden, November 22, 2004, http://www.alternet.org/story/20571/how_to_end_the_iraq_war
[8]Stewart was eventually convicted and sentenced to 28 months in prison. She was resentenced in July 2010 to 10 years in prison for committing perjury at her trial and showing no remorse for her crimes.

10

Oliver Stone's
Communist History

In the winter of 2012, the Showtime channel began airing a ten-part, multi-million dollar series called the *Untold History of the United States*, which was written and directed by Academy Award winning filmmaker Oliver Stone with the help of Peter Kuznick, a history professor at American University. The series and the 750-page book on which it is based are a ludicrous encapsulation of the Kremlin's view of the Cold War beginning with the capitalists' determination to strangle Lenin's revolution at its birth. This narrative is extended to include the Fidel Castro-Ho Chi Minh-Daniel Ortega-Hugo Chavez-Hamas version of the decades that followed the fall of the Soviet regime. In Stone's scenario every possible sympathy is extended to America's enemies, including not only Stalin's Russia but Germany and Japan, Saddam Hussein's Iraq and Ahmadinejad's Iran. Every step of America's way in the Stone-Kuznick chronicle is portrayed in the worst imaginable light, up to and including the Islamist attacks of 9/11, which are described as an excuse for a bigoted America to justify criminal wars "against two Islamic nations." According to the authors these caused "far more damage to the United States than Osama bin Laden ever could," while "shredding the U.S. Constitution and the Geneva Convention" in the process.[1]

---

[1]Mark Tapson, "Oliver Stone's 'Untold History' Comes to an End," *Front-Page Magazine*, February 8, 2013, http://frontpagemag.com/2013/mark-tapson/oliver-stones-untold-history-comes-to-an-end/

The hero of *The Untold History* is former president and Progressive Party presidential candidate, Henry Wallace who is presented as the visionary of a planet without capitalism and war, a symbol of Americans' lost opportunity to secure peace and prosperity for themselves and the postwar world. The historical facts tell a very different story. After being supplanted in the vice presidency by Harry Truman, Wallace ran as the candidate of the Communist-created and Communist-controlled Progressive Party, whose *raison d'être* was opposition to Truman's defense of the West and willingness to support Stalin's efforts to drag millions of Europeans into the Soviet gulag. Wallace even defended the 1948 Communist *coup* in Czechoslovakia, which decapitated that country's democracy and sealed the fate of its citizens for the next forty years. Wallace finally saw the light when Stalin's minions invaded South Korea in 1950. Two years later, he published an article "Where I Was Wrong," knowledge of which is suppressed by Stone-Kuznick. In the article Wallace acknowledged that he had failed to see "the Soviet determination to enslave the common man morally, mentally and physically for its own imperial purposes." He went on: "More and more I am convinced that Russian Communism in its total disregard of truth, in its fanaticism, its intolerance and its resolute denial of God and religion is something utterly evil," a perception that eludes Stone and Kuznick.[2]

How grotesque that Stone and Kuznick should have been able to revive at this late date, and on such a national platform, the myths that served the Stalinists in their conquests, and that still serve their successors engaged in a permanent war against the West and its freedoms. In the Stone-Kuznick narrative, the anti-Communist defenders of those freedoms are portrayed as racist, militaristic, imperialists of the right, motivated by a "blind

---

[2]Sean Wilentz, "Cherry-Picking Our History," *The New York Review of Books*, February 21, 2013, http://www.nybooks.com/articles/archives/2013/feb/21/oliver-stone-cherry-picking-our-history/?pagination=false&printpage=true

devotion to private enterprise."[3] It is a formulation that could have been lifted verbatim from *Pravda* in the heyday of the Kremlin.

To have revived a discredited enemy mythology is one thing but to receive a warm reception in the process is a cultural moment of some significance. As historian Ronald Radosh observed in a series of devastating critiques of the Stone-Kuznick effort, the warm embrace by leading intellectuals of this Communist fantasy was on display in a full-page promotion that appeared in *The New York Review of Books*. Rutgers historian Lloyd Gardner praised it as one that "many would consider impossible." *The Huffington Post*'s Glenn Greenwald called it a "counter-narrative to the enormous tide of hogwash that dominates most public discussion of America." Ann Hornaday of the *Washington Post* judged it to be "grounded in indisputable fact." Historian Doug Brinkley described its authors as grappling "with the unsavory legacy of American militarism," while Pulitzer Prize winning historian Martin Sherwin deemed it "the most important historical narrative of this century," and "a carefully researched and brilliantly rendered account."[4] It is with some confidence that Stone and Kuznick could claim that their historical view was already "the dominant narrative among university-based historians."[5]

It is true that there were dissents. *The New York Review of Books* published a critical review by historian Sean Wilentz. But it was an exception that proved the rule, treating the authors with an undeserved respect routinely denied to conservative authors who supported America's Cold War efforts.

---

[3]Daniel Greenfield, "The Death of Oliver Stone's Good Soviet Union," *FrontPage Magazine,* January 29, 2013, http://frontpagemag.com/2013/dgreenfield/the-death-of-oliver-stones-good-soviet-union/

[4]Ron Radosh, "The Real Henry A. Wallace: The Truth About Oliver Stone and Peter Kuznick's 'Unsung Hero,'" *PJ Media,* January 6, 2013, http://pjmedia.com/ronradosh/2013/01/06/the-real-henry-a-wallace-the-truth-about-oliver-stone-and-peter-kuznicks-unsung-hero/

[5]Sean Wilentz, op. cit.

Almost as impressive as the acceptance of Stone's anti-American fiction was the silence of the liberal lambs whose one-time icons it attacked. This was in striking contrast to the reaction that greeted the appearance of Stone's equally fact-challenged and conspiracy-ridden film about the Kennedy assassination, *JFK*. When that anti-American screed appeared twenty years ago, there were thunderous denunciations of its falsehoods by leading Democrats. But no such dissents from Democrats greeted Stone's Stalinist revival, no outcries over the libels committed on the memories of Harry Truman, John F. Kennedy and Lyndon Johnson, nor the country they served.

Some years ago I made a case for using the term "neo-communist" to characterize the progressive left. This seemed a reasonable choice since there was no discernible difference between progressive views of American capitalism and America's global exploits, and that of the Communists: capitalism is bad, America is an imperial aggressor and its militarism, racism and overseas investments are the root causes of international conflicts.

Of course, time will change everyone to some degree. Progressives and liberals do not call for the creation of Soviet-style gulags and they are even critical of the late Communist system, albeit well after the fact. But Lenin and Trotsky didn't set out to create gulags either. Their ambition was to achieve economic equality and social justice—goals identical to those progressives pursue today. Even Communists like Khrushchev, who was personally involved in carrying out Stalin's purges, eventually found it politically wise to become anti-Stalinists. So with the neo-Communist progressives. They may decry Communists who have been dead for fifty years but they are busily burnishing the Communists' ideas and preserving their legacies and passing them on to new generations in the curricula of our schools and on cable TV.

It also true that few people on the left still talk about establishing a "dictatorship of the proletariat" or "taking over the means of production"—at least not in those precise words. But the left has a history of studied and disciplined mendacity in the pursuit of its goals. Moreover, these goals visibly shift with its accretions of power. It has been to school with Saul Alinsky, whose manual, *Rules for Radicals,* is admired by President Obama, Hillary Clinton, the National Education Association, and progressives generally, and it has absorbed Alinsky's two main lessons: deceive the public about your agendas; remember that the end—the destruction of American capitalism—justifies any means.

In light of these considerations, the term "neo-Communist" seemed to me an apt description. It seemed at least as appropriate as the terms "neo-Nazi," or "neo-conservative," which are widely accepted terms for comparable political developments. The production and reception of Stone's work is concrete evidence that the spirit of Communism is alive and well in America and is now the heart of a mainstream movement. And that does not bode well for the American future.

PART IV

Identifying the Left

I

Discover the Networks

etwork, *noun:* An openwork fabric or structure in which
cords, threads, or wires cross at regular intervals.
DiscoverTheNetworks is an online guide to the polit-
ical left.[1] It identifies the individuals and organizations that make
up the left and also its sources of funds; it maps the paths through
which the left exerts its influence on the larger body politic; it
defines the left's (often hidden) programmatic agendas and it provides an understanding of its history and ideas.

The site is made up of two principal elements along with a
search engine to locate and explore the information stored. The
first of these elements is a database of "profiles" of individuals,
groups and institutions, which can be accessed through the heptagram on the home page or directory on the navigation bar. More
than 2,600 groups and individuals have already been delineated in
the profiles sections of the base. The information has been culled
from public records readily available on the Internet and from
other sources, whose veracity and authenticity are easily checked.

The second data-element consists of a library of articles, which
analyze the relationships disclosed in the database and the issues
they raise. These analyses are drawn from thousands of articles,

On February 15, 2005, I put an encyclopedia of the left on the Web and
called it Discover the Networks. In the first few days, a quarter of a million people visited the site, many of them outraged leftists. This is the
introduction and guide to the site.
[1]http://www.discoverthenetworks.org

both scholarly and journalistic, that have been entered into the base and linked in the "resources" columns that appear on the profiles pages. The judgments that inform these analyses are subjective, reflecting informed opinion about the matters at hand. In every case possible, their authors and sources are identified so that users of the database can form their own judgments and opinions about the reliability and value of the analyses.

DiscoverTheNetworks is an ambitious undertaking that would not have been possible before the creation of the Internet, with the storage capacities and data-linkage features that digital space affords and such an undertaking requires. As a result of the information these technologies make available, a user of this site can follow the networks described in the database to arrive at a new understanding of forces that define our social reality and shape our collective future. The database will readily answer many questions that previously would have required volumes of printed text to establish.

The primary question is: "Is there a left?" In the early 1970s, radical activists began referring to themselves as "liberals," in part to distance themselves from their failures as a socialist left. A sympathetic media culture went along with this deception, with the result that the word "left" has all but disappeared from the political lexicon. The spectrum of views is now regularly described in the media culture as extending from "liberal" to "moderate" to "conservative" or "right," as though a left did not exist or was so marginal as not to matter.

Thus Howard Kurtz, media critic of *The Washington Post*, explains in his 1997 book *Hot Air: All Talk, All The Time:* "There is ... no real left wing in today's talk show environment largely because the left has faded as a political force in America." Wrong on both counts. The National Public Radio network features plenty of leftwing talk shows and the left, as this database demonstrates, is alive and well. This doesn't prevent former Clinton Labor Secretary Robert Reich from agreeing with the proposition that there is no significant left in American politics. In his book

Reason: Why Liberals Will Win the Battle for America, Reich asserts: "Now it's hard to find any Sixties lefties, except maybe in the rarefied precincts of a few universities where aging radicals still debate Marxism and deconstruction. Most of the political passion and intensity these days are on the radical conservative right." These words were written in 2004—well after Sixties radicals like Leslie Cagan, head of United For Peace and Justice, had organized the antiwar demonstrations in which a million protesters with publicly-articulated leftwing agendas participated, and which fueled the antiwar presidential campaigns of Sixties veterans Dennis Kucinich and Howard Dean. Reich wrote his book as head of the Social Justice and Policy Program at Brandeis University, a leftwing enterprise, and is a leftist himself. The pervasive presence of a political left on the liberal-arts faculties of American universities is documented in the "academia"[2] module of discoverthenetworks.org.

By browsing this database, and familiarizing oneself with the agendas of the individuals and organizations it contains—the scope of their activities and the tens of millions of dollars available to support them—a user of this base will find ample evidence for the existence of the left and for the fact that it is a major player in the political destinies of this nation. (See in particular the organizations and individuals associated with "antiwar" or "peace" groups[3] and the Shadow Party.[4])

The movement to protest the war in Iraq reconfigured the presidential campaign of 2004 and has affected American policy not only in Iraq but in the War on Terror generally. What is the nature of this antiwar movement, who are its leaders and what are its agendas? The features of this database allow for definitive answers

---

[2]http://www.discoverthenetworks.org/guideDesc.asp?type=aca
[3]http://www.discoverthenetworks.org/viewGroups.asp?catId=9
[4]http://www.discoverthenetworks.org/groupProfile.asp?grpid=6706. Subsequently, I wrote a book with Richard Poe called *The Shadow Party: How George Soros, Hillary Clinton and Sixties Radicals Seized Control of the Democratic Party*, Thomas Nelson, 2006

to these questions. They provide a comprehensive guide to the principal groups responsible for organizing the national protests against the war, their leaders, their core agendas and beliefs. While the database cannot account for the motivations and beliefs of all the individuals who participated in these protests, it can describe with reasonable certainty the identities and agendas of all the principal antiwar groups and leaders who initiated these protests, organized their events and shaped the political debate. Inspection of the database shows that the agendas of these groups and the individuals who ran them were anti-corporate and socialist, and often Marxist-Leninist, rather than pacifist or nonviolent or merely "liberal," which is how the principal media present them. Their opposition to the war goes well beyond the issue of the war itself.

The relational aspects of the database reveal the paths by which these radicals were able to influence institutions like the Democratic Party. Using the information provided in the base, one can thus trace the progress of a radical menu of leftwing policies and complaints into the heart of the American political mainstream. The database also provides group profiles of the organizations engaged in organizing opposition to the Patriot Act,[5] as well as to frontline homeland security defenses such as border control and the linkages between them. Following the network of these organizations and individuals through the base reveals that they have agendas and perspectives that range far beyond legal issues and are rooted in their radical opposition to the American economic and social system.

The information entered into the database has been scrupulously assembled. The sources for the facts entered and the interpretations based on them have been made as transparent as possible, so they can be checked by users of the base. Textual analyses of the data contained in this site and attached to the

---

[5]http://www.discoverthenetworks.org/guideDesc.asp?catid=101&type=issue

profiles, or provided separately under the "issues"[6] module in the search heptagram and in the specific guides on each of the search pages, are identified by author and source so that they can be independently evaluated by the individual user.

We are aware that this base may raise legitimate concerns about the effect of categorizing and labeling individuals and organizations, and that such an enterprise entails the possibility of inaccuracies creeping into the data. We share these concerns and have provided a contact link on the homepage of this site ("Contribute Information"[7]) where corrections can be submitted. We will take immediate steps to correct any and all factual inaccuracies that are brought to our attention.

By the same token, we will not react to veiled expressions of distress over the factual information revealed on the site. A cry of such distress has already greeted a perfectly reasonable database called Campus Watch, created by the Middle East Forum.[8] This site records and analyzes the views of leftwing academics concerning terrorism in the Islamic world, views that can fairly be described as apologetic and even sympathetic to the radical Islamist cause. Critics of Campus Watch, many of them with views identical to those reviewed on the site, have claimed that the very enterprise of posting such reviews is "McCarthyism" and an Internet "witch-hunt." Such responses reflect an anti-intellectual attitude that seeks to embargo the political debate before it takes place.

We are familiar with such attitudes because they have already been directed at DiscoverTheNetworks in advance of its publication on the worldwide web. Almost a year before the official launch, a radical group in Colorado broke into the site under construction and supplied information about it to several journalists. One of the latter was Gail Schoettler, a former Democratic

---

[6]http://www.discoverthenetworks.org/issue.asp
[7]http://www.discoverthenetworks.org/contribute.asp
[8]http://www.campus-watch.org/

lieutenant governor of Colorado and a regular columnist for *The Denver Post.* In her column of January 11, 2004, Schoettler wrote: "Attorney General John Ashcroft and right-wing gadfly David Horowitz no doubt share many views. They also have one dangerous common goal: They want to turn us into a nation of snitches. Just like the good old days of … Senator Joseph McCarthy, they want Americans to spy on one another.… Horowitz is seeking funds to develop a huge database of so-called 'leftist' and 'liberal' individuals and organizations, a massive snitch file."[9]

This bizarre outburst reflects not only the partisan hysteria of the 2004 presidential year but also what appears to be a normal hypocrisy of partisans on the left, who react with outrage to practices that they themselves have pioneered. There are in fact more than a dozen political databases parallel to DiscoverTheNetworks that have been created by the left to map the political right, and they have existed for years. Among the most active are: Media-Transparency,[10] Namebase,[11] SourceWatch[12] (formerly called Disinfopedia) and MediaMatters;[13] this last a site created by Democratic Party funders and operatives led by George Soros and former Clinton chief of staff John Podesta. These dedicated "watchdog" sites are supplemented by other leftwing sites that post extensive lists of conservative organizations, accompanied by profiles designed principally to stigmatize them. People for the American Way, for example, is an organization whose principal activity is falsely tarring conservatives as "racists" on the basis of their dissent from leftwing positions. PFAW features a "Right Wing Watch"[14] section on its website which applies the same loose principles of characterization to a wide range of conservative

---

[9]http://mailman.lbo-talk.org/2004/2004-January/000865.html
[10]http://www.mediatransparency.org/
[11]http://namebase.org/
[12]http://www.sourcewatch.org/index.php?title=SourceWatch
[13]http://www.mediamatters.org/
[14]http://www.rightwingwatch.org/

organizations and individuals. People for the American Way also funds the MediaTransparency site.

In contrast to these shoddy practices, every effort has been made in the creation of DiscoverTheNetworks to avoid conflating subjective judgments about policy differences with factual descriptions of attitudes expressed by the individuals and organizations listed on the site. Individuals and organizations identified as "Marxist" or "socialist," or as having agendas sympathetic to America's adversaries, are so identified on the basis of their explicit commitments to these agendas. Their profiles are generally linked to analytic articles whose authors and sources are clearly identified. If any errors have been made in characterizing individuals or organizations, the editors of DiscoverTheNetworks will correct these as soon as they are brought to our attention.[15] As already noted, a form is provided on the homepage of the site for this purpose.

DiscoverTheNetworks is not by intent or design or consequence a "snitch file," as the former lieutenant governor of Colorado has maliciously suggested. To whom would the site be snitching and about what criminal activity? Is the lieutenant governor implying that the leftists identified in this site are hiding something that should not be submitted to public scrutiny? Is she aware of some governmental authority with an official list of forbidden viewpoints, ready to impose penalties on the persons in this database for having offensive ideas? How would the lieutenant governor know in advance of actually viewing the site what its nature and intentions might be? Isn't her accusation an example in itself of the guilt-by-association and innuendo she claims in her column to fear?

The purpose of the DiscoverTheNetworks site is not to stifle free speech but to clarify it. We recognize that people are not always candid in what they say in public life, particularly in the arena of political discourse. "Truth in political advertising" would

---

[15]http://www.discoverthenetworks.org/viewSubCategory.asp?id=1601

be a more accurate description of our intentions in assembling the data. The problem of deceptive public presentation is common enough to all sides in the political debate; but it applies with special force to the left, which has a long and well-documented history of camouflaging its agendas. The Communist Party, for example, operated through front groups which concealed the radical agendas of those who controlled them. In the 1948 elections, the Party created an entire electoral front—the Progressive Party—to field a candidate, Henry Wallace, whose purpose in running was to oppose the Cold War against Stalin. During the congressional investigations into the covert activities of the Communist Party, its leaders appeared before government panels to proclaim their patriotism and to describe themselves as avid defenders of free speech, denying that they had any radical agendas at all.

The disingenuous tradition of the political left has continued into the present. In the 1960s, the radical organizers of the mass antiwar demonstrations pretended that their only interest was to "Bring the Troops Home," when in fact their agendas embraced a radical menu that was anti-capitalist and welcomed a Communist victory in Vietnam. In the campaign against the war in Iraq, a similar pattern has emerged, as the information provided in this database clearly demonstrates.

2

The Left Strikes Back

It is now nearly a week since we launched our new website, "DiscoverTheNetworks: A Guide to the Political Left." This is the first Web attempt to define the left and to map its networks of funders, organizations and individuals along with their agendas (both overt and covert). We are gratified by the initial comments we have received in some quarters for this effort in building a taxonomy of the political movement. We wish to stress that it is still a work-in-progress, and that we expect to make it even better.

As we expected, the left has not taken the news presented on our site well. A writer for Alex Cockburn's CounterPunch regards it as "David Horowitz's Smear Portal" and objects to our linking noble champions of social justice like himself with the "resisters" in the Sunni triangle he supports.[1] But others of the leftist persuasion with less extreme positions have weighed in with similar objections. This article is designed to provide an answer to their complaints.

In the first place, it should be pointed out that even though discoverthenetworks.org consists of thousands of files, and is the product of years of work and decades of experience, these critics have launched their attacks within hours of its appearance, before any serious person could have digested a fraction of its contents. It

February 22, 2005, http://archive.frontpagemag.com/Printable.aspx?ArtId
=9493
[1]Kurt Nimmo, "DiscoverTheNetwork: David Horowitz's Smear Portal,"
Press Action, February 15, 2005, http://www.pressaction.com/news/
weblog/full_article/nimmo02152005/

is difficult not to regard such attacks as politically-motivated attempts to stigmatize and, yes, smear the new website, and thus bury the enterprise in a way that would preclude having to deal with the information and analyses it contains. Thus, instead of addressing the detailed profiles of individuals and organizations and their links to networks defined in the site, these critics have seized on a quirk in the format—in particular an index, an otherwise innocent feature—as a target for their attacks.

This is the "Individuals" search page, which functions as a table of contents for one section of the site. (Other sections focus on "Groups," "Funders," "Issues," "Media," "Politics," "Jihad," "Arts & Culture," "Books," and "Academia.") The specific target of their attacks is a picture-grid on the "Individuals" index page, which was intended as a kind of visual enticement to search the profiles on the site. Thus, if one were to click on the picture of Barbra Streisand or Abu Musab al-Zarqawi or Michael Moore, one would be taken directly to the individual profile.

The mere listing of these figures in the database was not intended to suggest that there are organizational links between these individuals. Nonetheless, Michael Moore has in fact called the "resisters" in Fallujah "patriots" and "revolutionaries," while denying that they are terrorists. Do the terrorist Abu Musab al-Zarqawi and Michael Moore have a common agenda? Evidently Michael Moore thinks so. Let's name it: defeating the Great Satan—the imperialistic, invading and occupying war-machine of the United States. It should be obvious that even the relatively innocent Barbra Streisand would be thrilled by an American defeat in Iraq, which would be a victory for the aforementioned Zarqawi, even if—as we are sure—she deplores some of his methods. She also is a fan of Moore's anti-American propaganda film, *Fahrenheit 9/11*, and is not on record (so far as we know) dissenting from Moore's sympathies for the terrorists. On the other hand, if one were actually to read the profile of Ms. Streisand in the database, as our critics have not, one would never make the mistake of regarding her as a Muslim fanatic bent on exterminating infidels.

Here is a typical reaction from the blogger who calls herself "Rox Populi": "Listed along with Bill Moyers, Barbra Streisand and Cornel West, you'll find the Ayatollah Khomeini, John Walker Lindh and enemy-of-the-state Pete Seeger on the 'Individuals' page. Read it for a good laugh. I must admit I haven't had this much fun since I was handed a Lyndon LaRouche tract that tied the Hapsburgs to the Challenger explosion." Of course, there's nothing to "read" in the picture-grid on the "Individuals" page. The laugh, in other words, is self-reflecting. The picture-grid is only a sample of the contents on the site and does not make connections in the manner of LaRouche. It is an enticement, not a thesis. It does not suggest any tie between these individuals, except that they all belong in a database about the left. Is their inclusion in the same database so unreasonable? Would Trotsky and Stalin belong in a database on Communism? Yet Stalin denounced Trotsky as an "enemy of the people" and put an icepick in his head.

Within the political left, as in the right, there can be differences that are both deep and also final. To exclude either Trotsky or Stalin from a database of Communists, let alone leftists, would preclude creating a comprehensive database of Communism or the left and ultimately reduce it to the description of one faction, which is evidently what our leftist critics want. In their view, any attempt to identify the spectrum of the left is to indulge in guilt by association. It is another way of denying that there is a left at all. Or, to approach this another way: is it conceivable that a leftist would attempt a comprehensive portrait of the right, and include such media conservatives as George Will, Pat Boone and Bob Hope, but leave out David Duke or—inevitably—Mussolini or Hitler? Conservatives might then point out that Hitler was a socialist and Mussolini a disciple of Lenin, so they properly belong on the left.

None of our critics, it seems, has bothered to look at any of the actual profiles. None has argued that a single profile is inaccurate or makes invidious or unreasonable connections between the individual in question and other individuals or organizations or ideas. If the profiles of Bill Moyers, Cornel West and Barbra Streisand are fair and accurate, what is the problem? In our introduction to the site, we made a specific pledge not to do what we are now being accused of—smearing individuals through guilty association (something the left does instinctively, relentlessly and all too well): "We are aware that this base may raise legitimate concerns about the effect of the categorizing and labeling that such an enterprise entails and the possibility of inaccuracies creeping into the data. We share these concerns and have provided a contact link on the homepage of this site (Contribute Information) where corrections can be submitted. *We want to assure both the public at large and those individuals and organizations whose names appear in this base that we will take immediate steps to correct any and all factual inaccuracies that are brought to our attention. The integrity and accuracy of this database is as important to us as it is to anyone.*" (emphasis added)[2]

Although the site is less than a week old, we have been true to our pledge. A blogger friend of *The Nation*'s editor, Katrina vanden Heuvel, sent her the bullet-points which appear at the head of each profile in the site and asked her for her reaction to hers. These are the points:

- Editor and co-owner of the left-wing magazine *The Nation*
- Limousine leftwing daughter of William J. vanden Heuvel, who worked for the founder of the CIA and for Robert F. Kennedy, and Jean Stein, whose father founded MCA-Universal
- Married to New York University Russian scholar and Gorbachev enthusiast Stephen F. Cohen
- Fluent in Russian. Worked as reporter for state-run *Moscow Times* in U.S.S.R.

---

[2]http://discoverthenetworks.org/guide.asp. This is the first essay in this section, "Discover the Networks."

Vanden Heuvel objected to the statement that she was fluent in Russian and a reporter for *The Moscow Times.* (It was *The Moscow News.*) More importantly, she pointed out that she was a reporter only for a few weeks to cover Russia's first democratic elections. The bullet-point (and related text) had insinuated that she worked for the press of a Communist police-state, which she hadn't. When apprised of this mistake, we removed the inaccurate point.

Similarly, when ABC's Jake Tapper called us directly to complain about a passage referring to him in our profile of the American Broadcasting Company, we immediately altered it and made it accurate to his satisfaction.

In our introduction to the site, we pointed out that there are several already- existing leftwing sites whose clear purpose is to smear conservatives by mislabeling them "homophobic" or "racist" on the basis of policy differences (e.g., support of the Clinton military policy of "Don't ask, don't tell" or opposition to racial preferences). These sites include People for the American Way's "Rightwing Watch," the report on conservatives compiled by the Southern Poverty Law Center,[3] and David Brock's MediaMatters. In contrast to DiscoverTheNetworks, it is the intention of these sites to misrepresent and smear those whom they include. That is why they refuse to correct defamations when they are pointed out by their conservative targets. (Exchanges exemplifying this problem between MediaMatters and myself[4] and also the Southern Poverty Law Center and myself[5] are available at frontpagemag.com.[6])

In constructing discoverthenetworks.org, we resolved that we would make it an informational site useful for all, regardless of political persuasion. Consequently, we have adopted a policy of not using labels to misrepresent and stigmatize individuals or

---

[3]http://archive.frontpagemag.com/readArticle.aspx?ARTID=16213
[4]http://archive.frontpagemag.com/readArticle.aspx?ARTID=12503
[5]http://archive.frontpagemag.com/Printable.aspx?ArtId=16570
[6]For the Center's reply, see: http://archive.frontpagemag.com/readArticle.aspx?ARTID=16377; for my reply see: http://archive.frontpagemag.com/readArticle.aspx?ARTID=16378

organizations, and we are ready to correct any misrepresentations that have crept into our profiles. We are determined that this will be a resource useful to all journalists and researchers, conservative and liberal alike. We will make it as accurate and as independent of the editors' viewpoints as possible.

Confusions such as those sown by Rox Populi's attack on discoverthenetworks.org are hardly confined to the political fringe. Her canard against discoverthenetworks.org is actually lifted (with a "hat tip") from the blog of a well-known English professor at Penn State, Michael Bérubé:[7] "The latest product of the fertile mind of David Horowitz is finally available for public use! It's Discover the Network and no, it's not a cable channel that shows mammals doing the nasty. It's 'A Guide to the Political Left'—that's right, a comprehensive introduction to some of the world's leading traitors, terrorists, and useful idiots!! And be sure to check out the 'Individuals' page, kids! Because before today, you could plausibly say that you just weren't aware of the connections between: Bruce Springsteen and Mohammed Atta; Sheik Omar Abdel Rahman and Roger Ebert; Martin Sheen and Ramzi Yousef; ... and, of course, Barbra Streisand and the Ayatollah Khomeini—but now you can't use that excuse any longer! So, kids, join the global war against the American entertainment industry and its alliance with Islamist religious fundamentalists whose beliefs about women, sexuality, and secularists only *appear* to be similar to those of Christian religious fundamentalists but are *really* allied with the decadent Fifth Columnists who introduced soul-sucking concepts like 'the weekend' and 'the minimum wage' into American life! Remember, *everyone* can fight in this war—even Sean Hannity and Jonah Goldberg! Enlist today!"

This is a pretty fair rendering of the paranoid fantasies of the left. Needless to add, no such connections are made in the database under attack.

---

[7]Michael Bérubé, "International Leftist Network Exposed!," February 16, 2005, http://www.michaelberube.com/index.php/weblog/international_leftist_network_exposed

Even my good and talented friend Sherman Alexie emailed me this stinging rebuke:

David
Your DiscoverTheNetworks site is disgusting. Placing the photo of Ayatollah Khomeini beside Barack Obama, Castro beside Kucinich, Mohammed Atta beside Mike Farrell? It's propaganda of the crudest sort. And it's lazy. Where are the right wing billionaires connected to Saudi oil money? Where are the right wing independent arms dealers who sell to any buyer?

I'm betting that most independent arms-dealers are driven by mercenary rather than ideological motives and sell their wares to all comers. But those that are "rightwing" aren't in this database because it is a database of the *left*. The same goes for rightwing billionaires connected to Saudi oil money. Sherman Alexie knows this. His letter is not an appeal to logic but a cry of the wounded. I accept that juxtaposing those images might be misleading if the reader doesn't proceed to the content of the profiles behind them.[8] Still, the inclusion in one database of radical Islamists with American leftists who organized an opposition to the war against Islamists in Iraq, or who participated in coalitions with organizations advancing the Islamist cause in the Middle East, is justified by these facts. Jimmy Carter was an enabler of the Islamist revolution in Iran, bringing the Ayatollah Khomeini out of exile and unseating the Shah of Iran. He has come down squarely on the side of Palestinian Islamists who want to liquidate the Jewish state. How does Sherman Alexie propose to deal with *these* facts?

I have described the interface between major elements of the left—though not *all* elements of the left—and radical Islamists as an "unholy alliance" and have written a book about it with that title: *Unholy Alliance: Radical Islam and the Radical Left.* The database merely fills in the particulars. Another way of viewing the database is to see it as an extension of *Unholy Alliance,* an

---

[8]We eventually dispensed with the picture-grid.

Internet version of a text I would have written about the left if it had been doable by one man and presentable between the covers of a book. The "alliance" between radical Islam and the left is generally not formal, but it can be easily identified in the profiles of individuals such as Michael Moore and Ward Churchill, both of whom regard Islamic terrorists as freedom-fighters resisting an illegitimate occupation in Iraq. Organizations that share this view and are represented in this database include CounterPunch, the Center for Constitutional Rights, the National Lawyers Guild and leading "peace" organizations like International ANSWER and Code Pink. And this is just the tip of an ugly iceberg.

Michael Moore has been celebrated and supported by leading figures of the Hollywood left and of course by leaders of the Democratic Party. They may not share his more radical views, but they are willing to stand closer to him than they are to President Bush and those who are leading the war against the terrorists. Thus the inclusion of various Democrats in this base along with Michael Moore and Islamic radicals is appropriate, and the connections we make are not the caricatures suggested by critics.

Sherman Alexie's complaint on this score is misguided, as is his complaint that the database slights the humanity of its subjects. He wrote: "I know many of the lefties on your site, and find them to be, by and large, fragile and finite and compassionate and intelligent and misguided and honest and hopeful and hateful and loving, just like most of the righty folks I've met and know." Well, if we were just to go by these generalized human qualities of political actors we would have no way of explaining political conflicts and why some people line up consistently on one side of the arguments. Alexie's categories are offered from the perspective of a novelist, not a political analyst.

I also know several of the lefties in our database. Moreover, I was part of this left for 25 years and thought of myself and my comrades as "by and large, fragile and finite and compassionate and intelligent," etc., too. But that is just the beginning of an understanding of the left. Compassionate and intelligent people often wind up supporting agendas that are neither.

3

The Left Defined

Professor Michael Bérubé is one of many ferocious and shallow critics of our new Guide to the Political Left at discoverthenetworks.org. In a recent attack on our site, he reveals once again the intellectual laziness of the left when it comes to engaging its opponents.[1] Of course, tenured radicals like Bérubé have lifetime jobs and captive audiences, and operate in an environment which has been purged of conservative influences, so what is their incentive *not* to be lazy? When discoverthenetworks.org was unveiled on February 15, Bérubé was one of many leftwing bloggers to answer it with a mindless tongue-in-cheek assault, focusing on a single page that contained a sample of individuals profiled on the site that represented them by their images alone. He thus ignored the hundreds of thousands of words in the profiles, which actually described the politics of the individuals concerned.

To a man and woman, the left wasn't interested in addressing the argument presented in the website. In a collective hissy fit, it responded to the posting of discoverthenetworks.org with howls of

---

In a further attempt to clarify matters and assuage some of our critics, we took the step of introducing categories of leftists into our list of individuals, which previously had no order at all. This essay was written to explain the distinctions we made. March 14, 2005, http://archive.frontpagemag.com/Printable.aspx?ArtId= 9276
[1]Michael Bérubé, "Rediscover the Brand New Network," http://www.michaelberube.com/index.php/weblog/rediscover/

ridicule and cries of anguish, fixating on the thumbnail picture grid that represented a partial index of the site, and nothing more. The grid committed the unpardonable offense of "lumping together" a small sampling of the individuals profiled in the base as part of the broad international left at war with the capitalist democracies of the West. As it happens, these individuals were selected because they were famous and therefore recognizable, and thus likely to entice browsers to enter the interior pages and view the actual profiles; each thumbnail served as a link to a profile. The enticement seems to have worked, since more than a quarter of a million people visited the site in the first few days it was up. But it apparently didn't induce leftists like Professor Bérubé to look at the actual contents.

Bérubé's assault was typical. It was conceived—ineptly—as a satire and intended as ridicule whose purpose was to dissuade others from taking a serious look at what was being said. Bérubé and other leftists chortled over the presence of Barbra Streisand and Katie Couric on the site, as though no one could take these women seriously. (Imagine if conservatives had proposed the same.) They objected in particular to the inclusion of these figures in a database containing profiles of terrorists like Sami al-Arian and the "Blind Sheik," Omar Abdel Rahman. Since Bérubé and his friends can't be bothered to construct an argument, I will pretend that they have done so and respond to what might be a reasonable concern.

Two issues come to mind. First, is there a legitimate rationale for compiling such an encyclopedia of the left, which includes the full range from extreme radicals to moderates—all of whom, by the way, are mislabeled "liberals" in the current political environment? Second, is there a rationale for including Islamic radicals and terrorists along with Americans who disapprove of terrorism, or with others like Bérubé who are selective in their disapproval and often apply the term "terrorist" to their own government? Obviously, the second question is the one that provokes the left's ire, so I will address it first.

Both Sami al-Arian and the "Blind Sheik," who are included with Couric and Streisand, are no strangers to the American left— as Bérubé certainly knows. Indeed, al-Arian's Orwellian-named National Coalition to Protect Political Freedom was the spearhead of the anti-Patriot Act movement.[2] He was a colleague and comrade of the leaders of America's legal left, which includes the ACLU and the Center for Constitutional Rights, two organizations spearheading the defense of captured terrorists at Guantanamo, and he was defended by the American Association of University Professors, in which Bérubé is a prominent figure. Now that al-Arian is in jail where he belongs, his coalition is headed by longtime National Lawyers Guild executive and fellow-radical Kit Gage. The "Blind Sheik," Omar Abdel Rahman, was aided and abetted in his terrorist enterprises by Lynne Stewart, a hero of the academic left and a stalwart of the National Lawyers Guild, the Center for Constitutional Rights and the ACLU. While under indictment, Stewart toured university campuses as a guest of their left-leaning law school faculties.[3]

How easy is it to be a guest of law school faculties like Stanford, as Lynne Stewart was? Ask conservatives like Supreme Court Justice Clarence Thomas and Judge Robert Bork. The reason an indicted terrorist can get such invitations, and conservatives usually cannot, is that law school faculties are dominated by leftist professors—political friends of Michael Bérubé, who are supporters of Lynne Stewart and thus are linked by one or two degrees of separation to the terrorists themselves. It is thus no great stretch to include them in a database along with active terrorists like Rahman and his Islamic Group. Are the degrees of separation important? Of course they are. Our database recognizes that fact, and has now attached categories to its index of individuals to make that clear. We have thus identified and distinguished totalitarian radi-

---

[2]http://www.discoverthenetworks.org/guideDesc.asp?catid=96&type=ind
[3]Erick Stakelbeck, "Cheerleaders for Terrorism," June 17, 2003, *FrontPage Magazine*, http://archive.frontpagemag.com/readArticle.aspx?ARTID=17670

cals like Stewart and Ward Churchill, who support terrorists, from moderate leftists like Bill Clinton and others who have fought them.

The New Republic's editor, Peter Beinart, who is not yet in the database, is such a moderate leftist. Beinart is currently leading a movement to get other moderate leftists, whom he refers to as "liberals," to dissociate themselves from leftwing individuals, organizations and publications like CounterPunch, which actively support the terrorists. In that category are prominent leaders of the broad antiwar left (like Leslie Cagan and Medea Benjamin) of which Michael Bérubé is also a part. We applaud Beinart's efforts and note that, if successful, they would create degrees of separation much healthier than the existing ones. We wait for Michael Bérubé to join him.

In *Unholy Alliance: Radical Islam and the American Left,* I have already made a detailed and extensive case for including Islamic radicals in our database. I even included in the book a lengthy collective portrait of progressives, which I called "The Mind of the Left," and which traced the continuities in radical thought from the generation of Stalinist intellectuals like Eric Hobsbawm, Noam Chomsky and Todd Gitlin.[4] These people may despise each other, but they also share a common hatred of America—the actually existing America and not some fantasy of an American future to be shaped by radicals.[5] It is this common anti-Americanism that makes radicals *de facto* allies of the Islamic jihadists. Both elements in this alliance think of America as the Great Satan and Israel as the Little Satan, root causes of evil in the world. This common belief also makes those American radicals into allies of convenience with Arab fascists like Saddam Hussein. Osama bin Laden himself recognized the collaboration of these unlikely allies in a *fatwa* aired on Al Jazeera TV just before Tony

---

[4]"The Mind of the Left" in the present volume is a revised version of that section of the book.
[5]See Part I of this volume.

Blair and George Bush began their military actions to remove the Saddam regime in Iraq: "The interests of Muslims and the interests of the socialists coincide in the war against the crusaders."[6] Bin Laden had in mind the ten million leftists worldwide who went into the streets a month earlier in protests, which if successful would have saved Saddam's monstrous regime.

My contention that the left is currently defined by its anti-American and anti-Israel agendas was recently confirmed by an academic leftist, Andrei Markovits, in an insightful essay, "The European and American Left Since 1945," which appeared in the leftist magazine *Dissent*.[7] But radicals like Bérubé can't actually be bothered to read what they are attacking or respond rationally to anything that ruffles their progressive feathers, let alone be concerned about the fact that a main political focus of the left since 9/11 has been in getting our terrorist enemies off the hook. Doubters can consult the archives of *The Nation*, *The Progressive* or any number of leftwing sites on the web to confirm the negative posture of progressives towards the war on terror and its instruments. Inevitably, not a single leftwing journal, or blogger for that matter, so much as noticed the existence of *Unholy Alliance*, which makes these arguments, despite the fact that there is no better- known critic of the left among leftists themselves than myself. It is only because I have constructed a website with *pictures* highlighting the problem that they have bothered to notice.

People more thoughtful than Michael Bérubé were initially puzzled by the principle of inclusion guiding discoverthenetworks.org and its now-famous grid, which led me to modify it. I did this not by excluding any of the leftwing individuals already in the database, but by introducing five categories that differentiated

---

[6]Allan Erickson, "The Marx-Muslim Mojo & the Commie Caliphate," *The Examiner*, February 10, 2011, http://www.examiner.com/article/the-marx-muslim-mojo-the-commie-caliphate

[7]Andrei Markovits, "The European and American Left Since 1945," *Dissent*, Winter 2005, http://www.dissentmagazine.org/article/the-european-and-american-left-since-1945

the spectrum of the left for those who couldn't be bothered to read the actual profiles, or couldn't understand them when they did. These categories are:

1. Totalitarian Radicals: Ward Churchill, Alexander Cockburn, Omar Abdel Rahman
2. Anti-American Radicals: Katrina Van Den Heuvel, Jane Fonda, Mumia Abu Jamal
3. Leftists: Hillary Clinton, Bill Moyers, Ruth Bader Ginsburg
4. Moderate Leftists: Bill Clinton, Peter Jennings, Maureen Dowd
5. Affective Leftists: Barbra Streisand, Katie Couric, Martin Sheen

Of course I never deceived myself into thinking that Bérubé and the comrades would be satisfied by these distinctions. In their minds, the first two categories boiled down to "McCarthyism" and last three didn't describe "leftists" at all. To hard-core radicals, these are *liberals.* But are they? In fact, the entire database discoverthenetworks.org is in one sense designed to show that the common usage of the term "liberal" is a calculated obfuscation by leftists to gain an advantage in the political arena, one that conservatives until now have been obligingly ready to concede. The current term "liberal" was hijacked from actual liberals a generation ago.

One can see this by taking the career of John F. Kennedy as a point of reference. Kennedy became a liberal icon at the beginning of the Sixties, before the left gained the ability to redefine the term and, with it, the political spectrum. Kennedy's politics—militant anti-Communism, hawkish defense policies and tax-cut agendas—are indistinguishable from the politics of Ronald Reagan (who was also weak on civil rights and a former Democrat). In the 1960s, Hubert Humphrey was also a "liberal" icon. But he too was an *anti-Communist* liberal—as any liberal worthy of the name would have been at the time. This made him an enemy of the left, the same left which everyone refers to as "liberal" today. In 1968, the left set out to cause Humphrey's electoral defeat and end his political career. They condemned him as a "Cold War liberal" and organized a riot at the Democratic Party convention that nominated him for President. The riot tarnished the convention and its candidate, who went on to lose the general election to Richard Nixon.

In those years, Norman Podhoretz, editor of the then liberal magazine *Commentary*, had been dissociating himself from the "New Left" because of its support for America's Communist adversaries, and because after Humphrey's defeat the Democratic Party had come under the leadership of George McGovern, a veteran of Henry Wallace's Progressive Party campaign. In Podhoretz's eyes, the Democratic Party appeared to be joining the leftist camp. Podhoretz held onto his liberal views and, as he describes in *Breaking Ranks*, fought fiercely to keep the label for himself and those like him who were reacting against the Democrats' leftward turn. It was the Democratic Party's betrayal of liberalism—its embrace of racial preferences, its appeasement of the Communist enemy—that made Podhoretz support the Republican candidacy of Ronald Reagan.

Leftists like *Dissent* editor Michael Harrington would have none of this. The socialist Harrington coined the term "neoconservative" to identify and vilify liberals like Podhoretz, Jeane Kirkpatrick and other Democrats disillusioned with their increasingly leftwing party. If Podhoretz could be labeled a neoconservative, as Harrington desired, then leftists like Harrington could be called "liberals." Fortunately for Harrington and other progressives, they had allies in the arbitrating institutions of the political culture that could make such labels stick. Soon *The New York Times* and the network TV anchors were referring not only to Harrington, but to lifelong Communists like Angela Davis and pro-Communist radicals like Tom Hayden, who had organized the Democratic convention riot, as "liberals" too. The *Times'* example was followed by *The Washington Post* and other engines of the political culture in identifying Podhoretz and his colleagues—despite their protests—as "neo-conservatives." And they made the labels stick.

In this way, the entire culture underwent a shift to the left, so that today leftists like Michael Bérubé are themselves amazed that an ideological feminist like Supreme Court Justice Ruth Bader Ginsburg should be referred to as a leftist, although that is precisely what she is. But people who support the redistribution of income generally, people who believe that America is divided into race, class and gender hierarchies and support the redistribution of social resources on the basis of skin color and gender, people who support the relentless expansion of the state, people who refer to Republicans as "Nazis" (as, for example Bill Clinton, congressman John Lewis and Senator Robert Byrd have all done) and who can find nothing wrong with university faculties that are 90 per cent located on one side of the political debate—such people are not liberal by any reasonable definition of the word. They are leftists.

But leftists don't want to be identified as "leftists" because they don't want to be burdened with the history of the left's deplorable "mistakes." In particular, they don't want to be accountable for their support for and appeasement of our Communist enemies during the Cold War. Nor do they want to be accountable for their protection and support of anti-American radicals like Democratic congresswoman Cynthia McKinney and the 60-odd socialist members of the so-called Progressive Caucus. They prefer to refer to overt socialists and anti-American radicals as "liberals" so people won't connect them to the disasters created by socialists and anti-American radicals. Take a look at the information provided in discoverthenetworks.org, the alliances revealed and the common agendas disclosed, and learn why it is important to apply the term "left" to the individuals who have been included on this site. Or, if the site doesn't convince you, then *argue* why the case is not proved. Ridicule is not an argument, and Michael Bérubé and his comrades know it is not. They want to avoid an argument they cannot win.

In a recent blog, Bérubé has attempted a response to the newly defined picture-grid distinguishing the degrees of separation between factions of the left.[8] But he has done so in a manner as superficial and dismissive as ever. Seizing on the category "Affective Leftists," he wrote: "What is an Affective Leftist you ask? Don't ask! This humble blog does not know." Well, it's not for lack of our trying to explain it to him. If Bérubé remains ignorant, it has more to do with his inability to read plain English, or perhaps just his inability to look at himself. On the very page in Discover-TheNetworks where the picture grid appears, there is a description of the section that explains its principle of inclusion. At the end of this description one can read the following sentence: "For an explanation of this picture grid click here." This takes the reader to an essay called "Defining the Left," where the question is answered: "The term 'Affective Leftist' requires some explanation, and I am grateful to Peter Collier for the description that follows.

"These are people who are often in positions of influence, the media in particular, who are *bien pensant* in the extreme. In spite of their social status, they see themselves 'in opposition,' a legacy from the Sixties when the notion of 'The System' as a malign codeword for America was born. They are also involved in post-radical chic, glorifying people who 'authentically' represent oppositional ideas in a way they would not have the courage or really even the political inclination to do themselves. To these people, as opposed to serious leftists, political 'ideas' are the intellectual equivalent of a fashion statement, always adjusting to meet current trends, always meant as a sort of code to tell the world that they are good people. Obviously, this refers to people like Katie Couric and Robin Williams and almost all of Hollywood. (Some Hollywood people like Sean Penn with his Communist lineage are harder-core and should be distinguished from this category; but there aren't that many of them, and in any case as actors their politics are largely emotion-based as well.)

---

[8]Michael Bérubé, "Rediscover the Brand New Network," http://www.michaelberube.com/index.php/weblog/comments/rediscover/

"These affective leftists have as their bottom-line definition the fact that they want to feel that they are on the right side rather than any real commitment to a vision (or anti-vision) for the country. They are for 'freedom' when it is freedom to kill third-term fetuses or engage in same-sex marriages or stuff blow up their noses; they do not define freedom as having anything to do with captive peoples around the world having the chance to escape the tyrannies that constrain them. They like Fidel because he is a thorn in America's side and a sort of dime-store existentialist, and they rhapsodize about his spreading of literacy in Cuba without considering the fact that at the same time he teaches people to read, he tortures writers like Armando Valladares whose books he doesn't like."

Is this definition difficult to understand? In the end, what people like Bérubé don't seem to fathom is that politics is a serious business, and support for totalitarian causes has consequences. When Bérubé and his friends opposed America's Cold War with the Communist enemy, the consequences were dire. In Cambodia and South Vietnam, Bérubé and his fellow leftists—including John Kerry and Ted Kennedy—were accountable for making possible the Communists' slaughter of two-and-a-half million innocent people after U.S. aid was cut at their insistence. What if they had been successful in other campaigns? If the nuclear freeze movement had prevailed over its conservative opposition, it is very possible that a billion people in the Soviet bloc would still be under the Communist heel. If leftists like Bérubé and Kennedy had been successful in obstructing the effort of America and Britain to liberate Iraq, Saddam Hussein would still be in power; Iraqis would still be disappearing into plastic shredders and mass graves; and the world in general would be a more dangerous place.

The fundamental utility of discoverthenetworks.org is that it shows that the left is indeed a network vast in scope, and that it influences American policy at every level, with consequences that are troubling.

Index

Czechoslovakia, 113, 286
  Soviet invasion, 264

dailykos.com, 84
Daily Worker, 99, 137
Damon, Matthew Paige "Matt,"
  68, 224
Dartmouth College (*see also*
  Davis), 4, 97, 100, 103, 112
Dartmouth Review, The, 4
Daschle, Thomas A. "Tom," 224
Davis, Angela Y., 4 23 n., 97 & ff.,
  115, 139–40, 315
Dayan, Moshe, 198
Debray, Régis, 146, 149
Declaration of Independence, 71
Deconstruction, 72, 295
"Defamation, Zionist Style"
  (Said), 172
DeFreeze, Donald (*see also* Sym-
  bionese L.A.), 163
De Genova, Nicholas, 11–12, 14–
  15, 85
Dellums, Ronald V. "Ron," 90,
  108–9
Democracy:
  academia, 96
  adversary culture, 203
  Cold War, 232, 235
  developing world, 61, 70, 107,
    121, 235–36, 238, 254
  Eighties left, 93–94
  goal of socialism, 212
  Iraq war, 11, 21, 47, 54
  leftist double standard, 33, 36–
    37, 43, 47, 58, 203, 234
  leftists' hostility to, 21–22, 27,
    30–38, 40, 45, 54, 70, 73, 85,
    110–11, 113, 121, 151, 193,
    212, 234, 310
  leftist movements, 92–94, 243,
    246–47
  New Left, 27, 91–92

Democracy, *cont.*
  "participatory" (Soviet), 41, 243,
    246–47
  postwar Europe, 110, 234–36,
    286
  progressives, post-communist, 1,
    21
  "rice-roots" (*see also* Vietnam),
    51, 113
  socialist countries, 110, 252, 286
  subversion, 220
  treason, 19
  utopia, 37–38
  Vietnam war, 92–93
    young peoples' hostility to,
    223
Democratic Party (U.S.):
  anti-globalization, 192
  antiwar movement post-9/11, 3,
    77, 283, 308
  Chinese influence, 201, 204
  collapse of liberal center, 95,
    273, 288, 315
  discounting of leftist influence,
    182, 316
  communist/radical infiltration,
    99, 271, 296
  Islamic radicalism, 308
  leftist takeover, 5, 95, 273, 314–
    15
  McCarthy period, 185, 270, 273,
    277
  "McCarthy stratagem," 182,
    277, 297–98
  Progressive Party, 179, 271
  "progressive" terrorism, 163
  socialists, 81, 257
Democratic Socialists of America,
  110–11
Destructive Generation
  (Horowitz), 207
Deutscher, Isaac, 191, 211–12,
  251–52

Totalitarianism, *cont.*
Iran, 78
Korea, 70
leftist movements, 21, 43–44,
92, 94, 100
Marxism, 2
McCarthy, Senator Joe, 273
9/11 attacks, 231
progressive culture, 4–5, 11
progressivism, 212
Progressive Party, Wallace candidacy, 74, 273
"social justice," 247
socialism, 140, 243, 245
Western Europe, 85
Treason:
academia, 202
American tradition, 19
Chomsky, Noam, 64
ideology, 19
inversion of, 15–16, 18
Lee, Wen Ho, 200–202, 204, 220
legal left, 200, 202, 207, 220
leftist movements, 92–93, 220
liberal culture, 203
race, 18 n.
utopian idea, 17–18
Treason (Coulter), 269 & ff.
Tripp, Linda Rose, 156
Trotsky, Leon, 167, 211, 250–52,
288, 303
Trotskyism, 5, 45, 106, 137, 251–52
Truman, Harry S., 69, 183–85, 190,
270–71, 273, 286, 288
Truman Doctrine, 74, 190
Truth About Hungary, The
(Aptheker), 100
Tum family (see Menchú), 148

U2, 224
"Un-Americans, The" (Weisberg),
187

Unholy Alliance (Horowitz), 307–308, 312–313
United for Peace and Justice, 45,
295
U.S. Peace Council, 107
Untold History of the United States, The (Oliver Stone), 6, 285
& ff.

Valladares, Armando, 318
Van Patter, Betty, 126
Vanity Fair, 153
"Varieties of Patriotism" (Gitlin), 49
Venceremos brigades (*see also* communism, leftism), 42, 46,
122
Venona Project, 176, 183–84, 267,
279
Verso Books, 251
Vieques, P.R., demonstrations, 223
Viet Cong, 113
Vietnam:
gulag, 52
police state, 239
poverty, 239–40
utopian idea, 49
Vietnam War, 35, 44, 74, 133, 190
Afghanistan, 89–90
American betrayal of Vietnamese, 275
American inaction, 93
American "original sin," 49–53,
109, 138–39, 228, 239–40
British "peace movement," 122
communist domino, 44, 239
Eighties left, 92–96, 108
genocide, 239, 318
Hayden, Tom, 113–14, 122, 270
Iraq War, 105, 109–110, 300
leftist domination of universities, 72, 96
liberal center, 95